D0896808

Cyber
Business

Cyber Business

Mindsets for a Wired Age

CHRISTOPHER BARNATT

John Wiley & Sons
Chichester New York Brisbane Toronto Singapore

Copyright © 1995 by John Wiley & Sons Ltd,
Baffins Lane, Chichester,
West Sussex PO19 1UD, England

National   01243 779777
International (+44) 1243 779777

Reprinted March 1996

Other Wiley Editorial Offices

John Wiley & Sons, Inc., 605 Third Avenue,
New York, NY 10158-0012, USA

Jacaranda Wiley Ltd, 33 Park Road, Milton,
Queensland 4064, Australia

John Wiley & Sons (Canada) Ltd, 22 Worcester Road,
Rexdale, Ontario M9W 1L1, Canada

John Wiley & Sons (SEA) Pte Ltd, 37 Jalan Pemimpin #05-04,
Block B, Union Industrial Building, Singapore 2057

Library of Congress Cataloging-in-Publication Data

Barnatt, Christopher
    Cyber business : mindsets for a wired age / Christopher Barnatt.
        p.   cm.
    Includes bibliographical references and index.
    ISBN 0-471-95605-8 (paperback)
    1. Business—Communication systems.   2. Cybernetics
HF5548.2.B338   1995
658.4'038—dc20   94-48425
                                                    CIP

British Library Cataloguing in Publication Data

A catalogue record for this book is available from the British Library

ISBN 0-471-95605-8

Produced from camera-ready copy supplied by the author
Printed and bound in Great Britain by
Biddles Ltd, Guildford and King's Lynn

At the end of the twentieth century, nothing recedes like reality . . .

Mark Dery
MONDO 2000

Contents

Preface

THE TRUE IMPACT OF computer technology on human civilization has yet to be realized. Digital communications networks now en-sphere the globe and even reach out into space. Coupled with this rise in computer 'connectivity', the physical systems of organizations across the planet are becoming increasingly integrated and interdependent.

The impact of an emerging 'global hardware platform', both upon ourselves and upon our business activities, will be enormous. 'Virtual organizations' and other new working patterns may become as common as traditional corporations and employment structures as we delve into the next century. Corporate cultures and human social relationships will also be transformed as Mankind and his technology meet in ever closer harmony to share the awakening medium of 'cyberspace'. Additionally, 'software agents' will emerge as electronic slaves to serve their human masters across vast webs of information.

We already have a youth culture in the nations blessed with wealth who seek a large proportion of their entertainment via interaction with electronic media, and to whom close interrelations with technology are almost as natural as breathing. The communities, the businesses, and the environments (both real and virtual) they will come to shape around us are therefore likely to be very different from those that many people fight to comprehend even today.

* * *

The process of writing *Cyber Business* can be likened to having had a metaphorical vacuum cleaner directed at the back of the head for over fifteen months, its intention being to suck every possible thought and idea from the mind. Fortunately, as this preface is written, the bag is now full and thankfully the cleaner has been switched off.

Aside from maintaining a certain level of mental stamina, the other major hurdle encountered in completing this manuscript has been in deciding what *not* to include. *Cyber Business* was never intended as a technical manual or instruction pack to detail business computing, virtual reality, organizational construction, network telecommunications or computer user-interface design. No attempt is therefore made to try and reproduce that which has been covered previously and far more comprehensively elsewhere. In broadly focusing upon how 'cyberspace' developments will impact upon business organizations, however, *Cyber Business* does address the *interrelation* of all the aforementioned disciplines. It is therefore topics upon the synergistic boundaries of these subjects that receive the bulk of attention.

Ultimately, the purpose of this book is to make people *think*. Several of the predictions herein will take years to emerge, whilst some of the examples of new working practices and new technology will be approaching 'old-hat' status by the time *Cyber Business* comes to press. Fortunately, neither of these facts actually matters very much. As humankind continues to evolve fresh communications media and associated business and social structures and norms, what is most important is that we discover a new *mindset* rather than take on board any specific bodies of knowledge. Technologies, new forms of organization, and the futurists who write about them, will inevitably come and go. As demonstrated by the fiction review in **chapter 7**, however, *ideas* concerning the future tend to remain remarkably concrete, evolving only slightly as they propagate toward their realization across common reality.

In order for either individuals or organizations to plan ahead, it is vital that they embrace visions of probable futures derived from the cutting-edge practice and research of the present. Fortunately for those looking ahead the future is exciting. The future is about *connectivity*. The future is about crossing incredible frontiers toward new organizational and social patterns. The future is *Cyber Business*.

Christopher Barnatt

Acknowledgements

WITH MANY THANKS TO: Mark Allin, Simon Ashby, Steve Benford, Andrew Brown, Brian Chiplin, Mark Daintree, Jim Devlin, Stephen Diacon, Paul Dobson, Anna Duval, Christine Ennew, Ingmar Folkmans, Alison Hull, Fraser Johnson, Francis Kinsman, Alison McGregor, Alison Mead, Sandra Mienczakowski, Steve Moore, Claire Plimmer, Mike Shardlow, Alan Shirley, Ken Starkey, Diane Taylor, Helen Whalley and Pauline Wong.

Prologue
The Dream

GRANT HAD AN IDEA, a new world to experience and sell, and he wasn't even logged into the Net. Raising a hand to the sensor beside his bed, he soon corrected that. Donning a headband consolidated the link. Now he could think properly.

Space unfolded before him and he quickly coerced matter into shape. Just roughly. A basic infomachine would soon tidy the edges of his creation. Minutes later the basis was laid, and an agent had created his usual directory structure for the project. Now all that Grant needed was backing. Finance, marketing, sales, distribution. Not to mention federal clearance to enlarge his working domain. Four hundred gigabytes ought to be enough. No. Better make that five hundred. He was always running out of file space.

Even as his mind drifted to the nightmares of organizational bureaucracy, his agent was transferring a mailshot to the Net. Just a hundred thousand copies at first. No. Better make that two hundred thousand. He wanted this project finished by tea-time, and besides, Sunday wasn't a day for being greedy.

Almost as soon as he had registered patents, the agents of interested parties were responding and a network began to form. A Japanese bank offered finance, a sub-agent reported that the rates were favourable, and Grant accepted the deal. Marketing and distribution offers came from China and Canada. Their portfolios looked most impressive. Very impressive. There was little to choose between them, though a knowbot recommended the Chinese service. Grant was unsure, and walked through the portfolios a second time. The Chinese was just a little too flashy — surely morphing 3-D logos weren't coming back into style yet again? Then his personal agent reported that the Canadian offer came from a network centred on a twenty-eight-year-old female with favourable bio-records and eight hundred idle gigabytes. With a smile Grant thanked his personal agent and accepted the Canadian deal.

Clearance came through for his five hundred gigas. Perhaps he ought to have asked for six? Then he reminded himself that Sunday wasn't a day for being greedy. Some public domain freak addressed nowhere in the arctic hopefully offered a sales service. Feeling benevolent, Grant accepted, instructing his agent to cluster all parties and keep him informed. With a double-pulse his software servant instantaneously complied.

The toaster reported that breakfast was ready. Feet falling into furry-but-flagging old slippers, Grant got out of bed and headed for the kitchen. As he passed his main server he smiled. Daft as it seemed, there were still times when he found even basic technology amazing. All those people across the world all now working for him. All making yet another dream come true — adding a further destination to his low-cost leisure domain. Then he smelt burnt toast. As multiple devices informed him that the atmosphere was now contaminated, he decided that technology still wasn't that smart after all.

The future remains unwritten, though not from lack of trying . . .

Bruce Sterling
Mirrorshades

1
Prelude

IMAGINE A THIN CYLINDER, perhaps six inches long, more slender than your finger, and tapered at one extremity. Imagine in conjunction a thin and flexible sheet derived from wood pulp. Stroke the cylindrical implement across the latter material and fine polymers or dyes are excreted to leave marks. Such marks may convey thoughts or images, forming icons of language or sound or mathematics. They may thus encode ideas and shape the thinking of future generations.

Yet why should you be told this? Why indeed, when the concept of using a writing implement to mark paper or parchment, even stone, hide or T-shirts, is known to all Mankind. An explanation of the written medium is hardly miraculous. What is amazing is that you were not introduced to this incredible concept during formal education — not in a school, college or university, and probably not even by your parents or other adults in early life. Granted, others taught you the alphabet, numeric symbols and possibly musical notation. You were probably also assisted in your first attempts at drawing and painting. But the concept of marking surfaces to represent ideas and to store and convey information is so inbred at this stage in our evolution that it is both universal and obvious. So will it be in the future with the awakening global medium of 'cyberspace', the shared, computer-mediated electronic realm of information and communications to which we will all soon have unprecedented access both at work and at play.

CYBER BUSINESS

This book attempts to predict the short- and long-term implications for those in business of the ever-closer harmonization of people, computer technology and organizational infrastructure as we approach the next millennium. Unobserved by many, a technological transformation of our own artificial environment is now rapidly drawing to a completion that will radically alter the way in which people may conduct both business and social activity. Computers have been of increasing significance in the workplace and in the home for several decades. Indeed, paperless offices and homeworking ('telecommuting') were heralded as the future years ago by technologists enthused with square-eyed optimism. Yet their dreams failed, with paper mountains continuing to grow, and ever more powerful computers making life seemingly ever more complex and potentially stressful.

So what went wrong? The answer is nothing. A new age of work, organization and computer technology will dawn, delayed perhaps a quarter of a century from the early estimates glinting in scientist's eyes. What has held back the daybreak of this future has not, in many senses, been the pace of technological advancement in terms of computer processing power and capacity. More important have been the velocity of organizational infrastructural development and the introduction, reliability and acceptance of new, low-cost communications technologies.

PERSONAL COMPUTERS, NETWORKS & DISTRIBUTED PROCESSING

Personal computers (PCs) proliferated across the workplace in the mid- to late-1980s. Only in the early 1990s, however, have they been widely interconnected across *networks* to share both information and applications resources. The lag between computers occupying the office, and their interconnection, has largely been due to the time (and money) that has been required to equip workplaces with appropriate network cabling, and hence to permit computers access both to each other and to long-distance communications linkages. Reliable and user-friendly LANs (local area networks), allowing the interconnection of a plethora of personal computers across an office or building, are also a relatively new development. Their introduction was at first resisted in many organiz- ations, both by technophobic employees, and by information technology (IT) departments more keen to maintain their power base and the status quo.

For decades, most computer users had to rely on 'dumb terminals' to access centralized computing facilities based around very large *mainframe computers* that handled all the processing for the entire organization or portions thereof. The spread of desktop PCs and new technologies for their interconnection has inevitably decreased the reliance of many employees on such centralized computing facilities. Information processing may thus be said to have been *distributed* across organizations, with many users now having their data manipulated within PC hardware upon their desk, rather than within a distant, central-processing facility.

As the 'downsizing' trend toward distributed processing has gathered pace, the power and status of many corporate IT departments has diminished. It is therefore hardly surprising that those primarily skilled and employed to maintain large-scale computer systems will have little inclination to investigate alternative computing solutions based on new technologies that may rapidly put them out of a job. Indeed, those brought up on mainframes may be totally ignorant of alternative computing solutions, or may not even believe they are technically feasible.[1] However, with over 100 large banking and financial institutions, such as the Richmond Savings Credit Union in Vancouver, now carrying out *all* of their computer processing over a PC network,[2] the objections of the old-school are starting to subside. In a decade, many will wonder why the technical feasibility of distributing information processing away from mainframes to 'mere' PCs was ever even questioned.

IMPROVED TELECOMMUNICATIONS

A major overhaul of the global telecommunications network is also only now nearing completion to enable widespread data transmission in digital rather than analogue form. As well as increasing the clarity of telephone calls, and permitting new telephone services, this infrastructural investment will greatly improve the speed of access to the loose amalgamation of international computer networks known as the *Internet*, into which many users connect via telephone lines. Digital wireless communications technologies, now common in portable telephones, are additionally a recent development that will in future become commonplace in portable computing devices enabling international data communications from your pocket. *Information super-highways*, employing complex digital data compression techniques and utilizing the latest, high-speed optical fibre cabling, are also set to deliver the 'information explosion' in the years ahead, a concept which the popular press erratically reports with scant detail and rampant enthusiasm when column inches on wars or political scandals are in short supply. In forms such as integrated services digital networks (ISDNs), these new technologies and information infrastructures will facilitate the communication of information at far higher velocities and in a far greater array of formats than in the past.

As new information communications infrastructures come on line, services such as interactive television and home shopping will become widely available. Perhaps more significantly for business users, new *groupwares* and *multimedia applications* will permit remote individuals to work together via real-time video, data and audio links. Teams of workers will therefore be able to operate dispersed not only around an office block, but also across the country or even around the globe.

Whilst computers have had the potential to communicate with each other for decades, only in the mid- to late-1990s are global, high-speed networks allowing for their widespread and reliable interconnection becoming commonly available for the majority. Additionally, *connectivity* is being fuelled by new forms of software application, such as electronic mail, intended to be used by groups rather than individual users. Changing attitudes are also a significant causal factor driving connectivity advancement, with many users now embracing computer-mediated communication (CMC) and hence coming to view their computers as powerful communications devices as well as information processing tools. Already, computer networks are routinely used to exchange text messages, graphics images, financial statements, inventory details, credit transfers and full-motion video signals for video-conferencing. Indeed, electronic data communications is likely to be a $40-billion-a-year industry by 1998.[3] Already over 50% of all connections across the global telecommunications network are made to link computer systems rather than to connect human beings for vocal communication. By the turn of the century, over 80% of all telephone network traffic will involve data transmissions.[4]

CONVERGING TECHNOLOGIES

With computer and information processing technologies rising to enjoy the lion's share of communications network provision, it should come as no surprise that telephones and computer peripherals are set to combine.

Giant corporations from both sides of the 'old' industries — AT&T, Novell, Intel and Microsoft, for example — are now pushing their own solutions toward the impending marriage.[5] Rather than being littered with telephones, facsimile machines and personal computers, future work locations (be they in the office or at home), are likely be equipped with integrated data processing and communications devices through which all work may be directed. Many companies are now working upon the development of combination telephones, PCs and fax machines which are likely to be operated by pens or touch screens, and which will be known as *telecomputers* or *smart phones*.[6] Just one example is the 'Screen Phone' from Philips, which may be used to access a range of services including home banking.[7] At the other end of the spectrum, voice-mail answering facilities will soon be available upon PCs. These will allow both text messages and telephone calls to be manipulated on-screen, with the user being able to possess just one single electronic mail box that will cope with all forms of communication.

SYSTEM INTERDEPENDENCE
& LEVELS OF ORGANIZATIONAL ANALYSIS

With increasing business interdependence and computer connectivity, future analysis of organizational hardware and communications infrastructures is likely to occur at two distinct levels. At the first, micro level, organizations will be viewed, as at present, as discrete physical and contractual entities within their own industries and marketplaces. Their computer systems will therefore be isolated for analysis at the individual machine or closed-networks level, with managers and technicians being concerned with their abilities to run discrete, internalistic program genres such as accounts, stock control, design and document processing. Micro hardware analysis will accordingly be concerned with the software and hardware of stand-alone PCs and PC networks, together with mainframe and minicomputer systems accessed via dumb terminals. Organizations and their IT staffs are likely to view their hardware at this 'home system level' for purposes of maintenance, development and system control. However, in order to ascertain the *value* to be reaped from their internal systems, they will also have to view their own discrete facilities as one small element of a much wider hardware conglomeration spread across the business community.

This leads us towards the adoption of a new, macro focus for business and hardware analysis, concerned with interconnected webs and alliances of organizational and computing infrastructures as viewed at the level of an industry, country, continent or planet. In order to appreciate this concept, it is perhaps easiest to first take a broad overview of trends across the marketplaces of the 1990s, within which many organizations now find themselves far more reliant upon the facilities and services of others than in years gone by.

Analysts engaged in industrial, strategic and structural appraisal, are already having to take a far wider perspective of organizational delineation as markets become more complex and turbulent. No longer can the majority of companies operate in stable environments in comparative isolation. Instead, firms are being forced into more flexible modes of production, combining with others to offer their services as part of industrial alliances and production networks in order to remain competitive. In turn, business organizations cannot view their own production facilities in strict isolation. Some firms, for example, now operate 'lean manufacturing' techniques of just-in-time supply, with components delivered by suppliers directly to the production line. Whilst decreasing stock-holding costs, this in turn makes companies more reliant upon the organizations from which they are supplied. Joint venture partnerships for large projects, shared research and development costs, and complex sub-contractual arrangements, are now also both common and essential across many industries, with even the largest of firms being unable to act continually in isolation from other players.[8]

Gregory Stock, in his thought-provoking book *Metaman*,[9] offers a fascinating general commentary on the increased interrelation of Man, his environment, and his organizations. Within this tome's glossy covers, we are invited to step back and imagine looking down upon the earth from space, from where we may observe a brightly lit network of human construction resemblant of a single living entity. Individual human beings and organizations therefore come to be analysed as sub-components of a wider system, symbiotically interrelated as part of a planetary 'super-organism'.

A single, global perspective of organizations and their hardware becomes ever clearer when we consider how information technology is now being employed across the business domain. Many industrial sectors are investing heavily in EDI (electronic data interchange) technologies to permit computer-to-computer communications to replace mountains of printed, mailed and then re-typed paperwork. Independent financial advisers and brokers, for example, may now have direct access to insurance company computer systems, allowing them to conduct their business without constantly filling-in and posting back and forth paper documents.[10] Similarly, a supermarket's stock-control computer may automatically place orders back to suppliers when stocks run low, with payments passing back and forth between organizational bank accounts without laborious human intervention. EDI is set to take off in a very big way in the mid- to late-1990s, meaning that companies who refuse to play the game and invest in the technology may well become isolated with fewer and fewer customers. Supermarket chain Tesco, a trailblazer amongst the 10,000+ companies estimated to be using EDI in the UK, already trades electronically with over 1,200 of the suppliers who provide more than 95% of the products on its shelves.[11]

A GLOBAL HARDWARE PLATFORM

As electronic interconnection becomes the order of the day across industry as a whole, it will be unclear in some respects as to where one organization's computer system ends and another's begins. Certainly the data flowing across computer communications networks will meet no resistance when it passes from one company to another, and it will therefore become sensible in many circumstances to think of all electronic networks as being sub-components of one single computing infrastructure. In effect there will thus be just one *global hardware platform* of computer technology across which everybody's data and software will flow, just as there is effectively one global telephone network used by all organizations. Indeed, a key reason for investing in new computer hardware in the future will be to possess a greater stake in the global system.

No company today would purchase a new telephone exchange which could not dial outside of the organization, and attempting to prevent external access to its hardware (ie incoming calls) would be even more ridiculous. Thus, just as we would not think of assessing the value of installing a new telephone exchange purely in terms of the improved effectiveness of its internal facilities provision, so computer systems will equally have to be judged from both micro (internalistic) and macro (global-system) perspectives. Indeed, as we cease to employ computers simply as devices for processing information, and additionally adopt them for widespread communication purposes, so our attitude toward our hardwares will have to evolve. Standardization and interconnection will increase *everybody's* system value, and companies will want others to feed them with data just as surely as they will strive to transmit details of their own wares across electronic networks. As connectivity increases apace, individual businesses may therefore come to be analysed as software patterns running across an international hardware base. As previously noted, such a trend is in keeping with the broader ideas of many business analysts who already view the production processes across some industries by studying flexible networks of firms engaged in joint-venture and sub-contractual activities, rather than the individual companies that form part of these networks. The increased flexibility of organizational structures that is and will be supported by new communications technologies is mind-blowing, potentially leading us towards *virtual organizational forms* with no physical infrastructure whatsoever. Such developments, and the role of increased computer connectivity in patterns of organizational structure, are explored in **chapter 3**.

THE MEDIUM OF CYBERSPACE

With the increased connectivity now made possible by digital hardware advancements, and the rapidly advancing global information infrastructure, computers and communications devices are intertwining in the nexus of an ever-expanding data environment now referred to by many as *cyberspace*. Put simply, cyberspace is the *information medium* in which computer software resides and executes and within which electronic communications flow. It is a *virtual information space*, existing within the microchips of all computer systems, from large mainframes to the humblest PCs, and more importantly across all computer and telecommunications networks. Thus, although you may discover cyberspace most frequently discussed in popular literature as the medium in which complex and graphically impressive 'virtual reality' simulation systems reside, equally it is the home of all business data processing operations and communications, facsimile machine messages, and even telephone calls.

The invisibility of cyberspace exists *within* all live, interconnected electronic systems, whether they utilize satellite, microwave and wireless link-ups, or more 'basic' fibre-optic or electrical cable connections.

Cyberspace technologies already surround us in a world hell-bent on the utilization of electronic devices. In the United Kingdom we now spend far more on video game and home computer systems than we do on education,[12] whilst since 1991 companies have spent more on computing and communications 'info-tech' than on traditional industrial plant.[13] There can therefore be no doubt that the majority of people and organizations crave access to *cybertechnology*.

Today, the key concept surrounding the potential of cyberspace developments concerns mass hardware interconnection. Although we may analyse activities within discretely bounded cyberspaces (for example those found within isolated PCs), the term is now generally being used to refer to a common information processing and communications medium existing globally across and between all connected (networked) computer systems. Cyberspace is therefore a medium to which we will all soon be able to have access. It is a consequence of the emergence of our global hardware platform. Hence, although cyberspace may be argued not to exist, it will soon allow a limitless common mental geography, accessed equally from Vancouver, a New York taxi, or a lab on the moon, as it 'siphons the jangle of messages that transfigure the physical world into the realm of pure information'.[14]

Perhaps surprisingly, the term 'cyberspace' was first used by Hugo and Nebula award-winning author William Gibson in his futuristic trilogy of novels *Neuromancer*,[15] *Count Zero*[16] and *Mona Lisa Overdrive*.[17] Within these works, the medium is described as a 'matrix of bright lattices of unfolding logic' — an information space existing, insofar as it does exist, by the virtue of human agency, and offering access to the sum total of information in the human system via understandable maps of '. . . icon worlds, waypoints and artificial realities'. Whilst these lavish descriptions were primarily intended to lexically augment a lush world of science fantasy, they neatly capture the conceptual essence of cyberspace as the *medium* of electronic processing and communication, just as paper and pen (or any other marking implement and surface) are the *medium* of written language and communication.

An understanding of the cyberspace concept will prove crucial for those shaping organizations in the 21st century, serving as it does to embrace the notion of near-instantaneous global connectivity. Cyberspace will soon become the primary human communications resource, eliminating time, distance and administrative bureaucracy from all activities of information manipulation and exchange. Cyberspace is also destined to become the focus of many work activities, with some organizations in future perhaps being delineated by the connectivity patterns they will spawn across its electronic frontier. After all, the physical hardware of most companies is likely to render them less and less identity in the years ahead, with standardization forcing all firms to become indistinct sub-components across the global hardware system if they are to continue to trade. Organizations with strong images and cultures will thus have to foster these as much within cyberspace as across the physical world, being judged with respect to their softwares, their human-computer interface technologies, and their communications protocols. The potential impact of new working patterns upon community and corporate cultures is explored in detail in **chapter 6.**

It should be noted that, whilst most leading theorists and software engineers are quite happy to be associated with the cyberspace concept,[18] a few influential writers still dismiss it as a 'brilliant fictional idea' 'bandied around when it does not exist'.[19] Perhaps this is because they see no value in assigning a label to the invisible nothing world of electronics inside and across computer systems. If this is the case they are seriously perceptually blinkered, for without tokens in language to enable the discussion of radical but abstract concepts, there is little hope that research and development into their exploitation and application can proceed apace.

CROSSING THE CYBER FRONTIER

The realization of a common cyberspace across and between most organizations, coupled with far more powerful computer technologies, will soon permit the creation a range of virtual environments within which we may choose to both work and render ourselves leisure. Commonly, 'virtual reality' (VR) is defined as a simulated cyberspace environment of artificial 3-D objects (rendered in computer graphics) with which people may interact. However this definition of computer-created virtuality is rather narrow. A computer-based electronic mail (e-mail) system in which memos and documents are 'posted' over a computer network is just as virtual a representation of a physical world construct as a graphic image of a proposed new building or atomic reactor. The near-infinite forthcoming cyberspace domain will only ever be bounded by our own mental and cultural blinkers and aspirations. An open mind is therefore essential in any discussion of virtual 'realities', 'systems', 'organizations' or other mental constructs within its non-existent bounds. Within this book, 'virtual reality' will therefore be taken to encompass any structured representation or metaphor of the physical world, encoded in computer software, with which human beings may freely interact.

The common PC graphical user interface Microsoft® *Windows*™, for example, presents a virtual representation of business and computer functioning. Users do not have to type in complex and oft-confusing programming instructions as under the more primitive DOS (disk operating system) *command line interface*. Rather, they can simply use a mouse to move a pointer arrow to highlight their desired application and file selections on screen. To write a letter, for example, the user may highlight and activate an *icon* (graphic image) of a pen, which will then take them into a word processing environment. Similarly, if the user wishes to alter computer settings, they just have to click upon a picture of a small computer to bring up a graphically operated control panel.

Stemming from work at Rank Xerox's PARC Labs,[20] the graphical 'desktops' now available across all PC platforms provide virtual metaphors of the real world to help us interact with computer technology. Modern electronic mail systems do exactly the same, giving the impression that we are actually creating letters that will be *posted* to the addressee, and which they may choose to keep in one of their document 'folders'. When running PC applications under *Windows*, or using electronic mail, we are therefore interacting with computer-generated virtual realities just as surely as if we were twisting and turning within the latest 3-D graphics simulation. We therefore come to appreciate that virtual realities encoded in cyberspace have been with us for some time. The concept of virtual reality systems will thus not be *introduced* into the business arena over the coming years, but instead will simply be *expanded* in its productive application.

LEVELS OF VIRTUAL REALITY

The interaction of human beings with virtual realities can presently be divided into encounters between man and machine at two distinct levels: *non-immersive* and *immersive*. Non-immersive VR involves the use of conventional HCI (human-computer interaction) hardware such as a VDU (visual display unit) monitor, a typewriter-style keyboard, and usually a mouse to map 2-D surface movement. The freedom of interaction with any virtual reality accessed via such input and output hardware is clearly limited. It should be noted, however, that keyboards have been common in the office for decades, and that 2-D text and graphics displays still form the basis of most information storage and communication media. Screen and keyboard therefore provide a natural means of interacting with virtual document processing or electronic mail systems. It is also worth remembering that high-resolution animated computer displays interactively accessed via mouse-controlled pointer movements are a very recent development. Ten years ago the level of interaction with office information technology now possible with modern *Windows*-based systems on bog-standard PCs would have been thought miraculous. Cyberspace access via conventional hardware should therefore not be dismissed out of hand, even though it does not provide the level of 'immersion' of new peripheral hardware forms.

Immersive VR, as the label implies, enables people to be placed right inside virtual computer worlds which they experience with a range of senses as if they were 'real'. The most basic hardware necessary for VR immersion is currently a *head-mounted display* (HMD) that positions small, colour screens before both eyes in order to give an impression of 3-D vision. The operator's cranial position is also 'tracked' so that when they turn their head the pictures before their eyes alter to give the impression that they really are 'looking around' a virtual world. *Datagloves* that track the movement of an operator's hand and fingers may also be used to allow complex interaction with virtual objects, with some gloves even offering tactile feedback (a sensation of touch) via a range of tiny air bladders or exoskeletal structures placed within or upon the glove. Thus, even in some of today's systems, an operator can view objects in a virtual world of computer graphics, pick them up, and feel them in their hands. Even more complex bodywear, allowing all of the movements of an operator's body to be utilized in data input, is also now in development. Such input clothing (perhaps worn as jewellery) will enable people to roam free in virtual realities and explore new worlds. Suits are even being prototyped with hundreds of strategically placed air bladder devices to offer physical tactical feedback to the whole body so that cyberspace will feel real to its biological visitors.

The development of *teledildonics* systems, allowing geographically distant individuals to meet in cyberspace for virtual sexual encounters, has also been widely discussed.[21] In future, such hard and softwares may perhaps allow 'physical' relationships to blossom between people who have never actually met, and whose rendezvous in cyberspace will occur in bodies and locations of their own choosing.

Complex soundtracks to accompany ventures into virtual realities are already comparatively easy to synthesize, and may add greatly to the overall immersion effect. In addition to the background sounds of the office or the jungle or whatever location they choose to be transported to, future VR participants may additionally be able to enjoy individually tailored, motion picture style musical scores along with their cyberspace experiences. The Biomuse™ system developed at Stanford University, for example, uses sensors to pick up signals from the brain, muscles and eyes which are then used as the basis for, or to govern, musical tones.[22] Imagine a board meeting held in virtual reality with an accompanying computer orchestration conveying the CEO's emotions as he hears each director's monthly report!

Today, virtual reality, particularly in its immersive guise, is still very much in its infancy: starting to toddle, perhaps, but definitely not up to long-distance walks. Government and commercial interest in the new medium is rampant, however, with VR being seen as a key future technology which may revolutionize both business and social activity. The US President's Office of Science and Technology has already identified many areas of national interest involving virtual reality. These include medical and training applications, engineering and design, and improving the quality of life for the disabled and the elderly.[23] An annual growth rate of 65% has been predicted for the virtual reality industry, with revenues in the US alone expected to exceed $1 billion by 1997.[24]

THE SYNTHESIS OF MAN & MACHINE

Sceptics of the development of immersive virtual reality systems tend to base their arguments on the inadequacies of the current and potential future interface hardware required to 'port' or 'jack' individuals into the cyber realm. Considering current advances and research into biotechnology and microelectronics, and our increasing understanding of human physiology, such criticisms will prove hard to uphold in the long term. HMDs, datagloves and body suits are merely today's immersive computer interface peripherals, based upon the crude principle of stimulating the body organs which in turn convey an impression of coherent reality to the brain. As discussed in **chapter 5**, tomorrow's hardware will quite possibly be much more subtle than today's, by-passing our 'natural' human receptors and instead being fused directly into the systems of our bodies. For example, instead of placing two small, colour display screens before our eyes, future VR peripherals may write images directly onto the retina, or may even feed their data signals directly into our optic nerves. When such systems for immersive VR are developed, the divide between the realm of human thought and reality and the electronic domain of the computer will sharply narrow, and may even disappear altogether.[25] Simultaneously, the distinction between reality and virtual reality may become impossible to delineate if that is what we wish. A wild fantasy? Research indicates to the contrary:

> . . . the first steps towards linking powerful sensory devices directly to the brain have [already] been taken. Electrodes have been implanted in the cochlea of the ear to stimulate the auditory nerve and enable the deaf to understand speech . . . [and] . . . with less success, electrodes have also been placed directly in the visual cortex . . . [Indeed] . . . by monitoring and stimulating brain cells and also communicating with external devices, it might eventually be possible to establish complex links between computer circuitry and the human cerebral cortex. This would give humans direct mental control over various machines and also expand mental capabilities with powerful enhancements of memory, communication and computation.[26]

The idea of highly-micro electronic implants being connected to our bodies in order to facilitate computer interaction and communication may at first sound ghastly, but already we accept false teeth, contact lenses, pacemakers and other prosthetic devices as 'natural' additions to our forms. When the placing of an array of electrodes into the brain becomes a simple and safe surgical procedure, many people may opt for the operation in order to enjoy near-infinitely widened possibilities for virtual business and personal relationships. This may be especially true for those caught in over-populated, parasitic 'mega-cities' whose metabolisms suck ecologies to barren wastes.[27] For such individuals an increased quality of life will become unattainable if they continue to need or desire an urban existence. Impossible, that is, unless such city dwellers turn to spending portions of their leisure time in computer-generated virtual realities. Alternatively, they may choose to live in comparative isolation and enjoy instant transportation to virtual metropolises when they desire the hustle and bustle of the city — a city, perhaps, of their own population and design.

THE RESIDENTS OF CYBERSPACE

Thus far we have considered cyberspace as a largely passive information processing and communications medium to be explored and exploited by Mankind and his organizations like a desert, forest, ocean or other resource. What we must also consider are the *active* residents of cyberspace on whom we will come to rely. The most common cyber-resident software-entity will at first be the 'agent', the development of which will be crucial to the realization of many of the concepts presented within this book.

At a basic level, agents are software routines that represent their masters in cyberspace to aid in the accomplishment of their desires and to protect humans from technical complexity or repetitive drudgery. Effectively agents are slaves encoded in computer software — virtual servants programmed to undertake the wishes of their masters, from whom they will be self-taught. When sending an electronic communication across the world, for example, a myriad of networks and data transmission protocols may be involved. As James White, a Director of Apple Computer spin-off, General Magic, explains, an agent could therefore be dispatched with your electronic communication to:

> . . . wander through the postal system, in and out of this building and that building, hopping aboard the trucks as they're passing from city to city, finding your intended recipient, obtaining for you the particular services that you want for a particular piece of mail.[28]

As well as acting as virtual guides and recipients for communications through cyberspace, agents will also increasingly undertake activities for both individuals and organizations. In the near future, rather than asking an assistant to check on travel arrangements and book the cheapest hotel in New York within a certain radius of the airport, you may simply request a software agent to make the preparations. With all business organizations connected across a common global hardware it will be comparatively easy for software routines to access any information their masters may require, sift it into the desired format, make decisions based upon known operator preferences, and organize bookings, contracts, sales, purchases and monetary transfers through the cyberspace medium. At first this concept may seem far-fetched. Will people actually trust software routines to undertake important operational decisions and critical arrangements in their work and home lives? The answer, of course, is that they already do.

Nobody in their right mind employs an assistant to watch their bedside clock all night and wake them at the appointed hour in the morning. This task is simply delegated to an alarm clock. We also commonly trust central heating systems to turn themselves on and off, video machines to record programmes to our orders, and smoke alarms to check the atmosphere and inform us of impending danger. The idea of telling a piece of software to find you a hotel or airline reservation, to manage your bank accounts, to write letters, pull files, arrange meetings, or even negotiate deals, may thus not be that abhorrent to the vast majority of people already dependent on technology to maintain the quality and bliss of their current working and domestic lives.

Programming personal computers to extract share price fluctuations from teletext information subject to certain criteria, for instance, is now comparatively straightforward. Once this is achieved it is only a small step to the scenario where your software not only constantly monitors share prices whilst you engage in office banter, but also buys and sells stocks and commodities when certain price parameters are satisfied, or perhaps when certain other statistics become available across the computer network. Agent software routines that will shop electronically, pay the bills, locate and book the cheapest holiday, or send your birthday cards, are not that far away. They will also become more and more useful to individuals over time as they learn the likes and dislikes, the skills and the failings, of their human masters.

As with other developments explored herein, the widespread adoption of agents hinges primarily upon increased global connectivity as much as upon applications development. Software agents can only live and work in cyberspace. Thus, although they may be of some use 'trapped' within our personal computers or internal organizational networks, they will only come into their own when they can communicate with external service and information facilities and other agents with as much freedom of movement in cyberspace as human employees enjoy in the physical 'real' world.

The entry of agents as active manipulators of the cyberspace domain (as opposed to passive information patterns within the medium) will further present us with possibilities for virtual and cybernetic organizational networks centred upon human beings but employing perhaps thousands of constantly active virtual employees in the unseen world of electronics. The scope for complex, destructive software routines descended from today's strains of computer virus to wreak havoc with the actions of other agents and computer data will hence be enormous. 'Virtual policemen' may therefore need to be programmed to seek out and erase potentially or actually troublesome software routines. A discussion of software 'agents, ghosts and other virtual monsters' takes place in **chapter 4**.

The question of the ownership of agents, either when the individuals whom they serve move between organizations, or when their masters take that one-way shuttle lift to the great cyberspace in the sky, may also create difficulties in the future. In both cases, will the agents of such individuals be the property of the organizations for whom they have worked, or the individuals themselves? This may be of great significance if, for example, an agent that has learnt to negotiate via studying the patterns of a CEO is engaged in finalizing a takeover deal when the CEO dies. Should such an agent continue with negotiations in its master's absence? Would this be ethical? And if so, would it imply that the CEO has achieved some form of cyber-immortality and may continue to be involved in the running of his or her organization when he or she no longer physically exists? Again, pure fantasy? In the long-term future almost certainly not. We readily accept that the likes of Walt Disney and Henry Ford played critical roles in forming the strong cultures of their great companies. Leaving an electronic legacy in the form of an army of software agent routines capable of running the show after the founder's death simply takes this notion one step further. Organizations are clearly more than the sum of their individuals, but equally they are all conceived by individuals, elements of whose parental guidance remains with many throughout their term of corporate existence.

WORK & PLAY IN VIRTUAL ENVIRONMENTS

With increased infrastructural connectivity, coupled with the refinement of immersive VR systems based upon tactile body suits and complex visual and audio headsets, the possibilities for working or playing with remote individuals in virtual locations will explode. Forward-looking software engineers Steve Pruitt and Tom Barrett talk of Corporate Virtual Workspaces (CVWs),[29] with employees awakening at home to don customized computer clothing in order to log-in to fibre-optic networks via their 'home reality engine'. They will then find themselves in a Personal Virtual Workspace (PVW) generated from computer graphics, and analogous to a physical office along a network of corridors in their employer's CVW. Herein employees may choose their own graphical bodyshell, as well as having the freedom to alter their 'physical' surroundings. Other workers may, as in any other office complex, freely drop in for impromptu idea sessions during the working day. That is, of course, unless the occupier has chosen to make his or her PVW graphical office selectively invisible, perhaps to obtain some privacy whilst catching up on any 'virtual-mail' messages 'received whilst away in the physical world'.

Other writers have even considered the notion of virtual 'come-as-you-aren't' parties,[30] where people in high-tactility data suits attend social occasions in software-edited bodies such as those of famous film stars or sex symbols. The experiences possible within cyber worlds via immersive technologies will be limited solely by our imaginations. People will almost certainly be able to appear as they wish rather than as they are in both their work and social lives. We may even be able to project different physical appearances to different people viewing us simultaneously. These possibilities may lead many individuals to prefer virtual cyber worlds to real physical environments. Almost schizophrenic lifestyles, where people work in the physical world to support play in cyberspace (or perhaps the other way around) may perhaps be commonplace one hundred years from now.

Science fact or madman's fiction? To many eminent writers and researchers, the realization of the above is now firmly a matter of when rather than if. In the UK a project entitled Virtuosi is currently bringing together several industrial partners and universities to pilot environments for computer supported cooperative work (CSCW).[31] The resulting virtual reality systems will enable employees to link together across the forthcoming network of global information highways in order to share a common working environment populated with familiar working tools. Participants will, for example, be able to draw upon a virtual reality whiteboard, the contents of which may be copied to the boards or desks of other parties.

One particular Virtuosi pilot scheme concerns the construction of a virtual reality environment spanning a set of geographically isolated cable makers. The aim is to allow workers and management in sites spanning several countries to cooperate as if they worked in a single 'virtual factory'. A second Virtuosi project, for the textile and clothing industry, will allow designers' computer visualizations of new garments to be viewed on mannequins parading a 'virtual catwalk' before remotely-linked clients attending a virtual fashion show.

Another interesting business VR initiative has been spawned by Advanced Robotics Research Limited (ARRL), which offers companies access to applications development facilities in return for a comparatively small annual membership fee. Via this membership coalition, organizations who would otherwise be unable to explore the possibilities of virtual reality find themselves well placed to develop applications for the future.[32]

Illustrations of current cyberspace business application already abound in their multitude, with many to be presented throughout this book. With the largest financial resources available to any current VR player, the US Army has long been developing and using a simulation system called SIMNET into which up to 1000 tanks, helicopters and other fighting vehicles may be networked for battle simulation and training under the control of geographically distant would-be killers. On a more down-to-earth level, some companies now use a PC VR software package to design their customers the perfect kitchen.[33] Other low-level VR systems allow British Telecom engineers to fly through a virtual model of their physical network, Marks and Spencer to examine new store layouts, and Rolls-Royce to work upon engine designs in cyberspace.[34] Systems are also available allowing fund managers to manipulate international stock and bond movements within 3-D VR landscapes,[35] whilst American doctors may use a VR system from NASA to study the anatomy of the human leg, or even to guide them during brain surgery.[36] Indeed in any situation where remote individuals need to work together in complex patterns, and/or must have access to materials, mechanisms and models that would be difficult or prohibitively expensive to physically prototype, cyberspace technology will soon be applied. With the cost of computer processing power continuing to spiral downwards, for most large organizations it should therefore be a question of *when* rather than *if* they will embrace computer simulation and high-level digital communications technologies into their corporate echelons.

Returning to Pruitt and Barrett's notion of the corporate virtual workspace of graphical corridors and programmable body shells, we may already find enough substance in the reality of current research and practice to counter those who dismiss their future workplace predictions as puerile fiction. Far from this, Messrs Pruitt and Barrett are simply noting that businesses will invest in any technology that will allow remote individuals to more easily capture, share, analyse and disseminate information. The concept of people in the next century porting into a virtual working domain, rather than driving to the office, *will become a reality*. Repetitive, stress-inducing travel may thus come to consume less of our lives, leaving more time for work or relaxation in either real or virtual environments. The likely drawback, however, is that social and cultural problems will abound. Paradoxically, these are likely to be experienced most critically by the forward-looking organizations who choose to be the first in adopting radically new, technology-dependent working patterns.

When surveying the characteristics of a range of 'excellent' UK companies, for example, Management Science America reported that none of the firms sampled chose to be first movers in the adoption of new information technologies. Instead they were 'early followers' — allowing others to run the highest risks and incur the costs of teething troubles.[37] They did not want to be guinea pigs — yet somebody has to be. Prototyping the technology and systems that will enable virtual working practices presents scientists from many disciplines with a tremendous challenge. Adopting the results of their labours for business use, and managing and motivating employees within and across virtual organiz-ations and workplaces, will present an even mightier crusade. Yet is it surely a crusade that has to be undertaken if we are to reap the full advantage of new cyberspace technologies before our competitors. How to rise to such challenges, and the environment in which they will take place, is what this book is really all about.

***

CYBER BUSINESS & THE FUTURE

So just what is *Cyber Business*? The answer is that it is many things. At one level, it is concerned with organizational forms created within cyberspace and perhaps accessed via immersive, virtual reality computer interfaces. On a more immediate level, *Cyber Business* relates to how organizations increasingly dependent upon the high-level interaction of human beings and computer systems may in future be managed, and what challenges may lie ahead as they 're-engineer' and evolve. Across some corporations, the hottest buzz-term is becoming 'management by wire', with IT-networks viewed as the 'tendons that hold the skeleton and muscles of the company together'.[38] Indeed once computer network links saturate business data centres, a path may well lie open for expert 'enterprise models' and software agents to be created that will manage day-to-day business operations for managers just as autopilots now guide aircraft during the routine portions of their flight. When and if such systems are created, the very *nature* of management will undoubtably change.

As this book progresses, the focus broadens to include a study of how industrial civilization in general may alter as cybertechnologies proliferate. After all, when any new technological developments impact upon human societies and cultures, so markets, industries, working practices and employee expectations invariably also change. It is therefore important for managers to reap a broad knowledge of cyberspace-related developments if they are to become the champions of the future, rather than to just concentrate on the immediate progress that will most rapidly be delivered to their doorstep. No apology is therefore made for the sections within this book which may initially appear to have no immediate relevance for the manager. *Cyber Business* is very much a book intended to broaden the mind, for almost all of the developments explored within will change the world that forms the environment around all of our business organizations.

Cyberspace is still narrowly perceived in much popularist writing as 'merely' an artificial 3-D environment wherein humans beings may freely interact with computer graphics. Yet the frontiers it tempts before us offer far, far more. A common cyberspace across a global hardware platform will present us with new media for human communication, the potential for virtual organizational forms, will trigger radically different social and cultural patterns, and may perhaps even permit global consciousness and forms of network-resident immortality.

Mankind is an information species. Since the dawn of civilization his survival has been dependent upon the acquisition and subsequent communication and utilization of knowledge. Whereas learning to hunt, to forage for food, is paramount in an infant's early life for most species, for human beings learning how to read and write, to communicate in an abstract form, has arguably become more important. Computer-based technologies — cybertechnologies — are already rapidly becoming integral to many people's lives, with computer interaction likely to become as natural as reading and writing for future generations. Indeed, some individuals already feel naked without a digital watch and databank strapped to their wrist, cell phone in their pocket, or microlight digital headphones linking them to a laser disk player in their pocket.

The worlds of business and cyberspace are hurtling towards each other, with new technology permitting fresh forms of organization capable of negating time and distance, whilst business demands are increasingly driving evolutionary progressions in computing development. Many are and will remain oblivious to the future on offer to those willing and capable of changing attitudes and competencies, and discarding old concept sets, in order to capture the potential of the next frontier facing humanity. Those who will adapt are now at the crossroads of a segment in history wherein the nature of civilization itself may be called into question. Like the Americas several hundred years ago, cyberspace offers a new territory to tame and explore. Its current cowboys may be bleary-eyed technofreaks married to their screens, yet these keyboard-hungry individuals will quickly become information barons with more power over people's lives than governments or multinationals if today's managers and corporations do not awake to the new connectivity age of the third millennium.

As an artifact and amplifier of thought, technology is not exclusively about rationality . . .

Brenda Laurel
Computers as Theatre

2
Embracing the Technology

THE COMPUTING AND TELECOMMUNICATIONS technologies of the future will be wondrous. Finally we will be granted infinite freedom to walk and to fly in the cyberspace realm of pure information, to create the physically impossible, to reach out to other human beings as never before, and to augment our own mental capabilities as one with machines. As science fact and once-science-fiction increasingly mingle in a concept jungle of new electronic media, the possibilities for Mankind afforded by his technological creations will be breathtaking.

In its exploration of computer hardwares past, present and future, this chapter effectively cleaves into two sections. Firstly, the development of computing machines from their very beginnings will be accounted, allowing the many apparently insurmountable hurdles ahead to be viewed in context. Already we have overcome enormous challenges in realizing today's generation of relatively cheap, compact, reliable and powerful computer systems. It would therefore be unwise, if not a little arrogant, to look too far into the future without at least a cursory glance back to the progression of machines that have already transformed many people's working lives.

After the presentation of the history, the nature of computers, and their key input, processing, storage and output technologies, will be addressed. Fear not, this chapter does not degenerate into a plethora of technobabble. That said, certain hardware genres and developments need to be appreciated as a background to the more organizationally centred analysis that follows in future chapters. After all, unless the capabilities and limitations of grass-roots technologies are embraced, any analysis concerning their impact on people at work, and on business organizations in general, will be missing a key anchor to the already murky seabed of future reality.

THE RAMPANT PACE OF CHANGE

Electronic computing has grown from nothing into one of the world's largest industries in just half a century. American businesses alone have spent over two trillion dollars on computer programming over the last fifty years,[39] and around one hundred million machines, mainly desktop personal computers, have now been sold. Glancing back across the rampant evolution of computing's adolescent generations therefore serves, at the very least, as a reminder of the advances humanity is capable of achieving in a very short space of time. After all, machine capacities and capabilities now taken for granted were hopeful pipedreams five or ten years ago, and decades previously were nothing more than idle fantasy.

In the late 1970s customers withdrew money from their bank accounts over the counter at their own branch. If you had told them that a decade later they would instead be served with cash and their balance via a computing device sunk into the wall of their local high street, then you would almost certainly have been greeted with a high level of scepticism. If you had subsequently informed them they would be able to use *any* such ATM (automatic teller machine) at any time of day, and that cheques would become secondary to debit cards automatically linked to their bank accounts, it is unlikely they would have even truly appreciated the *concept*, let alone accepted its future application.

Scepticism concerning the potential life-style transforming capabilities of new technologies remains to this day. A cashless society, video telecommunications as the norm, work and modelling in virtual environments, interactive-software entertainment, and intelligent software slaves to do our bidding; all these and more really *are* on the near horizon. To the majority, however, their widespread realization seems implausibly remote. For even when we accept that some boffin in some lab has prototyped the hardware, we still find it difficult to relate these mind-twisting concepts back to our own day-to-day routines. I mean, let's be honest, most people's business and domestic lives, and the nature of customers and organizations, can't really change that much over a decade or so, can they? Look back and they already have, and several times, thanks in recent years to technological advances spearheaded by our new friend or foe, the computer. So now try, for a few pages, to forget what life *is* like, and instead attempt to appreciate how it once was. The impact of how computer technologies have already transformed human civilization and its business communities may then become apparent, leaving you more receptive to the potential impact of current and future developments as explored herein.

FROM HUMBLE BEGINNINGS

For thousands of years human beings have dreamt of creating machines to assist in their mental as well as in their physical labours. As early as 3000 BC, the Mesopotamians were using the abacus to store numbers as an aid in mathematical calculations. Over four and a half millennia had to pass, however, before Blaise Pascal, French scientist and tax collector, created the first mechanical calculators in 1642. Like many technological developments since, his devices were met with fierce opposition by those who believed that such mechanisms would put people out of work.

It was over one hundred and eighty years before the next significant development in calculating machine technology arrived, with Cambridge professor Charles Babbage creating his famous 'Difference Engine' designs in 1823. His device was intended to aid in the calculation of astronomical, ballistics and engineering tables to an accuracy of up to twenty decimal places. Unfortunately, due to problems with funding and engineering accuracy, it was never successfully completed. In 1990, however, a team of researchers at the London Science Museum, using Babbage's initial drawings as a blueprint, successfully built a working Difference Engine, thus illustrating the validity of his designs. The completed machine was composed of over 4,000 machined parts and weighed three tons.[40]

After abandoning the Difference Engine, Babbage went on to a more ambitious project — his 'Analytic Engine' (1882) — which sought to use punched cards for storing instructions, a technique pioneered in 1804 by Joseph-Marie Jacquard in the control of a infinitely programmable weaving loom. With the adoption of interchangeable cards to sequence instructions into the Analytic Engine, the notion of 'computer programming' was effectively conceived. Indeed, Lady Ada Augusta, working on the Analytic Engine with Babbage, developed several of the programming techniques still used extensively by programmers today. The Analytic Engine was also the first machine to represent symbols by codes and capable of making logical comparisons. Unfortunately, as with the earlier Difference Engine, attempts to build a successful prototype were frustrated by the accuracy of the mechanical engineering of the day.

It is thus interesting to note that pioneering developments in computing were limited more by technological capabilities than by conceptual hurdles. Today the reverse may be argued to be true, with many potential users of computers and new communications media unable or unwilling to cross the conceptual barriers necessary in the adoption of new technologies and resulting working practices.

In 1887 American inventor Dorr Eugene Felt patented a simpler but far more successful calculating device christened the 'Comptometer'. Later developed by William Sears-Burroughs, who added a printing mechanism, this machine was adopted by the United States Treasury and evolved to become the most widely used accounting machine of the early twentieth century. Another early pioneer of a similar period was Herman Hollerith, whose punched-card systems for large-volume data sorting were being developed and marketed in the early 20th century by a consortium known as the Computer Tabulating-Recording Company, or the C-T-R. In 1914 C-T-R took on one Thomas John Watson as its General Manager. Ten years later came the change of name from the C-T-R company to International Business Machines, with IBM remaining the single biggest corporate icon of computer hardware development and production to this day.

COLOSSAL DEVELOPMENTS

By the 1940s, electromechanical and electronic technologies were increasingly being utilized in experiments with more and more complex calculating devices. In 1942, a team headed by Alan Turing at the General Post Office (GPO) Research Establishment in London began work on Colossus Mark 1. In many respects this was the world's first electronic computer, although its designers did not attribute it with such a label. Colossus went on to play a crucial role for the allies in World War II, deciphering the apparently impregnable German Enigma codes in 1943. A more powerful Colossus Mark II soon followed, using 2,400 thermionic values and capable of reading a then-amazing 5,000 characters per second.

Across the Atlantic in 1945, the Electronic Numerical Integrator and Computer (ENIAC) was created in the University of Pennsylvania to calculate ballistics tables for the US army. A mighty machine over thirty yards in length, weighing thirty tonnes, and programmed by 6,000 simple on/off switches that had to be manually reset for each calculation run, its 18,000 vacuum tubes drew so much power that the lights of Philadelphia were supposed to have dimmed when ENIAC was turned on.[41]

Having to have all of its switches painstakingly reset to perform a different type of calculation made ENIAC rather inflexible. John von Neumann, a collaborator on the project, addressed this problem by deducing that if a computer could store its own program in some internal memory then it would become far more versatile. Subsequently in 1949 a team at Cambridge University in England built the EDSAC (electronic delay storage automatic computer) as the world's first stored-program computer.

As the 1950s dawned, commercial computers built from thousands of the bulky, unreliable vacuum tubes on which ENIAC and EDSAC had been based heralded the start of the *first generation* of the modern computer age. On 14th June 1951, the first UNIVAC (universal automatic computer), was delivered to the US census bureau, the first machine built for business rather than scientific or military application. UNIVAC's memory was based upon thousands of tiny ferrous rings (or *cores*) laced on a matrix of fine wires. Each ring could be magnetized or demagnetized into either an 'on' or an 'off' state, allowing for the storage of one *bit* (or binary digit) of information. To supplement such storage (which was extremely bulky and very expensive), punched cards were also used to hold programs and data to be processed.

In the UK a couple of years later, the food giant Lyons became the first organization to operate a commercial data processing application when their LEO (Lyons Electronic Office) system ran the payroll for their chain of tea houses. Like UNIVAC, the original LEO computer was based upon vacuum tubes and processed data from punched cards. Also like UNIVAC and other first generation machines, the original LEO proved highly unreliable, with about 50 of its 6,000-odd vacuum tubes failing every week.

ENTER THE TRANSISTOR

Computers started to become faster, smaller and far more reliable when semiconductor components became available to replace the vacuum tubes which had been used as the electronic switching devices within all first generation machines. Although the first transistor was built in the Bell

Labs in the USA in 1947, it was not released to the world at large until 1952. By the mid- to late-1950s, transistors had begun to revolutionize the world of electronics, and the first all-transistor computer (the TX-0) was completed in the MIT Lincoln Labs in the USA in 1958. The TX-0 was also one of the first computers to possess a video display screen, and incredibly remained in use until 1975.

The *second generation* of computer adolescence, hinging upon the replacement of the vacuum tube with the transistor, also saw the introduction of *assembly languages*. These made computers far easier to program, as abbreviations were used to represent computer instructions rather than just reams of numbers. Higher-level languages such as COBOL (common business oriented language, 1959) were subsequently developed using even clearer English-style instructions. The development of these languages proved critical for the widespread adoption of computers across business, as at this time there was a dearth of skilled programmers capable of machine instruction at the most basic, mathematical level.

INTEGRATION & THE THIRD GENERATION

The *third generation* of computing was spawned in the mid-1960s with the introduction of integrated circuits. Previously each transistor within a computer or other electronic system had been a discrete physical component. Integrated circuit technology changed all this, with photographic methods being employed to allow many transistors and other components to be etched upon silicon layers within single microchips. In addition to transistor arrays used to perform logical calculations, integrated circuit memory chips were also quickly developed to replace the expensive iron core storage of the previous two decades.

As third generation developments continued, the large scale integration (LSI) of electronic components upon silicon chips made computer hardware far cheaper, more compact, and even more reliable. Manufacturers, most notably IBM with their highly successful System/360 range, were able to mass-market computers to small and medium-sized companies who had not previously been able to afford them. The computer industry thus began to grow apace, with machines being applied across an increasing range of business applications. In the first month after its System/360 range was launched, IBM took orders for computers worth over \$1bn.[42] Also of tremendous importance at this time were developments allowing computers to 'multi-task' several procedures simultaneously. Machines therefore became capable of running interactive customer service applications such as reservation booking and credit confirmation.

THE MICROPROCESSOR AGE

The large scale integration of components onto silicon chips continued into the 1970s, leading to very large scale integration (VLSI), with tens of thousands of individual components being etched onto some integrated circuits. This allowed component manufacturer Intel to introduce the first microprocessor (the 4004) in 1971. Heralding the *fourth generation* of computing, microprocessors included all of a computer's central processing components on one silicon wafer. With the speed enhancements that resulted, computers became capable of executing up to one million instructions per second, and thus machine power began to be measured in MIPS (millions of instructions per second), as it is to this day.

As well as permitting cheaper and more powerful mainframes, the widespread availability of microprocessors from the mid-1970s allowed for the birth of the personal computer (PC), an isolated machine with internal processing capacity and small enough not to consume a medium-sized desk. The first PC, the Altair 8800 (1975), was a simple box programmed via on/off switches. It didn't even have a keyboard or display screen, and only boasted 256 characters of internal memory (enough to store perhaps two or three sentences!). Sold for just \$397, however, the Altair did succeed in capturing the imagination of electronics enthusiasts across the USA.[43]

Not many years later, more practical, mass-market PCs with display screens and keyboards appeared from the likes of Apple Computer (1977) and Tandy (with Radio Shack's TRS-80 range, 1978). Machines from these manufacturers were aimed at the business market, unlike those from other successful computer manufacturers of the period, including Atari, Commodore and Sinclair, who concentrated on home computers primarily for playing games. The most significant computer to be launched at this time was the IBM PC, which saw the light of day in the summer of 1981 in the United States (and subsequently in 1983 in the United Kingdom).

Since the 1980s, the IBM PC has dominated personal computing. When launching their product, IBM carefully evaluated what business customers really wanted from their machines — namely reliability and after-sales support, coupled with the possibility for future expansion. These characteristics were and remain more important than technical excellence and innovation for most business users. After all, when an organization starts entrusting its data to a computer system, it has to be confident that the technology will work reliably, with help readily available should problems occur. IBM additionally guaranteed the success of their PC by permitting its architecture to become 'open'. In other words, they allowed other manufacturers to freely 'clone' compatible PCs and add-on, 'peripheral' hardware devices.

In contrast to IBM, most PC manufacturers in the late 1970s and early 1980s opted for 'closed' architectures and prevented other players copying their technology. Closed architecture policies proved to be unwise, however, as the majority of software houses which sprang up to publish PC programs concentrated on developing their wares for the open IBM PC standard. After all, by the early 1980s many closed architecture systems had already come and gone, and programmers didn't want to risk investing their time in the development of software for computers only produced by one manufacturer. The range and quality of programs available for the IBM PC (its 'software base') therefore rapidly became larger than for any other computer. In turn this made buyers more keen to purchase IBM-compatible machines, further increasing their market dominance. Today, over 90% of all PCs sold are IBM compatibles, with microchip giant Intel shipping more than thirty million microprocessors to the manufacturers of such machines in 1993 alone.[44]

THE FIFTH GENERATION

Arguably we are still caught in the final throes of the fourth generation of computing, even though the concept behind a *fifth generation* (to be realized in the 1990s) was announced by the Japanese in 1982. That the fourth generation has lasted twenty years may be attributed to the stiff hurdle for fifth generation realization as presented by the Japanese over a decade ago. By their definition, fifth generation computers will be extremely user-friendly, offering a far greater scope of application than fourth generation machines. Moreover, they will be able to accept input via voice-recognition systems, will understand 'natural' human language, and perhaps most significantly will process *knowledge* as well as raw data. True fifth generation machines will therefore need to possess some degree of *artificial intelligence*, a feat of software engineering which still eludes the mental capacity of human beings. *Smart* software 'entities' are now being conceived, however (as discussed in **chapter 4**). We are therefore still enveloped in the night of the fourth generation with the sunlight of the fifth yet to emerge over the horizon.

Progress is, however, being made apace. The widespread adoption of desktop, windows-based graphical environments, for example, has led to computer user-friendliness increasing in leaps and bounds. Additionally, limited voice-recognition systems do now exist (as discussed later in this chapter), and *expert systems* have been created wherein computers apply a complex set of rules (or *heuristics*) to a pre-programmed knowledge base in order to solve problems in a narrow field such as medical diagnosis or geological forecasting. We can therefore be fairly certain that a fifth generation of incredibly powerful, very-easy-to-use computers *is* just around the corner. When they arrive, we may finally begin to assign 'creative' mental tasks as well as repetitive, logical processes to the technology that now shares our offices. The real workplace revolution may thus be yet to come.

FROM CALCULATOR TO COMMUNICATOR

A historical backdrop has now been painted against which future advances in computer application and technology may be viewed in some developmental context. The hardwares and softwares necessary to breathe life into the concepts presented in the previous and subsequent chapters may still seem far distant, although perhaps not quite as challenging as they first appeared. It can already be appreciated that a 'staggering pace of change' in computer development has become the norm, with technological leaps being achieved about once per decade 'comparable to the four-thousand-year path from horse and cart to bullet train'.[45]

Some of the most fundamental mental hurdles for far more widespread developments in computer application are already starting to be cleared. Most people now accept the *use* of information technology at work, and equally the fact that they will have to use many *different* systems throughout their working lives. This is in sharp contrast to the attitude of previous generations, where the majority of the population would learn a single craft to be practised for life. Typesetting, for example, changed little for decade upon decade. Then, in the 1980s, new computer-controlled lithographic printers replaced systems reliant on the manual shuffling and placement of individual characters cast from metal. Now, in the 1990s, printing is facing yet new changes that will remove even more human involvement from the process of translating words from keyboard to page, or even keyboard to compact disk or information super-highway. As in many other industries, in the time it has taken for one new technology to comfortably replace the old, others have already arisen to take their place.

Today, therefore, it is not enough to simply *accept* new information technologies in order to remain competitive and employed. Rather, we have to accept to *continue to accept* them; fostering our knowledge and applying age-old principles in new ways as the hardware with which we work relentlessly evolves. Soon computers are likely to separate, even liberate, work from the technology of work. The administrative focus of most managers will therefore be able to shift toward the process — the *meaning* — rather than the *medium* of their endeavours. The data machines Mankind has created will have become catalysts for continual instability, creating environments across which we will have to be more certain of our priorities, values and abilities than ever before. For this reason if for no other, *everybody* in business needs to be aware of the nature of computer systems and their current and emerging technologies. As computers have evolved, so too has the make-up of organizations contingent upon their application (as discussed in **chapter 3**). To ignore the anatomy of the computer is to opt for ignorance of the most powerful force driving and permitting new patterns of work and organization.

THE NATURE OF THE BEAST

Flick through almost any book introducing and espousing the nature of computer systems, and you are likely to come across a graphical representation of a computer as a four-component data system. Such a model is illustrated in **figure 2.1**, and indeed the hardware of any system may be depicted in this fashion. Taking a modern desktop PC as an example, the input hardware will probably comprise a typewriter-style QWERTY keyboard and a mouse, output will be displayed on a monitor

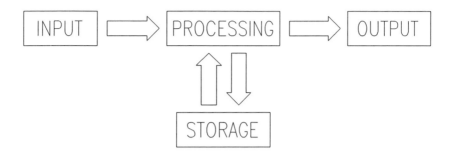

Figure 2.1 **The Classical Model of Computer Hardware**

screen or directed to a printer, long-term data storage will be upon hard and floppy magnetic disks, and finally processing will be carried out deep within the innards of the large, metal box that also serves to keep the monitor a comfortable height above the desk.

Whilst the above model proves useful in most basic introductions to computer hardware, it only serves to illustrate the system components necessary for data *processing*. As noted in the first chapter, computer systems will soon be used just as widely for *communications* as for data manipulation, with rapid developments occurring even today in areas like *computer telephone integration* (CTI). The value of many systems will therefore become partly dependent upon their ability to communicate with external systems across a range of information channels. Herein we will subsequently adopt an extended model of computer hardware as depicted in **figure 2.2**. Within this model, external hardware and facilities are included as a fifth element of the system, effectively representing all other interlinked computers that may be accessed. The importance of network hardwares and the required infrastructure for computer communications is thereby highlighted.

With the model in **figure 2.2** in mind, a broad overview of computer hardware will now be presented. In particular, emphasis will be placed upon emerging input, output, storage and communications devices, as it is these that will enable the realization of many of the developments in softwares, working practices and working structures discussed and predicted across other chapters. The focus within the following will also be directed in the main toward PC rather than mainframe computer

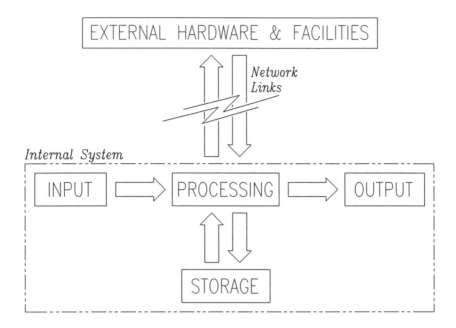

Figure 2.2 Computer Hardware: The Total System

technologies, as it is networks of interlinked PCs that will undoubtably form the backbone of the information infrastructures of the future, and to which the majority of managers and other employees will have immediate access.

AND THIS MEANS YOU!

A few readers may at this point feel a desire to skip ahead to **chapter 3**, somehow convincing themselves that it is not *they* who really need to be aware of developments on the hardware frontier. After all, isn't that what IT personnel are employed to take care of? There are, however, two important reasons for all of us to achieve a basic level of hardware literacy. Firstly, if you are not able to speak the jargon of the techies and the guy in the next office who can, then you may well allow others to get away with the installation of inappropriate technology. This may well lead to a loss of organizational competitiveness, especially if investments in critical new technologies (such as facilities for electronic data interchange

(EDI)) do not take place. Almost certainly, many organizations in future will refuse to trade with those whose systems they cannot access for electronic trading. Similarly, others may expect data super-highway connections for video-conferencing or virtual reality link-ups. The nature and capacity of an organization's information infrastructure will in future prove critical to its success or failure. Everybody should thus have some idea as to what is really going on.

Even if you fail to be convinced by the above argument, there is another reason as to why all managers should have some basic under-standing of the computer hardware lexicon. Increasingly, due to the cost of information systems and the accelerating pace of technological change, many large companies are outsourcing their IT functions to contractors in the marketplace.[46] It is therefore likely that many managers will find themselves negotiating with external IT suppliers regarding the specifica-tion of system requirements. Whilst this does not imply that in future we will all need extensive training in hardware engineering and software design, it does suggest that an awareness of computer peripherals and technologies would prove most wise.

If you turn up at a garage and simply state that you want to buy 'a car', then you are not very likely to be sold one with a towbar. If you know that trailers and caravans exist before you visit, however, and feel that you may purchase one or the other in the near future, then you can specify that you want a car with a towbar and a certain engine capacity. The vehicle purchased will not function any differently when you drive it away from the garage, but at some point in the future the fact that you explored 'expansion options' will save you both expense and aggravation. The same kind of argument applies when purchasing computer hardware. Sadly, many purchasers today only discover long after acquisition that their hardware is either unsuited for future expansion or will prove prohibitively expensive to upgrade. Managers therefore need to be have some awareness of both present and *potential future* hardware require-ments when faced with tech-spouting IT salesmen and enthusiasts.

COMMUNICATING WITH THE MACHINE

Before specific input and output peripherals and technologies are discussed, it is worth noting that just as computers in general have evolved through many 'generations', so have the range of interfaces that may now be employed for *human-computer interaction* (HCI). Different interface genres are particularly important to bear in mind when discussing the hardware (or *peripherals*) used to communicate with computers, as each interface type places different demands upon the devices required to facilitate communication between human being and machine. A brief summary of the generations of human-computer interface is illustrated in **table 2.1**.

As can be seen from the table, first generation human-computer interfaces require the user to type in specific, character-based instructions. They are therefore often referred to as a *CLIs* (command line interfaces), with probably the most common example being the DOS (disk operating system) CLI used upon IBM PCs. Under this type of interface, to copy a data file from one location to another, a user has to accurately type in a symbolistic command along the lines of:

COPY [location]:\MY-FILE.TXT [new location]

GENERATION	INTERFACE TYPE	BASIS OF INTERACTION
First	**CLI** (Command Line Interface)	**SYMBOLS** (Text commands)
Second	**GUI** (Graphical User Interface)	**ICONS** (2-D pictures activated within screen windows)
Third	**VR** (Virtual Reality)	**OBJECTS** (3-D representations directly manipulated within virtual space)

Table 2.1 The Generations of Human-Computer Interface

For those without an affinity for programming, the use of symbolic text strings for computer communication can prove troublesome. Because of this, the second generation of human-computer interface, the *GUI* (graphical user interface) is based upon clear, two-dimensional pictorial icons rather than symbols. Most people find icons easier to relate to than symbols, as they provide an interface based upon a metaphor of the real world (the computer screen usually being scattered with items common in the office such as a filing cabinets). Within a GUI, icon interaction takes place within movable, resizable display windows, with menus also being available to carry out certain operations. The most famous GUIs are Microsoft® *Windows*™ for the IBM PC, and the highly intuitive desktop found upon all Apple Macintosh™ computers.

Graphical user interfaces do, however, have their limitations. In particular, they provide a poor medium for non-linguistic human communication, not to mention being extremely cumbersome for applications involving 3-D visualization and design work. As a consequence, we have recently witnessed the development of various modes of virtual reality (VR) human-computer interface, wherein a user can work directly with identifiable virtual *objects*. Such objects are represented within a computer-generated 3-D domain, and possess readily identifiable spatial and physical attributes. Actions undertaken via a VR interface therefore more closely approximate to real-world human experiences than those employing previous-generation techniques for HCI. Effectively, VR interfaces allow their users to look *through* rather than *at* computer displays, or to become fully *immersed* within a simulated cyberspace environment. VR interfaces hence provide the ultimate, most natural means of human-computer interaction, and may in future be able to stimulate all of our senses in order to provide a man-machine medium indistinguishable from reality.

CLARIFYING DEFINITIONS

It is important to note at this point that it is possible, and often desirable, to draw a distinction between virtual reality *interfaces* (based upon the manipulation of *3-D graphics objects*), and virtual reality *systems* (which allow users to work with *virtual representations* of real-world phenomena). Whilst all virtual reality interfaces clearly involve the use of virtual reality systems, the converse may not necessarily be the case. As noted

in the first chapter, an electronic mail system offers a virtual representation of reality, allowing 'letters' to be 'posted' electronically over a
computer network. Such a *system* will probably not, however, involve the
use of 3-D virtual reality graphical *interface*.

The fact that we effectively have both broad and narrow definitions of
virtual reality can probably be attributed to the fact that 'VR' has for
many simply become a marketing term used in association with certain
technologies for immersing the user in 3-D graphics worlds. Indeed, as
the concept of VR began to 'flame out' around 1992, many of its
pioneers:

> . . . began scrambling to change . . . [their] . . . shingles from
> virtual reality to something roughly synonymous but less
> tainted — telepresence, augmented reality, immersion tech-
> nology. Anything to get some distance from the all too vivid
> spectacle of hype-fuelled, VR road-and-media show that
> rocketed VR pundits to the pinnacle of pop culture.[47]

It is equally important for the business user to cut through the 'hype',[48]
as it is all too easy to see VR purely as an interface technology for
training applications and video games when in practice it is a much wider
concept which will have a profound impact on organizational and social
structures over the coming decades. Therefore, as stated in **chapter 1**,
throughout this book the concept of 'virtual reality' will be taken to
encompass any representation or metaphor of the physical world, encoded
in computer software, with which human beings may freely interact.
Within the following sections concerning computer input and output
peripherals, however, the term will also inevitably be employed in its
narrower context to specifically refer to 'realistic' object-centred, human-
computer interfaces concerned with complex forms of human sensory
stimulation.

RECEIVING HUMAN INPUT

We have come a long way since computers only accepted data punched
onto cards or encoded across banks of switch combinations. For several
decades, most information to be input has been typed upon flat keyboards
laid out in the familiar QWERTY configuration adopted from the manual

typewriter. Although more ergonomically styled keyboards have become available (such as the Malatron model, curved around two human hands[49]), it is unlikely they will come to replace the *defacto* QWERTY layout. The first reason for this is the sheer expense that would be incurred in replacing all existing keyboards, coupled with the cost and hassle of retraining operators. Secondly, in theory at least, mass-typing will become less common as alternative methods of data entry proliferate.

After the keyboard, probably the most common computer input peripheral is the mouse. Moved over a flat surface, mice (so named because their cable resembles a tail!), allow a 'pointer' arrow to be moved around the computer screen. Mice hence enable the rapid operation of GUIs, as well as being reasonably effective in the control of many CAD (computer-aided design) applications and 3-D modelling systems.[50] Mice usually track operator motion by opto-mechanically registering the movement of two rollers trollied against a free-rolling central ball. Although usually encountered in the guise of a smoothly-rectangular little wedge, mice have now evolved into wand-like *pen mice* incarnations to be stroked against a smooth surface, as well as into the *trackballs* ('upside-down mice') often integral to modern portable computers. Indeed, even a *footmouse* is now available, based upon a directional pedal, and allowing coarse motions to be registered if both an operator's hands must be kept free.[51]

TRACKING MOTION IN 3-D

Whilst simple mice and trackballs offer a far more responsive means of computer interaction than available via punching keytops, they are less than ideal when motion within 3-D space needs to be conveyed to a computer system boasting an immersive 3-D VR interface. Various *gesture devices* are now available, however, allowing user motions to be 'tracked'. The most simple of these are *wands* or *flying-mice* which are simply held in the hand and moved freely in space. These usually record motion by sensing the relative strength of magnetic fields (and/or resultant eddy fields) across all three motion planes. Alternatively, a source may transmit ultrasonic signals to be decoded via a sensor into corresponding operator manipulations in 3-D space.

Also available as a 3-D VR control device is the SpaceBall™,[52] which provides a means of applying force and torque within a virtual environment. The device's palm-sized ball is mounted on a shaft that moves like a conventional video-game joystick except for the fact that rotation permits six degrees of motion freedom. Far more spectacularly, various *dataglove* gesture devices are also on the market, allowing all of the complex and subtle motions of the human hand and fingers to be fed into a computer.[53] When immersed in virtual reality graphics worlds, the use of a dataglove allows the user to grasp and accurately manipulate objects in 3-D space. The position of the hand is again tracked either electromagnetically or ultrasonically, whilst flexible fibre-optic cables or plastic strain gauges are employed to register the position of the operator's fingers. Datagloves are destined to fall in price rapidly in the next few years, and indeed a so-called PowerGlove™ has already been produced by Mattel for its Nintendo home-entertainment system.

Peripherals for tracking head movement are also essential in the creation of immersive VR interface systems, allowing the user to 'look around' a 3-D graphics world simply by altering the position of their cranium. Sensors for registering head movement are almost universally built into the head-mounted displays (HMDs) that provide the user with immersive 3-D vision (see subsequent section). As with other motion-sensing peripherals, HMDs usually rely on electromagnetic or ultrasonic mechanisms. Alternatively, electro-physiological sensors may be secured against the skin to detect muscle movement, although this can prove uncomfortable for the user.

Far more complex peripheral bodywear is likely to be developed as the corporate and leisure interest in VR interfaces grows. Technologies for registering the position of the body are already being applied in the development of entire body suits. As an alternative to wearing a suit, items of peripheral 'VR jewellery' for the wrists, ankles, fingers, waist, ears, forearms, neck and hair are also likely to become available as an alternative means of body-motion sensing. Either body suits or a jewellery sensor array will allow the complete orientation and motion of the operator's body to be tracked into virtual worlds within cyberspace, permitting the full and direct manipulation of data and other individuals on the human-computer interface.

CUTTING DOWN ON THE TYPING

Whilst the mouse is nearly indispensable for the operation of a GUI, and

3-D position tracking devices allow for the powerful manipulation of VR interfaces, neither do a great deal to reduce the drudgery of keyboard operations. Fortunately, for those tired of repetitive data keying, or who need to process graphic images, we now have a hardware family known as *scanners*. These devices, as the name suggests, directly capture images from pages of information. They also come in three basic variants.

Most expensive and most reliable are *flatbed scanners*, with a large glass plate upon which the material to be scanned is placed. For the more price conscious there are *hand scanners*, typically boasting a 4″ scan width (enough to accommodate one column of text, a small graphic or a photograph), and moved manually over the source item. Finally, scanning *wands*, such as bar-code readers, are also moved across an item by hand. Wands are also now available specifically for reading data from an envelope's address panel.

Whatever type of scanner is used, all that it will feed into the computer is a graphic image of the original source material. This may be all that is required if the user simply wants to display the image within a document. When a page of text has been scanned, however, it is more usual to require the input to be converted into words in a text format that can be manipulated in a word processor or *desktop publisher* (DTP) package. To convert a scanned image into an ordinary text file, *optical character recognition* (OCR) software needs to be employed. Only in the past few years have such OCR systems become reasonably reliable, cheap and widely available, and as they further proliferate the mass re-keying of previously printed data should become an extinct phenomenon. Thus, in future, those who live their lives at the keyboard will spend a greater proportion of their time editing, manipulating and presenting text rather than simply bashing it into the machine.

Another key area of development in non-keyboard data entry involves the application of a stylus to write directly upon a computer screen. Such *pen-based computing* is rapidly advancing, allowing portable computers to be created akin to conventional notebooks upon which the user can write and scribble. Some modern systems self-train themselves to read their owner's handwriting, and also respond to certain specific gestures and motions. To delete a word, for example, you can simply scrub it out, or to insert text you can sketch a caret mark at the appropriate juncture. Many people find pen-based (also called *gesture-based*) interfaces more natural to use than those involving mouse and keyboard, as they feel they are more directly manipulating items upon their computer display.

Already *personal digital assistants* (PDAs) using pen-based technology are available from a variety of manufacturers (the most notable being the Newton™ range of PDAs from Apple Computer and the Cassio *Zoomer*). Integrated wireless communications technologies are now also being incorporated into dedicated PDA hardware. The first such 'personal communicator' (the *Magic Link* from Sony) is due to go on sale in early 1995, with digital network support from AT&T. Wireless communications for Apple's Newton range are also soon to follow. Henceforth, employees will be able to stay in constant contact with their organization's computer system, accessing files and sending messages via pen strokes on pocket hardware with the dimensions of a medium-sized paper diary.

Other notable methods of gathering computer data include the use of *magnetic ink character readers* (MICRs), as employed to read the sort codes on cheques, and systems for voice or even vision recognition. Sadly, the latter method of input is very unlikely to become widespread for many years to come due to the sheer bulk and complexity of data that needs to be processed to analyse even a still camera image. When visual recognition systems do emerge, they will probably find initial application in areas such as security vetting, allowing authorized users and employees to be rapidly and uniquely identified.

Systems for voice recognition, on the other hand, are far less embryonic and have already been developed to the point where they are in use in applications where only a narrow control lexicon is required. One rudimentary but timesaving voice-recognition system, available for high-end Apple Macintosh computers, allows the user to place a telephone call by simply saying a name which the software then looks up in its telephone database in order to dial the number.[54] Other examples of voice-recognition application include systems used to control the inventory in a junkyard, to calculate anaesthetic dosages, to answer stock market queries, and to sort packages.[55] Voice-controlled video recorders are also in development. In fact, in any situation where a computer user is likely to have both of their hands employed, the application of a voice-recognition system may be of benefit.

Voice-recognition systems can also aid the disabled in their interaction with computers, as well as allowing writers and those collecting data upon the move to enter their thoughts and findings directly. This said, systems capable of recognizing continuous speech (rather than just isolated words) are still very much in their infancy, with most systems in use today only responding to a particular operator who has to clearly state precise instructions such as 'up', 'down', 'start' and 'end'.

Finally on the 'input' side, it should be noted that sampling hardware to simply *record* audio signals (rather than to *analyse* them into meaningful text and commands), is increasingly widespread. Many music studios, for example, now record directly into computer memory rather than onto magnetic tape as in years gone by. Similarly, techniques for digitizing moving video images are now extensively employed in the editing of visual material. The main advantage of such systems is that they allow non-linear, near-instantaneous access to the required material without having to spool through miles of film or videotape to find each shot as it is required.

GETTING THE FULL PICTURE

Technologies for computer output are clearly just as significant as those relating to data input. After all, it is what comes *out* of the machine that really matters at the end of the day. If data just disappears into bottomless silicon bowels never to be seen again, then it might as well not have been fed into the computer in the first place.

Most computer output still occurs in a visual format, with by far the most common display peripheral being the CRT (cathode ray tube) TV-style monitor. Most CRT monitors now boast excellent, high-quality colour displays. They are, however, bulky and power-hungry, making them unsuitable for inclusion within portable computer hardware. The latter therefore rely either on *liquid crystal display* (LCD) technologies to provide flat, low-power screens, or occasionally on gas plasma displays (although these do require mains power).

Potentially, LCD panels may one day replace all CRT monitors, saving energy and the environment, allowing screens to be hung on the wall, and removing the threat of health risks associated with the emission of electrostatic and high-frequency radiation from CRTs. In the short- and medium-term, however, the CRT monitor is likely to remain the dominant item of computer display hardware. This is mainly due to the fact that thin-film-transistor (TFT) LCD screens capable of producing high-quality colour images are extremely expensive to produce, especially in large sizes. Additionally, with the awareness of CRT-related health risks growing, many manufacturers are now offering 'low emission' monitors, whilst external screen filters to reduce electrostatic and high-energy CRT emissions are becoming commonplace. There has simply been too much R&D money invested over the years to allow the CRT screen to die without a fight!

TELEPRESENCE TECHNOLOGY

Whilst non-immersive virtual reality interfaces may be run quite successfully on conventional display screens (allowing the user to look *into* a graphics world), for immersion into a virtual world a head-mounted or *telepresence* display is required. 'Telepresence' simply refers to any system offering the user the illusion that they are actually present within another environment. Usually such an environment will be computer-generated, although systems have been demonstrated where an HMD-wearer experiences the images coming from two video cameras positioned within a similar headset worn by a second human being. With the latter arrangement, it becomes possible for many individuals to 'look through another person's eyes'. Such a facility can prove invaluable in applica-tions such as dental training, where ordinarily only a few people can see into the patient's mouth at any one point in time. However, with an instructor wearing a telepresence camera array and students using HMDs, as many observers as desired are able to watch the proceedings. Students do not even need to be in the same room (or even country) as the instructor if a network telepresence link is available.

Telepresence output peripherals operate by positioning small colour display screens before both eyes. A slightly different image is then sent to each screen, giving the wearer the impression of stereoscopic vision. Real feelings of space, size and depth can be portrayed to anybody wearing such a head-mounted peripheral, especially if (as in most systems) head motion is also tracked so that the images the operator is seeing are altered in sync as they physically 'look around'.

Many 3-D telepresence peripherals are now available, ranging from lightweight headsets through to goggles that 'consume the face' or even full-head helmets. A system called BOOM™ (binocular omni-orientated monitor) is also obtainable from Fake Space Labs. Unlike a 3-D headset, BOOM is simply looked into by the operator and pushed away when not required. Other variants of telepresence display come in the form of stereoscopic display glasses such as Crystal Eyes™, which allow the user to immerse themselves in a graphics world whilst simultaneously being able to see everything around them in reality.[56] There is even discussion of the possible development of contact lenses or lightweight glasses that will be capable of etching images on the retina using low-density lasers. A picture would therefore be formed directly upon the rods and cones that constitute the physiology of the eye, freeing VR interfaces of the limitations inherent in portraying images via display screen media.[57] Further immersive hardware technology developments are discussed in **chapter 5**.

THE PRINTED PAGE

Although being able to view computer output in splendid colour on a monitor screen or via immersive VR can be extremely important (if not entertaining!), today we still rely on the results of most computer-centred operations ending up on paper. In ten to twenty years the paperless office may finally be achieved, but until that point in time output peripherals allowing for the printout of documents and results will remain essential.

Over the past decade, many different technologies have been employed in the task of producing printed computer output, otherwise known as *hardcopy*. For many years, impact *daisywheel printers* fitted with a ring of cast letters, or *dot-matrix printers*, fitted with a row of minute pins, were most common, and thumped a fabric ribbon against a piece of paper to forge their printout. Nowadays, laser printers are more common for business correspondence, forming an image via the xerox process one complete page at a time. Dot-matrix machines are still required whenever multi-part copies need to be produced, however, as the laser printing process does not involve any physical impact to make an impression through sheets of ink-impregnated paper.

For low-end office and home use, *inkjet printers* that electrostatically spray ink onto the paper now dominate the market, being especially beneficial for cheap colour printing. New wax transfer mechanisms are also now emerging, which offer relatively cheap, high-quality colour printing to those who cannot afford to lash out thousands on a colour laser printer. By the turn of the century, colour options are likely to be available on the majority of printers encountered. This said, their productive application may be far more limited than it would be today, as paper-based communications cease to be of importance in a business world of e-mail, video-conferencing, EDI and virtual reality.

NON-VISUAL OUTPUT

Aside from screen and hardcopy images, the only other form of computer output likely to be encountered at present is in the form of synthesized audio. Programming computers to speak is far more straightforward than getting them to recognize the spoken word, as no 'understanding' is required. Today, PC sound cards are becoming widespread, and it is quite possible that the majority of standard desktop machines will be equipped with text-to-voice synthesis in the near future.[58] Such a facility may well be employed to allow PCs to read back typed documents, enabling their users to give their tired eyes a rest.

Finally on the output side, it should be noted that as immersive virtual reality technologies become more widespread and realistic, peripherals are likely to be developed that will offer physical as well as visual and auditory stimulation to the human body. Experiments have already been undertaken wherein tiny air bladders have been implanted into bodywear from gloves to full bodysuits. These can then be inflated and deflated as appropriate, to allow pressures and/or textures to be registered against the body as objects are encountered in virtual environments. The concept of *full-tactility datasuits* is most commonly discussed within literatures concerning the development of teledildonics (virtual sex systems), although applications for physical and tactile feedback from virtual reality experiences will be extremely diverse. Engineers, for example, will be able to *feel* materials in their hands, whilst doctors will be capable of operating in VR if they can be provided with a physical sensation of the virtual patient innards held between their instruments and virtual fingers.

To be able to mimic large forces against the body (as opposed to small-scale surface tactile pressures) peripheral mechanisms in addition to those relying upon air-bladder inflation/deflation will need to be developed. Indeed, force-feedback relying on air-bladder technology may not in the end be widely utilized, as more effective systems emerge based upon mechanical exoskeletal structures resemblant of lighter versions of the framework worn by Sigourney Weaver in the science fiction movie *Aliens*.[59]

WORKING IT ALL OUT

In the middle of **figures 2.1** and **2.2** we come across the 'processing' component of the computer system — the box of electronics into which all the other peripherals are connected and which forms the 'heart' of the machine. Some texts refer to the main computer housing as its CPU (central processing unit). This is, however, technically incorrect, as the CPU is simply the *microprocessor* chip upon which a computer is based. In contrast, the main housing of most computers contains far, far more — including the *motherboard* (main circuit board) on which the microprocessor, memory and other silicon chips reside, a *display card* to drive the computer's monitor, a power supply (to keep the machine alive!), and also hard and floppy *disk drives* (as reviewed in the next section). The microprocessor on which a computer is based does, however, provide the best indication of the system's raw power.

IBM PC and compatible personal computers, for example, are based upon a family of microprocessors manufactured by Intel. Inside most PCs today you will discover either an 80386, 80486 or Pentium microprocessor chip (the last being the most powerful), and hence people talk about '386, '486 and Pentium-based computers. At the time of writing an upgrade Pentium chip, the P54C, is just becoming available. Intel are also working on an even more powerful microprocessor code-named the *P6*.

Non-IBM-compatible PCs, such as Apple's Macintosh range, tend to be based upon microprocessors from Motorola, with typical CPU chips being the 68020, 68030, 68040 and 68060 (again the last listed being the most powerful). Motorola (in conjunction with Apple and IBM) have now also released a range of microprocessors under the 'PowerPC' banner, the first being the PowerPC 601, and with 'chips entitled the 603 and 620 to become available for use in portable PC and high-end workstations respectively.[60] PowerPC microprocessors form the heart of a new generation of PCs from both Apple *and* IBM, and are intended to provide direct competition for the Pentium and P6. Intel's 80% share of the microprocessor market[61] may therefore be seriously under threat over the next couple of years, with increased competition translating into keen prices for consumers.

The emergence of the PowerPC bodes well for users seeking widespread software compatibility. No longer will computer software packages be incompatible across different hardware *platforms* (you can't, for example, run Apple software on an IBM PC). Instead, with PowerPC software and hardware developments, new packages will have the ability to be 'platform-independent' — running on all desktop hardware variants. Business purchasers will hence not need to worry about system compatibilities and potential retraining costs if they change their PCs, leaving their attention free to be devoted to the peripherals and communications infrastructures available and in use across their organization.

Unfortunately, for computer users keen to explore cyberspace via virtual reality interfaces, the power of standard PCs still leaves a lot to be desired. Whilst 486 and upward PC systems are now capable of running some VR applications (most notably the SuperScape Toolkit from Dimension), in the mid-1990s most immersive VR systems still require a far more powerful (and expensive!) hardware platform. Workstations such as Silicon Graphic's Onyx therefore provide the processing *reality engines* behind most modern VR systems. Other platforms of note include SuperVison from UK VR specialist Division, Expiality from Virtuality (formerly W. Industries), and Pixel Planes, developed at the University of North Carolina. All of these hardware configurations rely on parallel processing (ie the ability of the system to perform many operations simultaneously), with the Pixel Planes hardware being so 'massively parallel' that it contains a separate microprocessor to control each of the 250,000 picture elements that constitute its display output! At the time of writing, such advanced VR set-ups can cost up towards £250,000,[62] although costs are continuing to spiral downwards.

COMPUTER DISKS & DATA STORAGE

The ability to capture, process and output data is largely irrelevant if a means for data storage is not available. Most modern media for data retention utilize some form of magnetic disk. These come in two basic variants — removable *floppy disks* that slot into the computer when required, and *hard disks* (usually resident within the main computer housing) which offer a far higher data capacity.

At present, the most popular floppy disk format is 3½" double-sided, high-density (3½" DS HD), storing just under 1.5 million characters of information[63] (around 400 pages of text) when used upon IBM PC or compatible systems. Modern hard disk drives (also known as *fixed disks*), using multiple disk layers in hermetically sealed casings, come in a range of sizes and with their capacity measured in *megabytes*. One megabyte

(1Mb) is equivalent to around 1 million *bytes* (or characters) of storage, and most hard disks today have a capacity of between 100 and 1000 Mb. A disk with a 1000 Mb storage capacity is more usually referred to as storing one *gigabyte* (Gb) of information, and thus techies involved in mass data storage will be heard talking in 'gigas'. At the time of writing, the largest hard disk listed in a supplier catalogue has a storage capacity of 4 Gb — over four billion characters of information, or enough to store the text of around three-and-a-half thousand average-length books.

As the demand for higher storage capacities increases (a photo-realistic graphic image can consume several megabytes of disk capacity), many standards for optical disks are emerging. These use lasers to permit a greater density of data to be written to and read from the disk surface. The most basic form of optical disk technology is CD-ROM (compact disk read only memory), allowing access to the 600 Mb of data that can now be pressed onto a 5″ CD. It must be appreciated that CD-ROM cannot be used to store user data (hence the term 'read only' memory), and that data on CD ROMS can only be accessed relatively slowly.[64] This said, CD disks are very cheap to produce, allowing for the widespread distribution of huge quantities of data. Whole libraries of books can be compressed onto one CD-ROM, with many interactive *multimedia* applications now available allowing users to access text, music, sound effects, still graphics and video images from a single CD. There is no doubt that CD-ROM will become a major publishing medium in the future. Already the 5″ CD is universal for the distribution of music, and with MPEG (motion picture experts group) standards for Video CD now firmly established,[65] and CD-ROM drives widespread across educational institutions, the cheap-and-cheery silver slices are set to enjoy a long life as *the* medium for *all* forms of digital data distribution.

For those wishing to both read and write data to optical media, *floptical disks*, identical in size to 3½″ floppy disks, offer 20 Mb of data storage. Faster and more expensive *magneto-optical* disks are also available, with capacities ranging from 128 to over 600 Mb. For those requiring even greater storage capacities, hardware allowing access to multiple optical disks can be purchased, offering storage capacities up into the multiple *terabytes* (thousands of gigabytes).[66]

In competition with optical disk media, high-capacity removable magnetic disks, coupling the storage capacity and speed of hard disks with the portability of floppy disks, are also now employed by those manipulating masses of data. At the time of writing, capacities range from 44 to over 270 Mb on disk cartridges as tiny as 1.8″ across. Externally boxed hard disk drives (that can be readily switched between different PCs) are also fairly common, offering employees eager to work at home an easy means of taking their own programs and data with them in their briefcase at the end of the day.

Non-disk-based 'solid state' memory storage on credit-card-sized media is also proliferating. Here, high-density memory chips store the computer data, with a tiny lithium battery preserving the contents of the card when it is removed from the computer. A standard for memory cards termed PCMCIA (personal computer memory card international association) has now emerged, ensuring compatibility between different systems. In particular, PCMCIA cards offer an ideal means of exchanging information between a desktop PC and a personal organizer, PDA or other pocket computer. When combined with microprocessor circuitry, solid-state memory cards are also frequently known as *smart cards*. These are already becoming common as a means of electronic identification, as well as being the potential currency medium across future 'cashless societies'. In the UK, tests are already under way to demonstrate the feasibility of an electronic-money smartcard entitled 'Mondex'.[67]

COMPUTER COMMUNICATIONS

As already discussed in **chapter 1**, world-wide computer *connectivity* will soon provide the information infrastructure and impetus towards new forms of work and organization. The actual practicalities of connecting one computer system to another, however, invariably prove both complex and laborious. *Networking* thus remains one of the areas of computing most shrouded in mystery and technobabble,[68] in turn leading to the potential benefits of interconnection being under-exploited by many users.

At a simple level, a computer *network* is created whenever two machines, be they PCs or mainframes, are linked together to pass data. Most networks, of course, comprise more than two machines, allowing many users to communicate, share data, and have access to the same software applications. In modern buildings and offices, *local area networks* (LANs) are now commonly used to interconnect scores of PCs, with a *server* computer controlling the network. The server is normally equipped with a large hard disk drive upon which data and applications programs to be accessed by all users on the network reside. With PCs connected to each other across a LAN, data can be swapped between users directly (without having to transfer it to floppy disks), and expensive peripherals such as laser printers can be shared. Communications facilities like electronic mail can also be used, saving on paper whilst permitting the rapid and certain communication of memos and other documentation to a great many recipients.

Whilst LANs increase user flexibility within the organization, for even greater benefits to be derived from computer interconnection the LAN needs in turn to be linked into a larger *wide area network* (WAN). Whilst most LANs rely on dedicated, machine-to-machine cabling technologies to interconnect every computer, WANs use a range of facilities to transmit signals between computers both nationally and internationally. Some WAN linkages take place over the global telecommunications network, using a device called a *modem* to access normal telephone lines. Standing for modulator/demodulator, modems allow individual PCs, or networks thereof, access to very wide scale networks such as the Internet, across which a whole host of communications facilities are available. As discussed in detail in **chapter 6**, Internet users may become embroiled in activities such as computer conferencing, electronic mail communications, or accessing programs and data 'posted' upon electronic *bulletin board systems* (BBSs). Many electronic databases can also be accessed and searched via an Internet connection, bringing a wealth of information to the fingertips of any user with a suitably networked computer.

In addition to using telephone lines, some companies have dedicated WAN connections between different plants and physical locations. These may take the form of electrical land lines (usually rented from telecommunications companies), or more usually fibre-optic cables. Links via satellite or microwave transmission are also used in the chain of computer communications nationally and internationally, with satellite systems in particular being destined to become widespread by early next century. Billionaire US entrepreneurs Bill Gates and Craig McGraw have plans for the creation of a $9bn global satellite communications system by the year 2001. Using 840 individual satellites orbiting at 400 miles above the earth, their Teledesic is intended to offer data, video and audio communication links across the planet using very high frequency transmissions from small ground-based antennas.[69] Whether this system gets off the ground or not, other similar ventures are surely destined to follow. The data patterns of cyberspace therefore really will be all around us early in the next century.

TRAVELLING BETWEEN GATEWAYS

The emerging data super-highways which receive so much journalistic attention these days are destined to utilize a great range of communications technologies in the transfer of data between their main information nodes or *gateways*. A gateway may be thought of as a railway station where data is sent by a computer user in order to catch the appropriate train through the information network. After catching its connection, the travelling data will navigate its own path from train to train across the system, eventually to arrive at the gateway from which it will be picked up by its intended recipient.

Most long-distance communications will pass through a great many gateways as they journey from one computer to another, making the route of most computer messages rather complex to represent, yet alone explain, in a non-technical manner. This said, **figure 2.3** attempts to illustrate how PCs in two different organizations may come to be linked for communications purposes. In the figure, the PCs used by *USER A* and *USER B* are both connected to local area networks controlled by a server computer. In most large companies there will be many such LANs and servers, all connected to a gateway which will allow data access into national and international network systems. To communicate between *ORGANIZATION A* and *ORGANIZATION B,* a wide area network will be formed across the various dedicated and public telecommunications connections that exist between their respective gateways. A message from *USER A* to *USER B* thereby flows from *USER A's* PC over a LAN to their server computer, out to their gateway, and across cyberspace to arrive at the gateway used by *ORGANIZATION B*. From here it will be routed though the appropriate LAN server to its recipient, *USER B*.

The above example is rather general, serving to indicate only one potential pathway for data communication between two simple PCs. It does, however, highlight the fact that computer communications is a highly complex field, making the emergence of the internationally interconnected global hardware platform we are beginning to witness all the more remarkable. Indeed, as years of research into data transmission

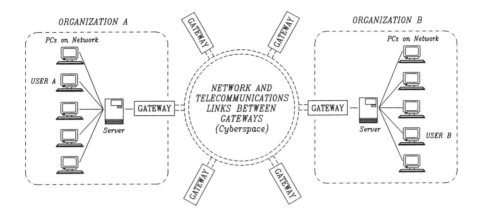

Figure 2.3 **PC Communications Across Organizations**

and compression finally bear fruit, and international standards emerge, most of us will simply be able to ignore the complexity of computer communications and just get on with our work. To get data from our PC to another will be as straightforward as directing our voice down a receiver to one of the 500,000 telephones interconnected worldwide.[70] What's more, computer communications networks will not only link us together for group working via text, sound and vision, or a multimedia amalgamation thereof. With developments in immersive virtual reality, high-speed connections will also permit instantaneous transportation into another person's virtual environment. Two or more geographically distant individuals will therefore be able to work (or play!) together in an intimate fashion, sharing and using physical space as they would if they had been brought together physically. We will, in a very 'real' sense, then begin to exist as entities *across* cyberspace, inhabiting electronic infrastructures as if they were physical, with distance becoming an arbitrary concept in human separation.

FROM PUNCHED CARD TO DATAGLOVE

This chapter has presented a broad and largely non-technical overview of the conception, adolescence and physiology of modern computer systems and their peripheral technologies. As a respected colleague once commented, however, the material has 'relied largely upon a "tower of Babel" approach', presenting categories of facts and ideas in progressions of lists that seem to go on forever without really getting anywhere. Unfortunately, any discussion regarding the essence and history of technology (as opposed to its application and wider social and organizational implications) tends to be like that. Perhaps, as new electronic media emerge allowing the non-linear communication of knowledge, so our exposure to the background material in front of which so many subjects parade will become more fulfilling and entertaining. After all, more advanced and widely interconnected computer systems should free human beings from repetitive drudgery, allowing our precious time to be focused almost exclusively upon the creative and the interesting. In the next chapter, we will indeed start to explore the real business implications of increased computer connectivity, looking ahead to a time when the structures of some organizations may become indistinguishably entangled within the data jungle of cyberspace.

The zaibatsus, the multinationals that shaped the course of human history, had transcended old barriers. Viewed as organisms, they had attained a kind of immortality . . .

William Gibson
Neuromancer

3
From Hierarchy to Virtual Organization

FOR CENTURIES ORGANIZATIONS HAVE been predicated upon the need to bring human beings together to cooperatively specialize in the production of goods and services. Across the vast majority of industries, workers have had to assemble within a common workplace (or visit the workplace of another) in order to undertake their role of productive activity or resource exchange. To make a car, for example, all assembly workers have needed to be present in the same factory, whilst to have a meeting all those involved have had to travel to a common location such as a boardroom.

For years organizations have also been able to operate in environments of comparative stability and predictability, permitting them the opportunity to invest in the extensive capital required for the large-scale mass-production of their products. With workers congregating daily at the physical locations housing these capital infrastructures, the boundaries of organizations have, to date, been clearly and uniquely defined. Joe Bloggs & Co., for example, has been the company resident at Unit 7, The Industrial Estate, Worksville, and known to employ Fred, Janet, Harry, Sally et al. in the production of 20,000 cardboard boxes, shovels, chocolates or whatever per year. However, with the emergence of new cyberspace technologies, and increasing product customization leading towards more flexible working arrangements in hypercompetitive market environments, this cosy state of affairs may be coming to an end. Indeed, in order to remain responsive to volatile market conditions, many organizations are discovering that they need to innovate new patterns of employee relationships. Frequently these are dependent upon the adoption of cybertechnologies. This chapter sets out to chart the evolution of organizational forms as new forms of working emerge. In particular, it describes how 'virtual organizations' may be spawned as connectivity continues across the global hardware platform.

THE EMERGENCE OF VIRTUAL ORGANIZATION

Books, reports and articles detailing 'virtual factories',[71] 'virtual companies',[72] 'virtual offices'[73] and 'virtual corporations'[74] now appear with increasing regularity. Although little coherence of definition has yet to emerge, all of the aforementioned *virtual organization* developments are associated with the use of cybertechnologies to allow people separated by time or distance to work together cohesively. The concept of virtual organization is therefore encapsulated in a desire to use information technology to enable a relaxation of the traditional physical constraints upon organizational formation and adaptation.

In addition to practitioner and academic interest, governments and other international bodies are now taking a distinct interest in virtual organizational developments. In the UK, an event entitled 'The Virtual Corporation' was held in mid-1994. This served as a launchpad for a Department of Trade and Industry initiative to back several projects charged with both realizing, and raising awareness of, developments in computer-supported cooperative work (CSCW). Across the European Community there are similar CSCW ventures, most notably the ESPRIT COMIC project. The buzz-term 'virtual organization' is consequently one likely to increase rather than decrease in popularity over the coming years. No manager should therefore remain ignorant of the plethora of new cybertechnology-enabled working practices now bundled together under the term's contentious metaphorical umbrella. In order to truly gauge the impact of virtual organization developments in context, however, it is important to first examine the general evolution of business organizations over the past few decades, and in particular the increasing trend toward the adoption of 'flexible' organizational structures.

ORGANIZATIONAL EVOLUTION

Technology has long played a critical role in driving the structure, size, diversity and complexity of the organizations that surround us. One hundred years ago technology was expensive and hence most industries were labour-intensive. As technological innovations accrued in the first half of this century, however, Western economies strengthened into previously undreamt of prosperity. In turn this led to a large-scale demand for consumer goods such as cars and domestic appliances. Organizations like the Ford Motor Company responded to the challenge with the creation of massive plants with dedicated technology that could produce the goods their customers were demanding. The products may have all been homogeneous (the Ford Model 'T' came in any colour so long as it was black), but then the new generation of mass-demand consumers had yet to be indoctrinated into the largely aesthetic whims of widespread differentiation. The same car — or washing machine or fridge — could be produced continually for ten years by the same dedicated plant and would still sell reliably to a content Mr. Smith and Mrs. Jones.

The logic concerning the mass-production of a few standardized products on dedicated production lines was simply one of scale, with cost-per-unit falling rapidly the higher the level of production. If a car manufacturer produced 200,000 rather than 100,000 automobiles a year, then it could sell them for less, as fixed overheads in both production and administration could be spread over a greater number of sales. Companies thus sought to be as big as possible. As noted by Alfred Chandler, however, there came a point when an organization was so large and unwieldy that it became impossible for a central management to run it effectively, as those in headquarters were simply too far removed from the breadth and scale of operations.[75]

From around the 1940s onwards companies therefore began to 'decentralize' in order to exhibit multidivisional structures. This allowed for the authority for the day-to-day running of different parts of the organization to be passed down the line to divisional management teams. The role of top executives in corporate headquarters subsequently became that of coordinating the actions of the divisional managers who reported to them. Expansive, multi-tiered *hierarchical structures* thereby came to be exhibited. First-line employees reported through ranks of supervisors and operational managers to divisional managers who were subsequently responsible to directors in the corporate headquarters, and ultimately to the managing director/chief executive officer. A representation of a hierarchical structure appears in **figure 3.1**, simplified to just three tiers for the purpose of clarity in illustration.

In general, classic hierarchical structures proved highly bureaucratic, with complex procedures and a great deal of 'red tape' to be encountered

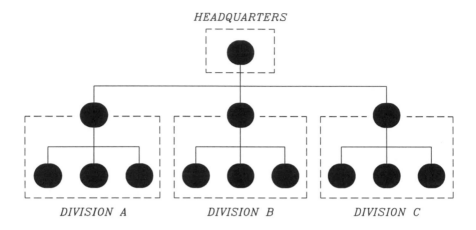

Figure 3.1 A Classic Hierarchical Structure

when passing information, authority and decisions up and down the organization. Sets of rules heavily dictated organizational processes, and:

> Depending on your position in the hierarchy of the organiz-
> ation, so were your communications patterns prescribed.
> Queens at the top could talk anywhere they wanted, whilst
> pawns at the bottom of the hierarchy were very controlled in
> their moves.[76]

Hierarchies therefore tended towards a 'communications gridlock', with new developments stifled as ideas could not easily permeate through their different tiers. Entire organizations, their rules and operating procedures, were therefore static and hardly predisposed to change. Many early management writer-practitioners, however, saw rigid, hierarchical and bureaucratic structures as the most appropriate form of organization, as they guaranteed *unity of command* (only one boss for each employee) and *unity of direction* (only one common plan) with employees treated impersonally (and hence impartially) as rational and interchangeable productive components.[77]

Indeed, such bureaucratic, decentralized hierarchies proved perfectly satisfactory when organizations were dealing with only a relatively small range of product lines, non-synergetic technologies and near-static markets. Divisions could be formed that were based upon product, production-process or production-function groupings, safe in the knowledge that the technologies and market demands upon which they were grounded would remain stable for relatively long time spans. Unfortunately, such *environmental stasis* has not existed within the industrialized Western economies for several decades, with the life cycles of many products decreasing and technological developments fuelling consumer demand for new products on an almost monthly basis. Programmable production technologies have also emerged such that production lines need no longer be dedicated to the production of a single, standardized product. As a result, today's companies can offer a far greater variety of goods and services to their consumers than in the past.

In order to keep up with changing tastes and technologies, modern organizations need to respond rapidly to new consumer demands. They must therefore acquire an ability to gear up for the production, marketing and distribution of new product lines in as short a space of time as possible. The traditional logic of scale has thereby come to be challenged. Rather than wishing to rely on standardized mass-production, modern firms are instead seeking flexible working arrangements that can rapidly adapt in the face of changing market conditions and new technological developments.[78]

THE MECHANISTIC – ORGANIC CONTINUUM

In 1961, after studying a variety of Scottish manufacturing firms, Tom Burns and his colleague G. M. Stalker suggested the notion of a *continuum* of organizational structures ranging from those that were *mechanistic* to those exhibiting a flexible, *organic* form.[79] Mechanistic organizations were characterized as those with specialized, standardized and highly rigid hierarchical structures (as in **figure 3.1**), whilst organic modes of organization, which produced a greater diversity of products, had broader and less-rigid authority patterns that enabled rapid decisions to be made. In organic firms organizational relationships could also be quickly reestablished in the light of new customer demands and technological developments, with project teams being formed and disbanded to cope with fresh initiatives as dictated by market and technological changes. A strict hierarchical structure was therefore not in evidence across organic organizations.

Burns and Stalker noted that firms such as fabrics mills exhibited rigid, mechanistic hierarchies, whilst those competing in more volatile business sectors, like consumer electronics, were more organic and predisposed to structural change. As the 1960s progressed, similar studies on both sides of the Atlantic lent further support to Burns and Stalker's propositions, with a general acceptance emerging of their notion of a 'spectrum' of organizational structures from a mechanistic to an organic pole.[80]

NEW MODES OF ORGANIZATION

Whilst the bureaucratic, hierarchical nature of mechanistic structures is not generally contested, the extent to which organic modes of organization have and will come to dominate modern industry, and what precise form they have and may take, is still highly debated. Indeed, it is likely that already there are ' . . . new beasts roaming around that we can't even identify'.[81]

The first clear organizational species to depart from rigid hierarchy was the *matrix organization*, as noted by Burns and Stalker in electronics manufacturing firms. Matrix organizations abandon the time-old notion of unity of command, and have employees placed within project teams responsible to two or more superiors simultaneously. For example, a project team would find itself responsible to a particular product manager, as well as to a manager with a functional responsibility such as research and development, production or marketing.

With their project teams formed and disbanded as required, matrix organizations are in theory highly flexible and capable of rapid structural adaptation in the face of new technologies and customer demands. In practice, however, within the large organizations that adopted matrix structures in the 1960s and 1970s, even the process of finding out what one should be doing and for whom proved unending.[82] It has also been noted that:

> To someone pitched into a matrix [organization] and left to find his or her own way the prospect is unsettling. It often appears unclear as to who is responsible for what, where the orders come from and how many bosses there are.[83]

Due to the inherent complexity resulting from its abandonment of unity of command, the 'success' of the matrix organization as the most appropriate organic organizational structure proved to be short-lived. It was not until the mid-1980s, however, that a widely recognized 'replacement' mode of organic organization emerged. Termed either the *organic* or *dynamic network*, this 'latest' structural model is based around slimmed-down organizations that have divested themselves of 'non-core' activities and who instead buy-in services and facilities from the marketplace in a 'subcontracting mode'. Organic/dynamic networks thereby consist of loosely connected webs of agents and brokers across industries, with a central core of staff setting a strategic direction and providing the operational support necessary to sustain the network. With all other services and facilities bought-in only as required, the boundaries of the organization therefore become highly fluid (dynamic) as the network at any given point in time:

> . . . operationalizes the "ideas" that the central group wishes to develop. For example, the organization may be in the fashion industry. It has created a name and image — "its label" — but contracts out market surveys, product design, production, distribution and so on [to the marketplace]. In the public eye, the firm has a clear identity. But in reality, it is a network of firms held together by the product of the day. It changes from month to month as different ideas and products come on line, and as the core organization experiments with different partners. The firm is really a system of firms — an open-ended system of ideas and activities, rather than an entity with a clear structure and definable boundary.[84]

Due to their policy of outsourcing and sub-contracting non-core activities, network organizational structures prove highly flexible, with a wide tolerance toward environmental uncertainty as they have few commitments to either production capital or non-core personnel. **Figure 3.2** depicts a common representation of a dynamic network structure, here for a fashion industry organization as in the above example, with five agent parties scattered around a central broker core. Similar examples of networked organizational practice may now be encountered across a range of industries, from soft-toy manufacture to publishing, large-scale building construction to film and television production. Across all of these

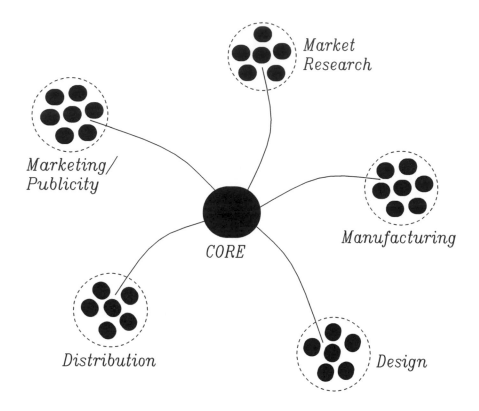

Figure 3.2 Example of a Dynamic Network Structure

sectors many small 'core' firms establish the purpose and identity of the 'organization', whilst enjoying the flexibility inherent in disaggregating themselves from the processes of production, marketing and so forth in which their suppliers (or agents) will specialize. The incidence of network organizational structures therefore goes hand-in-hand with the concept of *flexible specialization*, with:

> . . . the individual firms comprising the network being specialized, but the grouping as a whole being flexible with a potential mix of outputs that can be altered according to the mix of participants in any particular venture.[85]

FLEXIBILITY & ORGANIZATIONAL BOUNDARIES

With the emergence of networked organizational forms drawing together different parties into discrete contracts, licensing agreements and joint-ventures as required, distinguishing the boundaries of organizations in terms of discrete physical infrastructures, and the legal perimeters of their individual component players, clearly no longer provides a valid means of organizational analysis. For it is only when the range of specialists are brought together in the production *process* that 'organizations' in the more traditional sense can be viewed in operation. Dynamic network arrangements are therefore creatures to be delineated by contractual agreements *between* their discrete players, rather than by the physical plant and employees of more rigid, hierarchically structured organizations.

Indeed, existing with shifting, hybrid physical structures linked to the core only as required, the limits upon dynamic networks are solely those created via the problems inherent in contracting-in agents to perform task processes, as opposed to the more cumbersome physical, economic and legal constraints that limit the structural alteration of bureaucratic, hierarchical organizations. Within a purely hierarchical and rule-bound bureaucracy, if workload temporarily increases then it is unlikely that extra members of permanent staff will be employed. A dynamically networked production structure, on the other hand, may contract-in the services of additional parties on a short-term basis. Clearly this makes network organizations more flexible in response to the demands of their customers and changed market conditions.

It must be appreciated, however, that whilst dynamic networks have commonly been positioned at the organic extremity of the spectrum of organizational forms,[86] their degree of flexibility is not unlimited. Although dynamic networks exist with a shifting, hybrid physical structure linked to the core only as required, they *are* constrained by the problems inherent in contracting-in agents to perform task processes. Some tasks will always prove too complex, or too trivial, to consider outsourcing them at any distance externally from the dynamic network centre. In other words, there will be occasions when the cost of contracting-in another party will be greater than the benefit derived from its coupling into the network.

The specifications for some contracts may be just too complex to make them cost-effective, perhaps because their range of potential outputs is uncertain. Other tasks may require such a specialist knowledge of the core organization that the time cost of briefing another party would be too great. At the other end of the scale, a few hours of unforeseen administrative work may be undertaken by the network core, rather than by bringing in a temporary office worker, as even the temporary employment of one worker may entail an hour or so of administration in itself. Therefore, however fluid a dynamic network structure becomes, its flexibility will always be bought at the expense of time diverted into the contractual and administrative complexity of sealing and severing its required agent-broker linkages. However, contractual barriers preventing increased organizational flexibility are not unsurmountable. Indeed, as businesses start to utilize increasingly powerful cybertechnologies to allow remote working and to aid in the contractual process, new forms of *virtual organization*, freed of the flexibility constraints of even the dynamic network, will shortly begin to emerge.

FORGING BUSINESS LINKS ACROSS CYBERSPACE

By interfacing organizational computing resources, it is becoming possible to bring together (or 'entangle') production resources outside of the traditional arena of human contractual negotiation, a process already part-exhibited by systems for EDI. The dynamic network itself is a form dependent for its effective survival upon smoothly functioning communications linkages. The virtual organization is even more so, with electronic communications and processing technologies not only providing the primary or sole connection medium between member nodes, but also playing the key role in locating, attracting, interconnecting and severing parties to and from the core nexus as required. 'Contracting', inasmuch as it will take place across such virtual organizations, will occur transparently through cyberspace, with smart software routines known as *agents* automating the protocols for information and resource passage and payment between their master's computer systems.

The concept of software agent contracting is crucial to an understanding of the creation and functioning of the ultimate in virtual organizational forms. Artificial intelligence (AI) expert David Gelernter describes agents as dynamic *infomachines*, constantly being created and destroyed. Agents are the true native residents of cyberspace, and may even be thought of as virtual employees on the electronic stage of the global hardware platform:

> They make everything happen. They react to information and
> synthesize it, display it, study it, investigate it, double-check,
> analyze and digest it. Agents snoop for you . . . [whilst other
> agents] . . . do the main impersonal business — looking at
> information, answering questions, setting off alarms, painting
> the big picture.[87]

In future, agents (and associated 'infomachines' as detailed in **chapter 4**)
will be employed in their multitudes by busy individuals and organizations. Their job will be to gather any data that may interest their master,
to disseminate their master's outputs, and to generate new information as
they voyage through corporate cyberspace, dendrite tentacles ever-vigilant
for new patterns of connectivity. Agents will also forge contacts and make
and break contracts. They will *work* for you, and only *for you*, like
extremely diligent personal assistants whose loyalty is absolute and
guaranteed. Agents will also never need a holiday, a day off sick or a
coffee break.

With agents and other software routines representing the users and
providers of data services, wandering from one electronic building or
transportation truck to another,[88] utilizers of virtual organizational forms
will be able to create and disband their electronic networks of business
activity without ever having to bother as to exactly *how* the network is
formed and disbanded. Similarly, they will almost certainly be ignorant
of exactly *who* is involved in their particular virtual organization, *where*
they are, or *what* remuneration they will receive. Moreover, it is likely
that many human temporal organizational members will rarely know the
breadth or complexity of the virtual organizations in which they become
involved. If they want data analysis carried out, plans drawn up, graphics
images retouched, proofs checked, or simulations created, they will
simply issue instructions through their PC workstation or virtual
environment. All interconnections across cyberspace will be taken care
of by the software agents of the parties involved, who will bring them
together as required, deliver the work to those capable of undertaking it
(or with the knowledge and contacts to farm it out again), and return
completed electronic projects to the workstation of the person who
requested the service in the first place.

In future, drawing other parties into your own, individual project arena
may well be as easy as clicking on another application package on the
desktop display of your personal computer. Software will protect us from

bureaucracy just as it now shields us from complex operating systems and communications protocols; agents seeking out bargains, and selling our services, down an electronic global high street mirrored on our computer screens or around us in a simulated reality of photo-realistic graphics. Implausible? Impossible? A fantasy? Perhaps now. But in five or ten years . . .? This vision of virtual organizations as temporal working patterns across cyberspace, existing for perhaps only hours, minutes or seconds, lies not that far ahead. Indeed, over the past couple of years, several new cybertechnology applications have emerged that already indicate the pathway toward the virtual organizational structures of the future.

CURRENT VARIANTS OF VIRTUAL ORGANIZATIONAL FORM

What is clear from observation across industry today is that virtual organizational forms and patterns of cybertechnology-enabled working are likely to be encountered in a myriad of guises. By definition, the technology that may render them operable is itself highly flexible. It is therefore highly unlikely that the same patterns of adoption will be noted across different organizations, let alone different industry segments. There will therefore be no 'universal' virtual organizational forms. This said, isolating groups of like activity does enhance the process of analysis. The current application of cybertechnology-enabled working practices will therefore be explored within the following four broad and interrelated categories:

- ☐ The adoption of *homeworking*
- ☐ The development of *hot-desk* environments
- ☐ The increased incidence of *hotelling*
- ☐ The use of *groupware* to empower *virtual teams*

THE HOMEWORKING OPTION

Predictions concerning homeworking (or 'telecommuting'), with employees accessing their workplace via a home computer terminal, have been with us for well over a decade. Indeed pioneering experiments demonstrating the technical if not the social feasibility of homeworking operations were conducted at Rank Xerox in the UK way back in the early 1980s.[89] For many years the homeworking option was not welcomed and/or taken up, however, due in no small part to the inherent problems of social isolation that were shown to result from its implementation. For the majority, the difference between sitting at home at a screen and keyboard, and being part of the hustle and bustle of a modern open-plan office, was simply too great. There are now signs, however, that barriers toward the increased adoption of distributed, home-based working practices are receding on several fronts. Indeed in the US at least six million employees now have formal homeworking arrangements,[90] with a total of around twenty-five million people working from home in one form or another.[91] Across the UK there are now at least 300,000 active homeworkers, with the figure expected to rise to around two-and-a-half million by 1995.[92]

Current advancements on the homeworking frontier are being driven by new cybertechnologies, as well as by the evolution of existing workplaces and work processes. As an example of the former, by using ISDN telephone lines and PCs equipped with video image compression systems, it is now possible to provide homeworkers with rudimentary but effective video communications links. Whilst the development of these systems will soon allow wide-scale video-conferencing across the business community, more importantly for the homeworker they already permit the image of a caller or co-worker to accompany all casual and informal conversations if so desired. People working at home may, for example, be afforded the facility to chat with working colleagues viewed in a window on their screen whilst they getting on with their typing.

With PC video links available, homeworking/telecommuting clearly has the potential to feel less remote and therefore may be seen as more attractive. After all, when people can see other human beings, in addition to being able to communicate with them by telephone or keyboard, they tend to feel far less isolated and alone. Their productivity as homeworkers subsequently improves. At the time of writing, a PC camera and add-on board, together with ProShare personal video-conferencing software, was due to be launched by Intel in a price range of around $1,200 to $2,500.[93]

Homeworking is also becoming more attractive as traditional workplaces become less personal and are increasingly centred around international, electronic systems. With the spread of EDI, the bulk of the paperwork on which many computer-based office systems still rely is rapidly receding, meaning that is it less important to provide space where employees with a common function are located. Employ three more accounts clerks or programmers and, provided they have a computer workstation and an electronic mail address, you can locate them anywhere you like in any building. At the Microsoft Corporation in the USA, software 'gods and goddesses' work almost exclusively through the medium of electronic mail, which is even said to carry the organization's culture.[94] As more and more organizations route workflows through their information systems, employees will discover that even if they *are* physically at work, there will be no guarantee that they will enjoy a common location with colleagues. Homeworking, if offered, will hence become a more and more attractive proposition.

HOT-DESK ENVIRONMENTS

Hot-desk environments abandon the notion of having individual desks for individual employees. Instead, within these re-engineered workplaces, many communal desks or consoles with networked IT facilities are provided. In Digital Equipment Corporation's Stockholm headquarters, such an 'office of the future' has already been created. With permanent offices and desks scrapped, employees are presented with an open-plan area with terminals that drop down on flexibars. When an employee needs computer access they simply pull down a free terminal, and when they're finished they let it sail back up into the ceiling.[95] Any personal space in the office is confined to the capacity of one's own individual drawer in a communal filing cabinet.

At the British Gas Research Centre in Loughborough a similar hot-desk system is in operation. Here, staff arrive in the morning to be allocated a desk and terminal for a day, to which their telephone number will be diverted, and from which they can access their own computer files, e-mail and voice-mail.[96] As in the DEC environment, strong workplace ties are unlikely to be forged, as people are liable to be working at different (but identical) desks every day and hence alongside different colleagues. Under such a regime personal space, in so much as it exists, has become the *personal cyberspace* to be accessed within an employee's own computer files and directories.

Also in the UK, IBM now operates a new work/space allocation system entitled *Smart* (space, morale and remote technology). At Bedford Lakes on the outskirts of London, the company has divided individual workspaces into four distinct classifications. Traditional managers' offices and permanent workstations for administrative staff comprise the first two types of workspace, but additionally grouped and shared hot-desks for mobile consultants are provided, together with 'touch-down desks' for other staff visiting the office for brief periods.[97]

HOTELLING ARRANGEMENTS

Closely related to hot-desk developments, where enough desks will only be provided to accommodate the number of staff likely to be in the office at any one point in time, are *hotelling* arrangements. This system of working, as adopted by consultants Ernst & Young,[98] relies on the notion that many consultants, accountants and so forth spend the majority of their working lives out with clients. They therefore have no need for permanent desks or offices back at base. Hotelling employees are instead provided with portable, state-of-the-art computers, and rely on their clients to provide them with a desk from which they stay in touch with base via computer network links and voice-mail.

When 'hotelling employees' do need to work back at base, they simply call in to a 'concierge', letting them know when they will be arriving and for how long. A cubicle is then allocated for the duration of the employee's 'visit', on which their nameplate will be displayed by the time they arrive. Like its sister hot-desk working arrangement, the hotelling concept relies on organization-wide communications networks and high specification computer hardware through which all work is directed.

The financial benefits of hotelling arrangements can be considerable. At Ernst & Young, the adoption of hotelling across their New York and Chicago offices has led to space savings of 25%, with only one desk per three employees. Once it adopts hotelling across the US, the company expects to save in the region of $40 million per annum.[99]

GROUPWARE & VIRTUAL TEAMS

Playing a key role in the empowerment of virtual teams of homeworkers, hot-deskers or hotelling employees is a new generation of computer applications known collectively as *groupware*. At its most basic level, groupware is simply any form of computer software that empowers team working. Groupware has grown out of the 'individual-ware' of office automation, such as the word processing and database packages that have been employed for over a decade on stand-alone desktop PCs. The most obvious and widespread groupware application to date is electronic mail, which commonly increases the speed, coherency and immediacy of organizational communications, as well as allowing for a diverse and certain communications reach.

There is, however, much, much more to groupware than electronic mail. In its broadest context, groupware is concerned with all computer systems that allow multiple resource access, as it:

> . . . aims to help people work together through communication with each other and through access to shared information, whether they are processing invoices, involved in a major engineering project or discussing corporate strategy.

> [For example, groupware allows for] . . . the automatic storage and retrieval of document images by any number of people at the same time . . . incoming correspondence, forms, drawings and other documents that cannot be keyed-in through word processor systems [being] scanned in to be held on disk and called to a screen in seconds rather than hunted down in a filing cabinet or on someone's desk.[100]

Today, across many organizations, groupware systems have already been adopted with an 'almost unbounded enthusiasm',[101] with systems costing from only a few hundred pounds making major inroads into improved workflow management. Most commonly, the adoption of groupware means that time is not wasted when multiple individuals need to access and work upon the same documents and information sources simultaneously. Equally significant as a driving force in the 'groupware revolution' is the fact that many current groupware packages allow new virtual working practices to be spawned upon and across the interconnected PCs and PC networks that *already* inhabit the majority of desks within most large national and multinational corporations. The cost/benefits of groupware installation can therefore be enormous. Already a groupware application called Lotus Notes™ is used by an estimated 750,000 users spread over 2,500 companies, permitting its users multiple, interactive, on-screen dialogues as well as simultaneous access to corporate data stores.[102]

One example of a company using groupware applications to create teams of employees who work together even though they rarely meet is Mercury Telecommunications. In its bid to cope with the velocity of its growth and rapid technological change, Mercury has created many 'virtual teams':

> . . . people collaborating closely, but in a range of locations. They may work from home, in the car, at a customer's office, at "third-party sites", in a branch office of Mercury, or at head office — yet they work as a unified team. They are united by a strong sense of "mission", highly sophisticated IT, skilled team coordinators — and a base office that provides the right environment for anything from a "touch-down" visit to a full team brainstorming.[103]

All of the aforementioned working patterns and examples demonstrate how new technology can *empower* the cohesion of group working via new communications media. Individuals isolated by either geography or time can thereby work together (the latter facility made possible by the fact that e-mail messages can be sent and received even when the recipient is not present at his or her computer).

TOWARDS VIRTUCOMMUTING

Current and near-future groupwares, including remote video-conferencing facilities, will fuel the empowerment of an array of disparate but cooperative virtual working practices. The Advanced Media Unit at British Telecom's Systems Research Division, for example, is now working on a second-generation video-conferencing facility which will increase the feeling of being 'with somebody' over a video link. Their intended telepresence system will probably involve a huge round table bisected by a large screen. By using a system of cameras and high-definition images, a person sitting on one side of the table will see others on this screen *as if they were sitting across the table*. The ultimate aim is for people to be able to 'lose themselves' in such a system, with their awareness of the enabling technology falling to practically zero.[104]

Whilst British Telecom's intended telepresence system in itself sounds amazing, cutting-edge technologists are also proceeding towards the creation of far more advanced immersive virtual reality systems to enable *virtucommuting*. Put simply, virtucommuting involves transporting a number of geographically remote individuals into a computer-generated working environment that they will all manipulate and experience as a common reality. Many authors, of both fact and fantasy, have explored this concept, with propositions usually concerning individuals who don customized VR clothing (such as head-mounted displays and body suits) in order to enter their remote, graphically rendered, working location. Whilst five or ten years ago such ideas were pure fiction, today their realization seems far more credible. Indeed, with the level of sensory detail needed to sustain the illusion being more primitive, VR systems to permit cyberspace business encounters will prove far easier to develop than the systems that will one day offer us virtual leisure domains.

Consider a scenario where the directors of a company virtucommute together to meet in VR for a board meeting. So long as the technology enables each of them to see representations of all the involved participants, hear their contributions, and manipulate common objects such as papers and a whiteboard, then the meeting will be able to proceed effectively just as it would in the 'real' world. Granted it would be *nice* if tactile, force-feedback systems offered our business virtucommuters the opportunity to feel the surface of the table around which they all appear to be seated, but this stimulation will not be *essential* to the illusion's operational success. Similarly, it will not really matter if the involved participants, and the virtual boardroom in which they are located, look bland and 'unrealistic'. Very high level reality-engine hardware will therefore not be needed for perfectly acceptable business encounters in VR.

Now contrast this scenario with the likely desires of groups of people who will one day use immersive VR for non-work-related encounters. These individuals will almost certainly require a VR system which will blanket them with illusions across *all* of their senses, presenting a far more accurate representation of reality than required for 'simple' business meetings. In a leisure VR domain participants will want everything to look photorealistic. They will also demand peripheral hardware that will allow them to actually *feel* any sensation, from the moisture of the grass beneath their feet, to the warm caress of a virtual lover. It is therefore reasonable to deduce, due to technical limitations and the fact that relationships and encounters at work are socially, culturally and physiologically constrained, that VR business meetings will become commonplace long before more subtle genres of human cyberspace interaction involving activities such as virtual parties, virtual journeys, virtual fantasies and virtual sex.

Almost certainly over the next ten to twenty years, cyberspace and business will have the potential to become synonymous, with the medium offering organizations the chance to thrive in the hypercompetitive economy of the 21st century. Some employees may also end up working for corporations which exist totally within cyberspace, and which possess the revolutionary capability to interact instantaneously with both physical and virtual marketplaces.[105]

Indeed, the days when limited virtucommuting systems accessing multi-user domains become a reality may not even be ten years distant. Research teams are already accruing progress under programmes such as the UK Government's multi-million pound CSCW initiative, whilst military VR simulation systems (most notably the US Army's SIMNET) have been in use for several years. With many multinationals having already invested in the links for dedicated video-conferencing facilities, some of the communications hardwares are also already in place. We are therefore just waiting for the dawn when VR peripherals, software and reality-engine workstations permit the Japanese businessman taking over your company to meet with you not just *on* a flat screen but *in* a computer-generated VR body as you both 'virtucommute' to discuss terms.

Whether realization of the above takes five, ten, twenty or fifty years (and few in the fledgling VR industry believe the CSCW/virtucommuting vision to be fifty years away), immersive VR technologies will at some point allow many people to enter and manipulate common cyber-workplaces almost indistinguishable from reality. For many, the opportunity cost of travelling to work may therefore come to far outweigh the loss of real social interaction forgone in working from home. Homeworking (virtucommuting) across many occupations, from banking, programming and research, to marketing and most forms of management, may therefore become the norm. Although today's input peripherals for immersive virtual reality — HMDs, wands, datagloves and so forth — are fairly cumbersome, the corporate interest in their continued development means that more comfortable and easier-to-manipulate hardware must be on the near horizon. When this new generation of peripherals arrives — perhaps in the form of lightweight VR glasses and an armoury of VR jewellery that can unobtrusively (or perhaps even fashionably) adorn the body — it will allow employees to feel, touch, see and hear objects and other people in virtual reality as never before. The corporate interest in developing the VR technology (that will in turn enable virtucommuting) is massive.

Already Ford has its designers and engineers creating virtual prototypes of new cars with doors that can be opened to permit the user to get inside and grasp the steering wheel; the Co-op retail chain has created virtual supermarkets to try out new store arrangements; and Westland System Assessment arranges VR demonstrations of new helicopters.[106] The list of similar big-business ventures into cyberspace could already run on and on for pages. Ultimately, experiments in the direct stimulation of the human nervous system will lead to immersive virtual reality stimulations so realistic they will be indistinguishable from reality. When that day is reached, the desire to physically *go* to work may disappear altogether.

DEFINING THE VIRTUAL ORGANIZATION

Virtual modes of organization will continue to mean different things to different people as they embrace a widening galaxy of new technologies and working patterns, from groupware-enabled homeworking and hot-desk systems, through to immersive virtucommuting. Truly virtual organizations, however, may reasonably be expected to exhibit certain key characteristics:

- □ A reliance for their functioning and survival on the medium of cyberspace across a wide system of organizational infrastructures.

- □ No identifiable physical form, and only transient patterns of agent-broker (employee-employer) connectivity.

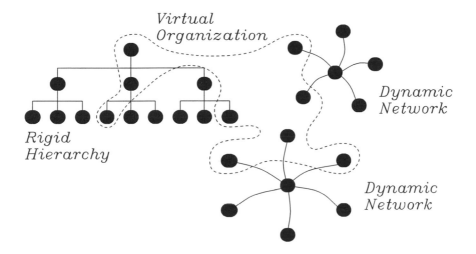

Figure 3.3 Hierarchy, Network and Virtual Organization

□ Boundaries defined and limited only by the available information technology, rather than by bureaucratic rules or cumbersome contractual arrangements.

By definition, virtual organizations will have to exist across the communities of 'real' organizations whose hardware they will utilize. **Figure 3.3** therefore serves to illustrate a virtual organization as an informal overlay across several conventional organizations (in this case a rigid hierarchy and two dynamic networks), with its members electronically and instantaneously connected across cyberspace when and if they choose to be so. This loose pattern of organization, brought together solely when required for productive work at the behest of any involved party, is hence virtual both physically and contractually, with no real or legal boundaries to indicate its existence save for patterns of connectivity across cyberspace. **Table 3.1** compares the make-up and nature of the rigid hierarchy, dynamic network and virtual organization, whilst **table 3.2** highlights their bounds, delineations, expansion constraints and physical characteristics.

Mode of Organization	Make-up	Nature
Rigid Hierarchy	Static/discrete physical entity Static/discrete contractual entity	Static (bureaucratic)
Dynamic Network	Flexible/virtual physical entity Discrete but dynamic contractual entity	Dynamic (flexible)
Virtual Organization	Virtual physical entity Virtual contractual entity	Transient (virtual)

Table 3.1 A Comparison of Organizational Forms

Mode of Organization	Bounded by	Delineated by	Expansion Constraints	Physical Form
Rigid Hierarchy	Rules	Physical and legal boundaries	Physical resources	Real (discrete)
Dynamic Network	Contracts	Tasks/ Processes	Limits of human agent/ contract negotiation	Hybrid
Virtual Organization	Information linkages	Tasks/ Processes	Available cyberspace	Virtual

Table 3.2 Structural Forms: Bounds, Delineations and Constraints

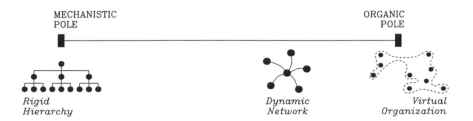

Figure 3.4 The Spectrum of Organizational Forms

Note that in **table 3.1** 'physical entity' refers to a clearly bounded infrastructural and human conglomeration that encompasses the organization, most hierarchical structures being largely delineated by rigid employee roles played within a specific physical geography. Also note that dynamic networks only partially exist as discretely bounded physical entities. They may have a central headquarters at the core, but the majority of the physical facilities they utilize will be coupled into the network only as required. Finally, note that as virtual organizations are primarily *transient* rather than *dynamic* (like the network form), they will not evolve over time, but instead will be created and disbanded extremely rapidly as required by their key individuals. Thus, whereas one individual may remain at the core of a dynamic network for many years (the structure shifting around them), they will find themselves creating and disbanding hundreds or thousands of *different* virtual organizations for their bidding over the same period of time.

Comparing the rigid hierarchy, dynamic network and virtual organization, leads us to consider again the theoretical spectrum of organizational forms spanning from the mechanistic to the organic. **Figure 3.4** illustrates this spectrum of organizational species with the rigid hierarchy at the mechanistic pole and the virtual organization at the organic. The dynamic network is then placed perhaps two-thirds of the way along from the mechanistic extremity of the spectrum, indicating that although it is a highly organic form, it is still bounded by certain physical and more notably contractual limitations with regard to the level of transience its patterns of agent relationships may achieve.

FLEXIBILITY, CONNECTIVITY & STRUCTURAL PROGRESSION

There can be little doubt that the emergence of organizational forms such as the dynamic network has been driven by the increased desire for flexibility on the part of previously more rigid organizations constrained by the limits of internal bureaucracy. We may therefore term the desire for increased flexibility the *change mechanism* driving one mode of organization toward another. In the case of the progression from the hybrid dynamism of the network towards the virtual organization, however, it may be argued that it is new forms of information connectivity that are the causal catalyst towards ever more temporal organizational forms. In future, those in business will be forced to adapt their very means of organization if they wish to take advantage of the instant multiplicity of communications linkages available across an expanding cyberspace. Thus, as organizational forms have evolved from hierarchy to dynamic network and beyond, so too has their medium of change from the *desire* to be more flexible to the *potential* to more greatly interconnect. This is reflected in the expansion constraints on new organizational forms, as illustrated in **table 3.2**, with the limits of agent/contract negotiation constraining the growth of dynamic network structures, whilst only the available cyberspace bounds the expansion of virtual organizations.

SYMBIOSIS OR PARASITISM?

Because virtual organizations, by definition, must utilize some of the hardware infrastructure created and maintained by more traditional organizations, they will exist at best symbiotically, at worst parasitically, across the whole spectrum of organizational populations. The implications of the emergence of virtual working practices may thus prove to be both positive and negative for business organizations as a whole.

By their very nature, virtual organizations will only ever be applicable to task processes concerning the movement and manipulation of electronically-coded information, although such data patterns may of course represent and/or control physical resources or processes. Being transient in nature, virtual organizations will also never have their own identifiable staff, and indeed most people caught up in such electronic webs will also be working simultaneously for more traditional organizations. There is therefore no question of all, or even a majority, of organizations becoming virtual in nature, and hence it is the *balance* between real and virtual organizations in future that will be of significance, as well as the impact of virtual working patterns on the functioning and efficiency of their 'host' organizational population.

Consider, for example, the role that may be played by a virtual organization. Harry, working in marketing, may discover that he needs some sales data on products related to his own brands. He does not possess the figures he needs, although he is aware that they could be pieced together from information known to many of his contacts across the industry, and from public, on-line data sources. Nowadays he may just pick up the telephone and make a few calls, or perhaps give an assistant the task of researching a report. With intelligent technology and global connectivity, however, he could instruct a personalized software agent to seek out the information he requires, pay for it via EDI if required, process it into a useful form, and bring in other parties for data analysis if appropriate. The connectivity pattern so formed may exist for only a few hours, minutes or even seconds, with its human players all being simultaneously employed by other organizations. In this example, the spawning of the virtual organization would clearly be to the advantage of the primary organization for whom Harry worked, closely related and interdependent across it in a symbiotic fashion. In such cases, virtual organization forms may be viewed as electronic combinations of the 'old boy network' and public information facilities, constructed to serve the needs of their key individuals, and in doing so oiling the wheels of the host organizations that provide their infrastructural habitat.

With wide-scale access to a globally interconnected hardware base, used both by organizations for business and by individuals for pleasure, there will also be the possibility for parasitic virtual organizations to form, drawing on the infrastructure of other business organizations without offering any payback. Indeed, the ease with which organizations constructed purely in software may be created could well become a problem for the very companies whose infrastructural investment permits their conception.

PERSONAL VIRTUAL ORGANIZATIONS

All businesses have to accept that their autonomous, organic factors of production — their human employees — are likely to exhibit social, economic and political aspirations which are unlikely to be fulfilled via the completion of the tasks they are assigned at work. This is, of course, perfectly natural, and most employers have no wish to impose regimes banning idle gossip in the office and all other non-work-related activities. Discussion of sports, personal relationships, complaints and current events makes life in the office more comfortable, as do social and charity events, and communications with family members organized and conducted from the workplace. Unethical — like walking biros — perhaps. But realistic. Employees are human; they can't suspend one task set completely and take on another for the duration of the working day. Indeed, they would probably function less effectively if they did so. Business and personal lives are inevitably *integrated* rather than *isolated* by the majority — with an estimate of one-third of any employee's time in the average office being spent on purely personal activities.[107]

Now, of course, when the infrastructure and technology of work and personal lives are largely separable (the telephone presenting the only common linking hardware element), the above is not a problem. What will be the implications, however, if your employees suddenly start spawning temporal virtual organizations not only in your time, but also across your hardware (or, more likely, across *everybody's* hardware)? Suddenly organizations could have a real problem on their corporate protuberances: global connectivity becoming a curse as much as a blessing.

Put an electronic mail system into any office and the level of inter-staff communication will dramatically increase, with by no means all messages being of relevance to the productive, official work of the organization. Now consider the scenario when data super-highways allow all employees easy access to their home systems, and to those of others, not to mention their friends in other workplaces. Employees will quite literally have at their fingertips the potential to shop and arrange their finances from work terminals, and to gain access to interactive entertainment. And this is before we ponder the possible actions of closet entrepreneurs who aspire to run their own business ventures dependent only upon access to the media of corporate cyberspace.

Access to our rapidly dawning global hardware platform has, by definition, to be as open as possible if those creating it are to reap the benefits of their investment. Granted, protecting your software so that users have to pay for access will be possible, but whether putting restrictions on hardware access, control and provision will be feasible, or even desirable, is quite another matter. Couple to this scenario the fact that flexible, temporary and contract employment is on the increase (with the technically highly-competent able to name their price), and the potential to control the conception of a temporal race of parasitic virtual organizations will prove nigh-on impossible. Indeed, even if the spread of virtual organizational patterns could be controlled, it has to be remembered that many such forms will be of enormous benefit to the traditional organizations over which they will thrive, with near-instantaneous, transient connectivity patterns allowing new forms of efficiency and innovation. It will thus not be in the interests of business to place obstacles in the way of the conception of virtual organizations. What's more, accurately isolating advantageous virtual forms from those simply drawing on corporate resources will almost certainly prove an insurmountable quest.

THE VIRTUAL ORGANIZATION, FACT OR FANTASY?

Many concepts of increased organizational flexibility have been discussed since the early 1960s, and in particular much attention has been focused on this area over the past decade. This chapter has drawn together key facets of literature, speculation and practice, concerning both modes of organizational operation and technological development, in order to present a variety of new 'virtual' organizational structures and working practices that may allow increased flexibility to be rendered to business organizations in both the immediate and long-term future. True virtual organizations may become transient both physically and contractually. They will undoubtably also be part-populated by intelligent software routines, and only capable of survival in the world of cyberspace created via the interconnection of the infrastructures of all other organizational species. This is indeed a vision of the future, but of a future not too distant — a future probably not even a decade away.

As computers across the planet continue to interface directly with others to exchange and process information and resources, and software becomes more personalized and 'intelligent', we will undoubtably be presented with the potential to release some work processes from the bureaucracy, complexity and mistrust of contracts negotiated by human beings. Managers, artists, researchers, writers and more will be free to concentrate on their *work*, rather than the *administration* thereof. On the one hand, this may increase the efficiency and fluidity of the corporations who employ them. More pessimistically, it may lead to the corporates that provide the majority of the hardware habitat of cyberspace being sucked dry by a plague of talented individuals sailing personal business activities freed from the echelons of contractual bureaucracy.

In practice, the truth is likely to come to lie somewhere between these two extremes. It will probably have to be accepted, however, that when organizations can be spawned in cyberspace, liberated from the constraints of contracts, that tidy delineations between employer and employee will greatly diminish. Everyone with the skills and knowledge required to perform administrative work for future corporations will be capable of becoming the nexus point of a virtual organization. Controlling their personal webs of interaction will also be as difficult (and probably as undesirable) as preventing biros walking and personal photocopies being made, or stopping Hillary, Sophie and George talking about the latest soap opera rather than getting on with that great mound of invoices. New ideas as to how to control, to motivate, and thus how to *manage*, will need to be sought.

Whatever technologies, patterns of connectivity and software developments the future holds in store, we have to accept that ' . . . old information processing capabilities aren't designed to meet today's challenge of managing an organization's knowledge and technological capabilities.'[108] All organizations therefore need to open their minds to new ways of working in order to take advantage of the increasingly advanced processing and communications infrastructures to which all players in most markets will soon have access. New patterns of connecting organizational nodes, and employees into organizations, will have a considerable impact on the structures and processes of organizational functioning in the decades ahead. The concept presented herein of the ultimate 'virtual organization', as a symbiotic or parasitic transient web of connected individuals and software over the hardware infrastructure provided by more conventional working structures, is just one idea of how some of the most flexible organizations forms may in future appear. Not all organizations can, or will even want or need, to aspire towards a state of total temporal existence rooted in the electronic-nothing world of cyberspace. Others most definitely *will*, however, and all managers should at least have in their mind the *idea* that transparent webs of 'software-only' organizational constructs may be working, perhaps unofficially, both for and against them, across *their* organizational infrastructure in the years ahead.

Monster: imaginary beast, usually made of various human parts . . .

4
Agents, Ghosts & Other Virtual Monsters

FEW PEOPLE WOULD WANT to take a computer to a party. After all, since the days of ENIAC,[109] all our computational companions have been good at has *been* computation. Any level of intelligence or common sense has been lacking from our machines almost entirely, whilst the ability of computers to communicate — with either each other or human beings — has been stilted and problematic. Computers have never made great conversationalists, and even today, in a world of instant, electronic communications, getting one IT peripheral to tolerate another's communications protocols can prove a frustrating experience. Faced with setting up a modem or network link, even the most hardened technocrat may occasionally discover clumps of tugged-free hair between their digits.

Fortunately, recent developments highlight a glimmer of hope for increased machine 'intelligence'. To ease communications difficulties, and to allow computer systems to manipulate data for their flesh-and-blood masters in a more enlightened fashion, developers are now conceiving 'smart' software routines. One of the most important of these new cyberspace-resident 'species' is likely to be the *agent*. As noted in previous chapters, agents are pieces of software capable of learning from human beings, and/or programmed with the 'netiquette' required to socially interact with the various classifications of computer network to be encountered as they serve their masters across our emerging global hardware platform. In the future, when you 'post' an electronic letter, it is therefore likely to be dispatched in the safe clutches of a trusted software agent that will negotiate the passage of your communication through the system. You will also be able to dispatch agents to collect and collate data, make reservations and electronic payments, negotiate deals and contracts, as well as any other number of business or personal activities that will in future come to rely on cybertechnology-mediation.

Agent software routines have already been revealed as critical to *Cyber Business* developments involving the birth of organic *virtual organizations*. Indeed, so important are agents and other emerging smart software 'entities' to the development of man-machine business systems that they have been granted the majority of this chapter all to themselves. However, as the discussion progresses from the beneficial to the detrimental application of so termed 'infomachines', the real 'monsters' of cyberspace also come in for some scrutiny. Known variously as 'hackers', 'crackers' and 'cyberpunks', these manic individuals may pose one of the greatest threats to stable business operations in the future as they continue to create more deadly *virus* programs and use more devious methods to illegitimately 'hack' into corporate computer systems.

MONSTERS & MACHINE INTELLIGENCE

The inclusion of the word 'monsters' in the title of this chapter serves two important purposes. Most obviously, it indicates that *smart viruses* are likely to appear which will engage in disruption, fraud and industrial espionage for their criminally minded masters. The choice of the term 'monster', however, should also serve as a reminder that any intelligent (or apparently intelligent) human creation will encounter a world of hostile ignorance. One man's software agent could quite easily be viewed as, or even become, another's monster or nemesis. Cutting-edge programmers may not be cut-and-pasting corpses from the graveyard, but as smarter and smarter *learning* software is developed they will almost certainly begin to encroach on the activities of one Dr. Frankenstein.

Whilst the line between fact and fantasy can at times appear extremely fine, it must be appreciated from the outset that this is not a chapter of science fiction. Agent-based computer communications and data retrieval systems will soon prove to be big business, with the market for software agents likely to be worth over $2.5bn by the turn of the century.[110] Smart-software development will therefore play a critical role in the success or failure of many current players in the computer and media industries. Research into machine learning involving developments in areas such as 'neural networks'[111] also manages to sustain a high profile, and may one day lead to the realization of true 'artificial intelligences' (AIs). Indeed even today, some American states already consider AI programs to be legal entities in their own right.[112] No apology is therefore made when terms like software 'entities', 'slaves' and 'virtual servants' are used liberally herein.

Philosophers and computer scientists have debated and will continue to debate what constitutes machine 'intelligence'.[113] For most of us, however, an answer to this question is largely irrelevant. In business, and in the home, we are primarily interested in what computers and new forms of software will actually *do* for us, and as smart software arrives across global networks it will empower computers to do a great deal more than they can accomplish today. Smart software entities will quite shortly *appear* intelligent, and for the majority that is all that will really matter.

AS TECHNOLOGY LENDS A HAND

The concept of machine intelligence is exciting. Once initial apprehensions have been allayed, the more information technology appears capable of, the more we are likely to employ it, and the more we are likely to enjoy working with that technology. In a wonderful manual for their Surefax Plus system, Mercury Communications ask the user to consider the system as:

> . . . a robot, working from home, with hundreds of fax machines in the bedroom. When the robot's not busy it watches TV. The robot is at your disposal. It is your metallic slave.

> Normally, you send a fax, it's delivered, life goes on and the robot continues watching 'Going For Gold', oblivious of what the humans are up to.

> However, the number may be busy, and you don't want to hang around the fax machine exercising your index finger for the next half hour. Or maybe you want to send the same fax to 96 people and you had other plans for the rest of the month. It's time for the robot to get off its ASCII processor and start dialling.

> Send your fax to the robot, with an instruction.

For example, 'Dear Droid, forget about Henry Kelly and send this fax to those 96 phone numbers I gave you last week.'

The robot obeys, lying in bed, dialling with its numerous robot arms, patiently re-dialling if a number is busy. You send the fax once, to the robot, and your fax machine is free again. The robot has its own phone lines.

At night, the robot sends the faxes you've told it to send at the cheap rate. Just before the continental movie at 1am, it faxes a report of everything it's done in the previous day to your office.

It's a great system. It's called SUREFAX PLUS.[114]

Few can fail to be drawn in by the above passage. The idea of something *within* a technological device becoming our *servant*, our *friend*, our *slave*, appeals to deep and megalomaniac human sensibilities. It is a concept that offers us power as the master. Drudgery and technical complexity can be handed down to menial but loyal and unquestioning patterns of electrons. And is this not as it should be? After all, computers were created to help human beings. Unlike the many facets of humanity that past power-minorities have enslaved to their selfish desires, they can also never demand to be free . . .

In his fascinating book *Mirror Worlds*, David Gelernter argues that software models within computer screen windows will soon not only provide us with *representations* of 'chunks of reality', but will also permit a degree of *control* over the real world.[115] We will, for example, be able to view a model of our city in virtual reality, and then by manipulating this model be empowered to influence city operations. With the data upon which all human business systems depend constantly rushing in and pouring out of computer networks, such *mirror worlds* of Mankind's physical systems are already springing into existence across cyberspace. This trend is in turn breeding vast data and software complexity, making cyberspace a jungle far too complex to be navigated solely by human beings. We will therefore *have* to rely upon the assistance of the natives of the world of information. These natives, such as software agents, are arguably most easily conceptualized as specialist *infomachines*.

INFOMACHINES & SOFTWARE ENTITIES

Any man-made structure that transforms its inputs into outputs of value constitutes a machine. An infomachine — an information machine — is simply one that manipulates information (meaningful data) into another form. Any *running* computer program may therefore be thought of as an infomachine; an entity given *embodiment* by the computer hardware upon which it is executing. When we watch computer programs execute, the machine we are watching is in fact not the computer itself, but rather the embodiment of the live program syntax that the computer empowers into operation.[116] In this sense, computers may be viewed as devices that *turn on* computer software, converting disembodied patterns of data codes into operational infomachines that will then perform their intended functions.

Even though active software routines do not possess *physical* bodies, this in itself should not prevent us from conceptualizing them as discrete operational *entities*. To think of live software infomachines as the inhabitants of cyberspace is in fact a very sensible proposition. Granted, live software can only exist as an entity *within* a computer system, but similarly fish can only exist in water, and we humans only within the subtle confinements of a suitable planetary atmosphere. Nobody would seriously argue that human beings are not real because we would all perish if exposed to the cold vacuum of space. All entities are dependent upon their native medium for embodiment. Therefore, why not consider active software programs as infomachine entities? After all, they are most certainly more than mere electrical signals chasing around live wires and silicon wafers.

SOFTWARE ENSEMBLES & SOFTWARE AGENTS

The infomachine concept only becomes really significant when we begin to consider *ensembles* of many software embodiments, rather than just single infomachines in isolation. If computer programs all keep themselves to themselves, then it is largely irrelevant as to how we conceptualize their nature and operation. When computer programs start working together, however — getting born, swapping data, and spontaneously self-destructing as they share information and task demands from their human masters — then the notion of infomachine *entities* within a cyberspace software *community* becomes critical.

Software agents are special kinds of infomachines that will need to work together in ensembles if they are to be of significant value to their human masters. Agents will work for specific individuals or organizations as information snoopers, investigators, analysers and digesters. Agents will sort out the nitty-gritty technicalities of *human* business activities across cyberspace. In order for this notion to be realized, however, a common set of standards and protocols for agent communication will need to emerge and be adopted internationally across the computer and telecommunications industry. After all, if you send an agent off on an errand (to compile a list of airline departure times, for example), then it will find itself totally handicapped if other agents (such as those representing the airlines) either don't speak its language or refuse to enter into conversation.

THE BUSINESS OF GENERAL MAGIC

California-based *General Magic* is one of the companies currently pioneering the conception of software agents, and in particular a communications standard for their widespread operation. An off-shoot of Apple Computer also funded by industry giants AT&T, Motorola, Philips, Matsushita and Sony, the company has created a software language — Telescript — for creating and dispatching agents into cyberspace, and which in the process defines a common communications standard. In order to make compatibility as wide as possible, Telescript has been designed to run across a variety of computer hardware platforms, including both IBM and Apple PCs. Telescript also permits agents to travel over both regular and cellular telephone systems to just about any form of computer database.[117] Thus, so long as all involved parties are running Telescript software, their agents will be able to communicate and hence work cooperatively in the emerging infomachine ensemble.

The hurdle before Telescript's potential success obviously lies in convincing as many other companies as possible to adopt the software as an international standard. To this end, General Magic intends to license

Telescript freely throughout the computer and telecommunications industry. Even this move, however, is unlikely to prevent a standards war in agent communications, with IBM, Microsoft, Hewlett-Packard and Rank Xerox having also emerged as leading players in the rapidly expanding marketplace and espousing their own agent communications standards. As witnessed during the video-standards battle between VHS and Betamax in the 1980s, consumers will need to be cautious in declaring their allegiances and committing their budgets. Almost certainly one standard for agent communications will become dominant over the next decade, but nobody as yet owns the crystal ball indicating which one it may be.

Whilst the complexity of agents themselves will depend upon the function or functions for which they are programmed, all genres of the species will be charged with protecting their human masters *from* complexity. In AT&T's Personalink messaging system, for example, due to have been launched by the time this book goes to press, the use of agents allows computer-to-computer messages to be sent without having to remember and key cumbersome address codes. A typical electronic mail address, for example (in this the author's) comes in a format along the lines of:

`lizcjb@lin1.nottingham.ac.uk`

Under Personalink, however, a user can ignore this style of computer gobbledygook and instead type in the telephone number of the person to whom they wish to send their electronic letter. Armed with this number and the message, an agent then nips off to a database to find the associated e-mail coding. The agent then uses this code to deliver the message, as well as reporting back to confirm its receipt if required. Personalink agents will also be able to filter incoming messages and search for information across computer networks.[118]

THE FACE OF THE FUTURE

Agent software will only be widely utilized by the masses if it can be made foolproof and user-friendly enough to appeal to even the most technophobic of employees. To this end, Apple Computer researchers are now experimenting with agents which are programmed with distinct 'personalities', and which present themselves on the computer screen as interactive 'characters'. When an agent is called up it will therefore be displayed with its own animated human or animal face. The 'Eager' agent, for example, which is designed to spot the occurrence of repetitive user operations so that it may offer assistance, appears on screen as a smiling cartoon cat.[119] Most agents are also likely to possess a distinctive synthesized voice enabling them to actually *speak* to their master.

The potential application of software agents is enormous. The emergence of virtual organizations and working patterns empowered via emerging cybertechnologies will also make their integration into most people's working lives completely seamless. Systems for loan and insurance processing, for example, are already in development, leaving users free to concentrate on the minority of cases that cannot easily be handled by active software routines seeking out their own background information and applying a base of pre-programmed rules. One of the companies hoping to grab a lead in the race is News International, which plans to turn its mass of newsprint into 'digital product'. Information from this database will then be extracted and configured according to individual desires by 'retriever' agents that will 'go and fetch' for their masters as if they had 'thrown a stick'.

The protocol and complexity of many mundane business dealings and negotiations will probably also be left in the virtual protruberances of software agents, a trend already exhibited by those organizations whose stock reordering is automatically linked to their suppliers' computer systems via EDI. Delegating task responsibilities to agents across networks, however, need not imply that humans will lose control. On the contrary, bureaucratic foul-ups will be less likely to occur when processes are carried out by tireless electronic servants which will automatically and consistently request human attention when complex decisions beyond their operational parameters need to be made.

It should be remembered that developments and associated benefits involving agents as 'virtual workers' will not be confined to the 60% of employees who spend their days in an office or other PC-populated location. With palm-sized, pen-operated personal digital assistants (PDAs) linked by digital radio links into cyberspace, even salespersons, buyers, construction workers and others out in the field will be able to join in and dispatch agents to do their bidding. Agents may therefore become the electronic glue holding *everyone* together within virtual business communities. Loyal, and programmed to be protective of their masters, agents will be very, very useful indeed.

HIS MASTER'S PROFILE

In order to obtain the services and data required by their masters — to selectively interrogate a database such as that to be provided by News International, for example — agents will need to be programmed with a *profile* of the human being they represent. These profiles will then be used like filters through which only information of value to the agent's master will be able to pass. If you wish an agent to book you a weekend away, for example, then your electronic servant will need to know where you want to go, how much you can afford to spend, as well as numerous other personal details. By comparing your known preferences against the holiday packages offered by the travel agencies listed on the network, the agent you dispatch will be able to report back with a selection of deals that come closest to matching your requirements. Upon instruction, the agent will then be able to make the necessary bookings and arrange payment electronically. A flowchart indicating the progression of steps that may be involved in utilizing an agent to arrange a vacation is illustrated in **figure 4.1**.

Whilst personal profiles will initially be built up on the basis of a user's responses to basic questions, over time profiles will alter as a result of the actual *actions* of the user. In other words, agents will learn what their masters like and dislike — how they *really* behave and make decisions, rather than how they *say* they will behave — and will use this information when locating and arranging future services and data. The concept of profile building is illustrated by John Evans, President and Chief Executive of News Electronic Data:

> An agent, Wanda, says: 'If you will tell me what you like and dislike about travel and fill in some forms — you'll only ever have to do this once — I can help you with subjects like airlines, and hotels, and restaurants. I will keep your information very safe and you'll only pay for the maps that we give you.'

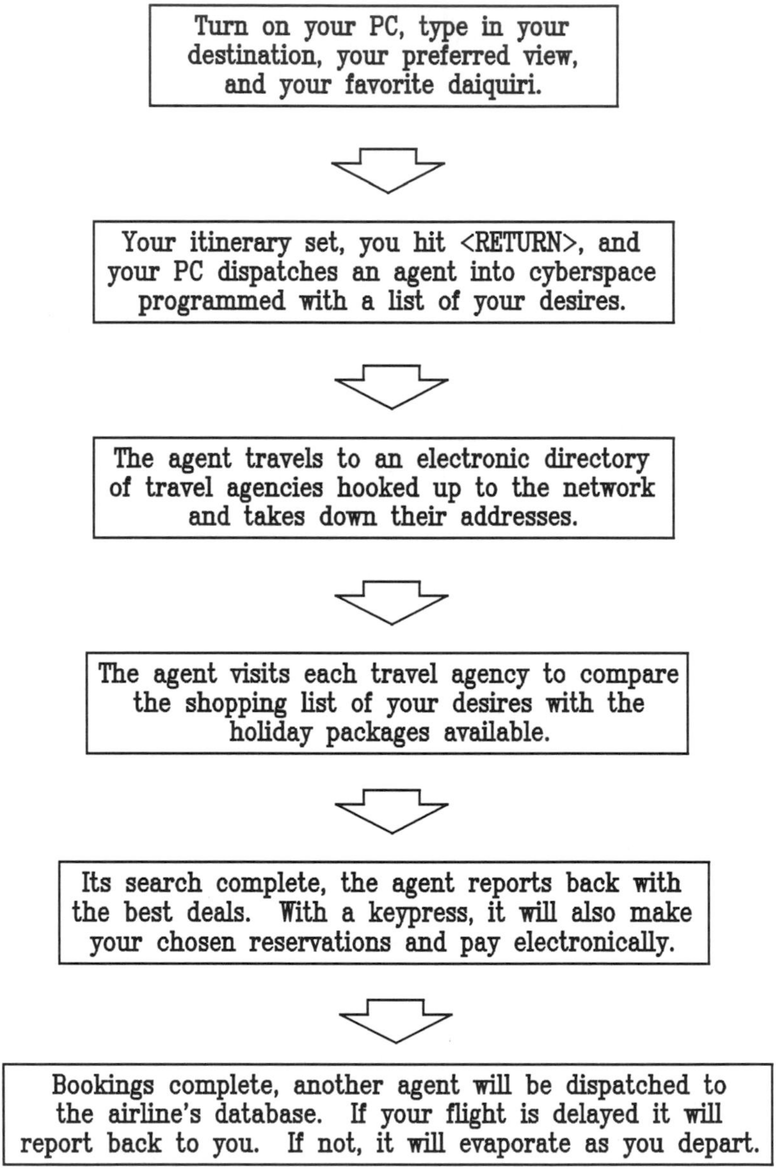

Turn on your PC, type in your
destination, your preferred view,
and your favorite daiquiri.

Your itinerary set, you hit <RETURN>, and
your PC dispatches an agent into cyberspace
programmed with a list of your desires.

The agent travels to an electronic directory
of travel agencies hooked up to the network
and takes down their addresses.

The agent visits each travel agency to compare
the shopping list of your desires with the
holiday packages available.

Its search complete, the agent reports back with
the best deals. With a keypress, it will also make
your chosen reservations and pay electronically.

Bookings complete, another agent will be dispatched to
the airline's database. If your flight is delayed it will
report back to you. If not, it will evaporate as you depart.

Figure 4.1 Booking a Break — An Agent at Work
[Adapted from Andrew Kupfer (*Fortune*, 24th January 1994: 54)]

> The interesting thing is that this profile we're building will stay upon the PDA or the device you're going to use and adjust itself: you may say that you'd rather have fruit in your room than alcohol, but in fact that may not be true, you may be guzzling on a bottle all night. And you may say that you're a vegetarian, but when you start to book reservations in steak-houses, your profile will adjust itself.[120]

AN ELECTRONIC LEGACY

The concept of the 'self-correcting' profile will have profound implications as agents become commonplace and relieve human beings of more and more laborious complexity and organizational bureaucracy. At work, many people will come to rely upon agents to such an extent that they will not be able to perform their jobs without them. This dependence in itself is not inherently a problem. Despite the objections of many worried technophobics, a reliance upon smart software will not be 'bad'. It will not dehumanize us. After all, we *already* rely very heavily on technology to maintain the quality of our lives and the fabric of Western civilization. Many jobs are already computer-dependent, and without complex technological infrastructures the concentration of human beings found in most cities could not be sustained.

The 'problem', if a problem it is deemed to be, may instead rotate around the fate and the ownership of agents either when their masters move between organizations, or more significantly when they've punched their last keyboard, kicked the metaphorical bucket, and ascended to an astral plane even more virtual than cyberspace. In such circumstances, will organizations own the agents of their deceased employees? And perhaps more importantly, will they continue to use these agents in the day-to-day operations of the company? If the latter proves to be the case, then the responses and business *personalities* of former human beings may continue to be enacted, via their agent profiles, perhaps years after their physical demise. John Brown could thus continue to negotiate the best deals, exhibiting the same nuances and judgements via the cyber medium, even when his body *is* lying a-mouldering in the grave. An horrendous and immoral concept? Perhaps not. Future organizations may simply claim that the only reason for employing certain individuals will be as software agent trainers. If people do come to be seen as a means to an end in this fashion, then their profiles will indeed become corporate property when they move on from this world.

If the above scenario proves correct, and agents are not deleted from existence upon the death of the human being they represent, then cyberspace may well come to be inhabited by tens of thousands of software *ghosts* (ie the agents of the dead). People may therefore come to achieve a form of corporate cyber immortality, with a legacy of their actions and reactions to countless past scenarios encapsulated in computer code and data patterns. Alternatively, organizations may in future choose to fuse the knowledge and experience of ghost software routines into some central corporate databank or profile store. In either case, it becomes clear that key individuals — especially key leaders, founders, innovators and negotiators — may continue to have an influence over the operation of their companies long after their death.

Whilst initially this concept may seem far-fetched, it is worth remembering the way in which the culture and hence operation of some companies has *already* been influenced by a founder long departed. Walt Disney and Henry Ford, for example, shaped the culture of their organizations and left a legacy across them in terms of their work ethic and spirit. To allow an army of ghost software entities to continue to be utilized after an employee's death simply takes this idea a step further. Indeed it could even be argued that it would be unethical to delete agents from existence upon the demise of their master. After all, who will be able to claim the right to destroy an infomachine encoded with a former human personality?

ASSOCIATED RELATIVES

Agents, and perhaps ghost derivatives, will not be the only smart software entities regularly cruising the data pathways of cyberspace city in the years ahead. Leaving aside the potential characteristics of any sentient machine 'intelligences' that may one day emerge (a topic that could easily consume a book in itself!), there are perhaps two key infomachine classifications of note to those keen to stay abreast of at least current terminology in this rapidly evolving field. Firstly, *knowbots* can be isolated as a particular form of analytical software servant. 'Inserted' into computer systems, these tiny, diagnostic infomachines are programmed to detect faults and then to report back to their human masters.[121]

Secondly, and far more interestingly, there is now also the classification of infomachines found under the conceptual heading of *artificial life*.

In a computer software context, developments in artificial life, or *Alife*, are concerned with the creation of software entities capable of replicating, and hence evolving into new forms. As Rudy Rucker explains,[122] in a typical Alife world each 'little critter' will carry a chromosome of binary information which will split and recombine with that of another during the mating process.

Alife populations are usually programmed in order to seek solutions to complex and seemingly unsolvable problems. Each Alife entity attacks the problem with a slightly different permutation, and a *fitness function* is defined such that only those Alifes coming close to a solution to the problem will survive. Over time the characteristics of the fittest Alifes are strengthened via cross-breeding (in an process akin to selective evolution), with the descendants of the first population mutating to provide the answer to the initial problem posed by the programmer.

One of the major variables determining success in Alife modelling concerns the choice of optimal parameters for mating and survival. A common approach is to employ *genetic algorithms*. These allow fitness and survival, and the choice of mate and gene combination, to be scored and selected toward the attainment of the optimal permutation of potential solutions to a problem. Alife applications are likely to skyrocket in the near future, particularly in areas such as financial forecasting where thousands of outcome permutations may impact upon any decision under evaluation. By assigning an Alife to each possible pathway and seeking optimal mutations over many evolutionary, machine-learning cycles, comparative information impossible to assimilate via normal arithmetic and computer programming techniques can result. The modelling of complex scenarios within Alife systems may therefore become a standard means of gaining quality decision information.

The genetic algorithms used in today's Alife decision and problem-solving systems may eventually be adapted to allow software agents and other infomachines to bear offspring. This facility could be utilized to allow the strengths of many employee's software agents to be combined (perhaps as they were 'added' to a central data store). Alternatively, when allocated complex data analysis tasks, agents may well learn to dispatch 'children' to scan cyberspace for information in a multitude of different ways. After a given interval, these offspring would be recalled, each child's progress reviewed, and the most successful children allowed to mate. Subsequent generations of the original agent population would then be sent out into cyberspace once more until the task in question was completed. In other words, agents may learn to conceive and control Alife systems. What should become apparent from this futuristic scenario is that cyberspace may soon be literally teeming with smart and/or sexually active infomachines. The potential for chaos will be considerable. Indeed, we can note the potential downside of increased computer usage even today. Few people may yet have heard of agents and Alife, yet *everyone* knows about the family of destructive, self-replicating software feared under the general banner of *computer viruses*.

VIRUS ATTACK!

Unlike *bugs*, which are unintentional errors in computer programs which may cause operational problems, *viruses* are deliberately crafted pieces of software with the sole aim of malicious computer disruption. The effects of viruses are wide-ranging, although in general they cause messages to appear and the screen to be disrupted, machine operations to slow down, data and program files to be deleted or corrupted, and/or computers to 'crash' and seize up altogether. Some viruses 'attack' computers as soon as infection occurs. Other more sinister forms wait until a certain date (for example Friday the 13th), or until a certain operation has occurred a certain number of times, before wreaking their chaos. The latter are potentially far more of a headache than the former, as they may lie dormant and undetected for months or even years, hence fooling the user into a false sense of security.

Viruses and associated disruptive programs are created by computer malcontents (as described in the next section) usually as a means of displaying their talents to the world, or as a massage to lonely egos. Viruses may also be created purely for espionage purposes, however, in order to corrupt competitors' systems and data, although at present such instances are thought to be rare.

In order to travel between computers, viruses are usually programmed to secretly copy themselves onto every floppy disk inserted into an 'infected' computer (although network links may also be utilized as the means of spreading a virus plague). Indeed, the first virus programs were a response by their creators to the growing number of personal computers which could not be 'hacked' into because they were not connected to computer networks. By creating virus programs capable of self-replicating themselves from floppy disk to floppy disk, computer malcontents thereby gave themselves access to the world of the stand-alone PC. Because of the potential risk of virus infection across their operations, many large companies now carefully control the suppliers of their computer disks (with some even having their own labels). Indeed in some organizations it is an offence meriting dismissal for an employee to use a floppy disk from outside the company on an office PC.

The first recorded computer virus was called 'Brain'. It first struck in October 1987 at the University of Delaware, rapidly infected hundreds of floppy disks, and destroyed at least one student's thesis.[123] Like many viruses that have followed, 'Brain' was written to destroy the *boot sector* of floppy disks. This portion of a disk stores file control information and its corruption effectively makes all data on the disk irretrievable. Today, a variety of virus detection programs exist that scan for the presence of viruses on disk and in computer memory. If these programs find viruses, then it is also sometimes possible to clean or 'disinfect' the floppy or hard disk involved. However, anti-virus software should not be relied upon as the only means of virus defence, as by definition such programs can only scan for *known* viruses. With virus killers constantly being updated in *response* to the emergence of new strains of disruptive program, the virus creators will always have the potential to remain one step ahead.

With computer viruses now so widespread, it is hardly surprising that some 'specialist' forms have been created and labelled. One of these is the *worm*, a form of virus that copies itself into computer memory and then replicates itself over and over. Over time this clogs up the system, causing the computer to run more and more slowly. Eventually the worm will cause the computer to crash, as its applications programs will have no space left in which to run.

Another variant of virus is the *trojan*. In one sense trojans are not true viruses, as they actually tempt the user to execute them. The first trojan appeared one Christmas linked to a piece of electronic mail and told the user to run the program to 'enjoy themselves'. When they did, a Christmas tree was drawn on their screen. Unbeknown to the user, the program then also looked up their electronic address book and mailed itself to thousands of other computers. Not many days later, the trojan had managed to spread across several continents. Effectively, trojans may be thought of as electronic chain letters.

Another type of destructive program form to be aware of is the *logic bomb*. These do not replicate, instead being pieces of coding that lie dormant until detonated by a remote password or a specific chain of events. They then 'explode' to delete files and corrupt computer operations, often launching viruses, worms and trojans throughout the system. When sacked, some computer programmers are reputed to have held their employers to ransom by placing hidden logic bombs in the system code which have only been 'defused' once certain redundancy demands (such as large, one-off payments), have been met.

Finally, it is worth being aware of the recent emergence of programs called *sniffers*. These are not viruses, yet are used by the criminally minded computer user. The purpose of a sniffer is to 'steal' computer log-in sequences and passwords as legitimate users tap them into their system. Thousands of corporate security access codes are now being pilfered in this way, allowing hackers illegitimate access to hundreds of supposedly secure computer systems. In May 1994, two sniffer programs had been reported in Britain, one in Australia, and 40 in the United States.[124]

BATTLES IN CYBERSPACE

The emergence of smart software forms, and agents in particular, has the potential to permit a new generation of smarter and far more destructive viruses. In order for agents to perform their functions, mechanisms will have to be in place to allow them to roam freely from computer to computer, and hence controls will be necessary to prevent disruptive and malicious infomachines accessing the same channels. In their attempt to counter this threat, General Magic have built safeguards into Telescript so that when agents arrive in a foreign computer they will be greeted and interrogated by its Telescript software to determine their purpose and content. Agents will then be barred access to certain program areas and issued with an 'electronic permit' that will be regularly checked by the host computer to make sure that there is no foul play. Agents exceeding their time and stated purpose in a computer they are visiting will be kicked out of the system. Similarly virus programs without the appropriate pass will be excluded.

Taking this scenario a stage further, it is possible that specialist 'virtual policemen' agents/knowbots may one day be created to seek out and destroy infomachines created with a malicious intent. A taskforce of such cyberspace defenders, perhaps bestowed with genetic algorithms allowing them to evolve as new viruses are created, could constantly patrol corporate computer systems to seek out offenders and delete them from existence. It is possible, of course, that virus strains could also be programmed with complex Alife reproductive capabilities, leading to a constant battle between two continually evolving camps of 'good' and 'evil' virtual monsters. However, this need not inhibit 'normal' cyberspace operations. Within our own bodies there is constant biological warfare between viruses and antibodies, yet for the most part we are oblivious to this battle and it has no major impact upon our lives.

THE REAL (VIRTUAL) MONSTERS

Malicious programs need malicious programmers. It really is science fiction to suggest that a piece of software will get up one morning and decide to electronically rob a bank or crash somebody else's mainframe. It still takes a person to do that. However 'evil' viruses, sniffers and associated disruptive infomachines become, they will only ever be tools used by criminals to exploit fellow users of the cyberspace medium.

Until recently, computer criminals, be they hardened fraudsters or disruptive malcontents, tended to be called *hackers*. As the first generation of hackers has grown up, however, a new breed known as *crackers* has emerged. Sometimes also described as *cyberpunks*, crackers are typically alienated cyberholics, specifically out to cause disruption, who believe that the old generation of hackers have become too establishment. Indeed it has been noted in some circles that the difference between hackers and crackers is that the former are now respectably employed by the computer companies they once battled against, and that in many cases they are actually *running* these companies! Whatever label computer malcontents are clustered under, they tend to share a common philosophy. They will argue, for example, that 'information wants to be free', and that when you copy information you don't steal it as the original still exists. The whole debate about digital information ownership is therefore argued to be irrelevant.

The majority of the adherents to the cyberpunk ethos are young men for whom computers, computer networks, and the control thereof, have become an obsession. Within the pages of their casebook *Cyberpunk*, Katie Hafner and John Markoff present a detailed history of three such individuals, all of whom became icons of the dark side of computing in the 1980s (and all of whom eventually got caught!).[125] Kevin Mitnick in the United States, for example, gained a reputation as a computer renegade capable of manipulating credit ratings and taking control of distant computers. Another individual, under the name of 'Pengo', operated as part of a group that played out outlaw fantasies over computer networks and then sold the fruits of their wanderings to the Soviets. It is perhaps comforting to note that in both cases these individuals were eventually brought down due to their own arrogance and through betrayals and vengeance wrought by former colleagues whom they had treated badly. In other words, without human social skills, even the most technically gifted criminals have found it impossible to go unchallenged forever. It is their *human* side that has always proved to be their Achilles' heel.

As cyberspace expands as *the* business medium, crackers and hackers cannot be ignored. They are the old cowboys of the new frontier. They know the terrain and the opportunities it will tempt before those with criminal and maladjusted dispositions, and who abhor bureaucracy and the establishment. To illustrate this point, the following passages by (ex?) hackers/crackers perfectly capture the ethos of these human 'virtual monsters':

> The more digital society gets, the more we'll be able to completely change money. We'll be able to change a date on a document. We'll be able to add a figure to a bank balance. We'll be able to change a 'no' to a 'yes'. How do you trace things like that? If you're a good programmer, there are no fingerprints.
>
> 'Emmanual Goldstein'[126]

> You know who was the most important president? Richard Nixon. You know why? Because he took us off the gold standard. Once upon a time, money in the bank had to be related to a real-world object. But suddenly the governor was

removed. Money was just a bunch of bits and bytes in computers. Money became the first exploration into cyberspace. This is why the economy is messed up. This is why the damage that can be caused electronically can be so great. We stopped using reality as the 'acid test' for what was represented in our machines.

Michael Synergy[127]

BLESSINGS IN DISGUISE

Whilst the above may charge fear into the heart of anybody leading their company further and further down the track of increased cyberspace reliance, it should be remembered that whilst most great discoveries can be perverted into weapons, the reverse usually also holds true. In the case of smart, evolving and self-replicating software, we have simply experienced the 'bad' long before the delivery of any 'good'.

Almost as soon as personal computers were created, the hacker generation strove to create viruses to disrupt their operation in a bid to display wasted teenage talents. Only twenty years later will most people experience the impact of beneficial software entities such as agents. Software agents *will* make life easier, aiding communications, undertaking repetitive and eye-straining tasks, and negating our need to cope with technology at its lowest, nit-picking level. Additionally, agents, knowbots and their descendants will also be created to *protect* us from viruses, sniffers, worms, logic bombs and the malicious electronic mail of the future. A cyberspace populated by agents, ghosts and other virtual monsters may have the potential to suck individuals and corporations down into a bytestream nightmare of data corruption, system crashes, fraud, espionage and good old-fashioned theft, yet it may also have a very *positive* influence on Mankind and his business systems. After years of struggle, we may finally have found the slaves to do the data-jobs that no individual desires. They will not need monitoring or paying, will be totally loyal, and will greatly improve the quality of our decision information. Indeed in ten years time, we will almost certainly look back and wonder how we actually managed to do business without the assistance of electronic servants across the global network of pure information.

It is not as important to know what to do with technology as to know what technology does with us . . .

Daniel Burrus
Technotrends

5

The Marriage
of Man & Machine

SINCE EARLY MAN FORGED crude implements from bone, rock, wood and hide, human beings have craved tools and technologies to aid in the accomplishment of their end desires. As a species, our survival and dominance across the planet has almost certainly been *dependent* upon technological advances and their integration into our society. Continually, a desire for invention has led Mankind to create ever more complex means of manufacture, distribution, storage and communication. The use of 'technology' — be it in the form of a rock bound to a branch or a computer linked into our own new frontier of cyberspace — is synonymous with our evolution. We can therefore note that computer systems and other cyberspace technologies are very natural developments when viewed within the frame of the progression of our race. Indeed, the most common and dominant *change agent* throughout human history has been technological advancement.[128]

THE DAWN OF A NEW ERA

There can be little doubt that humanity is now caught in the embryonics of a new era of technical and hence social evolution that will transform the nature of our businesses, cultures and societies. In previous chapters we have already noted how remote and 'virtual' working practices are encroaching upon the business nexus, allowing individuals to link together across cyberspace in order to undertake new forms of cooperative work. These trends will undoubtably continue, with key developments in broadband computer networking, groupware and virtual reality already well beyond the drawing board stage. The whole world *is* becoming electronically interconnected; electronic servants *are* being created to help us navigate the new realm of almost limitless information; and the working lives of many, many individuals (if perhaps not the majority) *will* evolve into radically new patterns over the next decade.

Thus far, this book has adopted a rather upbeat approach to *Cyber Business* developments, ignoring the potential downside of a cellular society of 'honeycombed individuals' (or 'console potatoes') linked solely via cyberspace and a myriad of electronic servants. Over the next two chapters, however, both the positive *and the negative* implications of increased man-machine 'synthesis' will be addressed. Specifically, this chapter will concentrate on technology adoption and the individual. **Chapter 6** will then broaden the scope of debate to consider the implications of *Cyber Business* developments for groups of individuals — for the culture and functioning of business organizations, society in general, and the social patterns of humanity. Some writers hurdle the individual man-machine interface issues in a leap and a bound, in order to collide as quickly as possible with the sexy, high-profile topics concerning the forthcoming 'global village' and 'virtual community'. There is, however, an inherent and rather obvious danger in such an approach. For how can we hope to understand how *Cyber Business* developments will impact upon business and society, without first questioning how they will impact upon the individual human beings that make up these wider human communities? Cybertechnology developments will not simply change the nature of work and employment relationships; they will also alter the nature of individuals as the *customers* of all business activity. We therefore have to study the evolving relationship between individuals and cybertechnology — *the marriage of man and machine* — so that we can at least crawl before we sprint into an investigation of the dawn of fresh cultural compositions.

LEARNING TO LIVE WITH TECHNOLOGY

> Don't like computers? Unamused by technology? For most people, technology is the ocean on a bright cool spring day. Sparkling in the far distance; breathtakingly cold; exhilarating once you've plunged in.[129]

Most people's lives, both at work and in the home, are now mediated, if not dominated, by electronic technologies. Even if we are unaware of it, computers play some role in most of our daily activities. Make a telephone call, use a debit card, shop in a supermarket, drive down the motorway, watch a television programme, cook something in the microwave, take a plane, write a letter, listen to music or work on a production line: in all these and more computer processing power is now used in at least one stage of the involved process. What may therefore surprise us is not the *resistance* to technology that some people exhibit, but the degree to which most people *have already accepted* new technologies over the past few decades. As researchers into human-computer interaction (HCI) have long known, most people don't mind 'squaring up to technology' as long as it's not intimidating.[130]

As you may expect, part of this chapter examines some of the cutting-edge technological advances that will undoubtably lead us to interact with computer and communications systems in radical, subtle and even exciting new ways over the coming decades. Before peeking into this Pandora's box, however, it is wise to explore the current impact of technology upon individuals. There are still many advocates of the 'old ways of doing things' — CEOs who refuse to use PCs, maths teachers who shun calculators, designers who stick with pencil and paper rather than converting to stylus and digitizing tablet — and their influence in some entrenched quarters can be considerable. It is therefore worth taking some time to investigate why a large, largely silent, and in many cases shunned minority, have embraced cybertechnologies to a level which at times borders on addiction. By studying the 'hold' that computers may have over the latter, managers can hopefully make progress in influencing the perceptions and fears of those who still shy away from adopting a computer as a 'co-worker' if not as a 'friend'.

WHY WORK WITH A COMPUTER ANYWAY?

Today, most managers argue that computers may be employed to improve cost-effectiveness, to further business growth, to enable better communications, and to aid in the decision process. The first of these advantages — improved cost-effectiveness — will clearly accrue when computers are used to automate repetitive tasks such as accounts processing and stock control. As a result business growth may also be enabled, as computer-based administrative processing systems frequently present organizations with an increased potential to reap economies of scale. For example, if processing a payroll manually, it would probably take twice as long to write out or type 200 cheques and pay slips as it would to produce 100. With a computer-based payroll system, however, printing the 100 additional cheques and slips would almost certainly only involve a minimal additional overhead, as most employee-time would be spent on tasks such as threading the printer and initiating the software, rather than in executing the actual print run itself. In general, once a computer system has been set up, throughput can usually be greatly increased with only minimal cost incurrence.[131]

As noted in previous chapters, computers may be utilized to improve organizational communications in a variety of ways, with options including the adoption of electronic mail and other groupware, computer-telephone integration and EDI. Finally, the fourth commonly cited argument for computer adoption — using the computer systems to aid in the decision process — will yield benefits in different ways depending upon what form of decision making is involved.

Many of the decisions that a manager has to take, such as reordering supplies when stocks fall to pre-specified levels, are routine and non-creative. In such instances, a computer can be programmed to actually *make* the decisions involved on the basis of set criteria. Routine decision making is thereby *automated*.

Other types of decision, however, will be more complex and will involve subjective and creative human inputs. Examples include choosing the design for a new office block, or deciding upon an opening bid when initiating a takeover. Most decisions of this type tend to be 'one-of-a-kind'. They cannot therefore be handed over to machines as there are no routine algorithms to apply. Such decision making may be *augmented*, however, with computers utilized to present data in novel ways, and/or to model potential outcome scenarios, in order that more informed choices can be made. By employing a computer, an architect can walk through a VR simulation of his or her new building before it is built, whilst a manager responsible for a takeover can prepare spreadsheets detailing the worth of the target firm under a range of financial scenarios. Therefore, even though creative decision making cannot be automated, computers may be used to improve its quality and effectiveness.[132] What's more, as more routine decision making is automated under computer control, there will be more time available to spend upon creative decision tasks.

On a purely economic level, organizations therefore have a very good range of arguments for requiring their employees to work with computers, as the technology enables the more efficient and effective monitoring, administration and control of operations. However, there are also other more subtle reasons as to why *individuals* may come to rely upon working with cybertechnology.

DRAWING PEOPLE IN

The benefits associated with using computers do not simply derive from the fact they are capable of performing calculations and accessing vast stores of data. Just as importantly, computer systems also possess the ability to represent *actions* in which human beings may participate, hence drawing us into dramatic engagements.[133] Inevitably, once the decision is made to 'computerize' a previously manual activity, the *medium* in which the work is carried out will fundamentally change. Rather than involving physical transactions and data handling processes, work tasks will instead be enacted upon or *within* a computer display window. New ways of thinking about and structuring work processes therefore need to be taken on board.

To appreciate this concept, consider how the job of an accounts clerk has changed. In pre-computer days, clerks meticulously wrote up, double-balanced, cross-checked and allocated figures in physical paper ledgers. The *focus* of their work was therefore these ledgers, together with the physical invoices, receipts and other paperwork that consumed banks of filing cabinets. To perform their job, clerks had to move around the office collecting and distributing paper. They had to physically find files and write-up ledger entries. They effectively manipulated a database store physically incumbent around their working location.

Today, with computer-based accounting systems, the job of an accounts clerk is very different. When an invoice is to be paid, a clerk will typically enter the details into a specific data entry screen within a particular module of the accounts software. The computer will subsequently print the cheque and make ledger entries as required. What's more, if further information is required, the clerk will frequently be able to obtain this again via software manipulation. The focus of the job has therefore *become* the computer system, with its display screen having taken the place of the physically distributed set of records and file information stored around the office. As a result, the *flow* of accounts work has radically altered. No longer is the job punctuated by physical requirements for moving and searching and filing. A clerk can process a whole mound of invoices without ever having to leave their desk, and with the minimum handling of physical material. As EDI and credit-transfer automatic payment systems proliferate over computer networks, the day may soon dawn when the clerk no longer has to handle *any* physical material. There will therefore be nothing to inhibit a continuous flow of work, with all the clerk's attention being focused into activity upon (or 'within') their computer screen.

WORKING WITHOUT PHYSICAL PUNCTUATION

When physical punctuations are removed from human activities, work intensity tends to increase. If you have to get up from your desk to go and look for something in a file, then you may well find yourself 'distracted' into an informal conversation with a colleague. Alternatively, you may nip off and get a cup of coffee. When engaged in any task that can be entirely completed upon a computer, however, such breaks tend not to present themselves. As *anybody* who uses a computer regularly will tell you, it is very common to sit down at the keyboard 'to do something for ten minutes', only to look up three hours later to discover that the afternoon has passed you by.

Computers draw people in. They entangle us in the *process* of what we are doing by freeing us from *distractions* that present themselves when work is not based around one physical location or technology. Writers are not distracted by having to turn the page or thread another piece of paper into the typewriter. A manager with a PC networked-up for electronic mail does not have to move from the keyboard to process his or her in-tray. In a very real sense, once you have started something on a computer, once you are *engaged* in technological interaction, you are likely to want to continue until task completion. And this is why working with a computer can become a highly addictive experience. Indeed, some 'technoholics' are reported to have found computer interaction more addictive than cocaine.[134]

Integrating task environments to make working with computers more fluid, natural and unified, is one of the key goals of software designers today. After all, if one sub-task leads directly into the next, then your flow of work is far more likely to continue uninterrupted than if you have to physically do something in order to proceed from one activity phase to another. Programmers who create computer games have known this 'hook' for years. At some point in their lives, most adolescents have sat for hour upon hour playing the same computer game over and over. When one game ends it can be *incredibly* difficult not to start another when the computer prompts you to do so, especially if your performance has been improving. Carefully programmed, computers rarely fail to capture human attention. A pile of papers scattered across a desk generally holds far less immediate and interactive appeal.

EMPOWERMENT & EXPERIMENTATION

The ability of a computer to catalyse the flow of an activity is only one of the concepts that draws people into seeking greater cybertechnological interaction. Perhaps equally important is the notion of *empowerment*. This is related to the fact that when using a computer, most people discover that they have more control over their work. When producing a newsletter with a word processor or a desktop publisher, a designer will enjoy far more freedom to try out ideas, and to manipulate the involved text, pictures and layout, than if they were working with traditional methods.

Adopting a computer can also be observed to increase individual aspirations. Most children, for example, give up on drawing and painting when they realize that they are incapable of using traditional art materials to produce the pictures they desire. Computer art and design packages, however, can make drawing and modelling easier, with perfect geometrics, colouring and multiple attempts available to every user. Similarly, computers used in sound recording and/or equipped with MIDI[135] interfaces can aid those with limited musical talent in the rendition of competent pieces of music that they would otherwise have been unable to produce.

In short, computers offer the freedom to experiment at no cost. Figures, colours, dimensions, notes, scenarios or whatever variables are involved, can be changed at will, and without destroying an original piece of work to which you can always return. No other medium offers such creative freedom. No other medium is as lenient when it comes to the correction and obliteration of human error or experimentation.

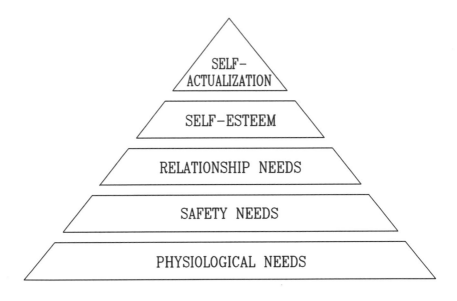

Figure 5.1 Maslow's Hierarchy of Human Needs
[Adapted from Maslow 'A Theory of Human Motivation' (1943)]

COMPUTER ADOPTION & THE FULFILMENT OF HUMAN NEEDS

In 1943 psychologist Abraham Maslow introduced his now famous *hierarchy of human needs*, as illustrated in **figure 5.1**.[136] Intended to encapsulate a theory of human motivation into a pyramid of five levels, the hierarchy assumes that people are wanting beings who have needs that they yearn to achieve sequentially. Initially people want their *physiological* needs fulfilled, including the satisfaction of thirst, hunger and maternal behaviour. When these needs are met, people move up a level and desire that their *safety needs* are met (the desire for security, the freedom from pain and danger, and so forth). Next to be fulfilled come *relationship needs* (to be loved and to interact with fellow human beings), followed by the desire for *self-esteem* as associated with the fulfilment of self-confidence, independence, prestige, status and recognition. Finally, at the apex of Malsow's pyramid is the ultimate level of *self-actualization*, at which point people realize their full and individual potential.

Whilst perhaps not providing a model to explain all patterns of human motivation, the Maslow hierarchy does highlight the spectrum of goals that the majority strive (and often fail) to achieve. In modern Western society, most people no longer have to worry about the fulfilment of the 'lower' physiological and safety needs, hence leaving them more strongly motivated by the desire for social relationships, self-esteem and self-actualization. Unfortunately, these needs can be far more difficult to fulfil. Looking again at the reasons as to why many people become 'hooked' upon working closely with computers, we can note that in doing so they may well increase their potential for achieving the three highest levels of the Maslow hierarchy.

Within large organizations many people now use computers as tools to enable them to foster relationships with a great many other individuals across the world. In pre-computing days such a wide range of contacts and colleagues would have been impossible to achieve. Nowadays, as discussed in **chapter 3**, electronic mail, video-conferencing and other groupware links can empower employees into cohesive virtual teams. Indeed, with advancements in computer-mediated communication (CMC), we now have the emergence of entire *virtual communities* composed of people who have never physically met, and whose relationships blossom solely over computer networks.

Moving up the Maslow hierarchy, it becomes apparent that, as computers offer improved work flow, control and the potential for infinite experimentation, their adoption in the accomplishment of tasks such as design, musical composition, painting, planning and forecasting may greatly increase an individual's potential for creative freedom and self-expression. Some individuals may also seek to build themselves power bases by becoming computer literate, hence further enhancing their own level of self-esteem. Finally, by connecting into cyberspace, individuals may find themselves liberated from their demographic and geographic bounds. They may, for example, engage in worldwide debates over a global network, or build up folklores of achievement in the only medium free of the prejudices of gender, race, age and social background. As noted by journalist and popular networking advocate Howard Rheingold, the technologies of cyberspace have the potential to bring enormous intellectual, social, commercial and political leverage to individuals.[137] The potential to self-actualize is thereby increased.

Without doubt, even today, computers empower many people to fulfil a greater number of their higher-level needs than previously thought possible. Computers allow us to be more than we are — to be liberated by the digital rather than constrained by the physical. As virtual reality systems are developed, millions of people are likely to find themselves in this position, with cyberspace offering the only medium in which the majority's highest aspirations are ever likely to be met. In reality only a few people can rule any country, state or organization. In virtual reality, *everybody* can have the opportunity to reign over a kingdom of their own. Just empowering a first-line employee with their own desktop PC may render them the satisfaction of being in control of *their own* complex data system. Granted there may be a period of trepidation as the employee comes to terms with what a computer may do for them, but this does not usually stop them being flattered by their trusted new status as a computer-literate being.[138]

In aggregation, computer media of all genres may empower people with more creative potential, in turn making them less frustrated and hence more able to satisfy inner needs left unfulfilled when utilizing conventional media. Additionally, computers now also offer individuals the information and resource power previously only available to a corporate player. In other words computers change the rules. It is becoming more and more difficult to restrict information supply to a narrow minority, and even if multinationals and governments can and do prohibit public access to many systems, individuals with powerful databases will still be free to conduct their own investigations in order to discover what they wish to know. If you have access to cyberspace then you will never be left out of the game.

THE PROS & THE CONS

What may now be concluded is that, over and above their economic justification to business organizations, computers impact beneficially upon individuals in a variety of ways. In particular, computers may:

□ Empower individuals with information.

□ Enable an uninterrupted work flow to be attained due to the removal of physical punctuation between task stages.

◻ Permit individuals more creative freedom, as mistakes can be tolerated and multiple scenarios can be easily explored.

◻ Lead to the fulfilment of higher-level human needs due to the satisfaction of increased creative freedom and empowerment, and to raised aspirations due to potentially and actually higher levels of achievement.

Whilst the above points paint a very rosy picture, it should be remembered that if you are reading this book then you probably already possess a very positive attitude toward the use of computer technology. There are, of course, many people — many employees — still openly hostile to technological change. Indeed there is a substantial minority who are actually afraid of computers. Managing this sub-set of the workforce whilst **Cyber Business** developments are taking place may perhaps be the greatest challenge to face many managers over the next decade. However advanced and user-friendly the technology that is installed, it will never fulfil its true potential if it is not positively embraced by *everyone* across the organization. There's no point in installing an electronic mail system if people simply print out every message and stuff the hardcopy into an already bulging filing cabinet. Training clearly has a vital role to play in allaying employee fears, as do particular managerial styles and actions directed toward changing the *perceptions* of the technophobic toward technological acceptance.

THE FEARS OF THE TECHNOPHOBIC

Technophobia, a fear of new technology that may result in a physical and emotional burnout known as *technostress*, generally arises from a reluctance to adjust to the structural and social changes that take place when new technology is adopted in an organization. When computers are introduced into the workplace, there is often a great deal of resistance from many employees, most usually associated with a fear of losing status. Many older managers may feel that they are being asked to perform the job of their secretary if they are expected to undertake any task involving the use of a computer keyboard. In turn, if such managers are unable to type, they may feel ignorant and embarrassed and hence may resist computer technology even further. The fear of such potential embarrassment is significant in that if such a skills-void is addressed in time, via a proper training programme, then further entrenched cybertechnology resistance may well be eliminated.

A second concern associated with a potential loss of status and/or control arises when employees fear that computers will actually take away or automate key parts of their job, hence de-skilling their occupation. In many cases this fear is accurately founded, with industries such as printing and car production having already witnessed the introduction of new computer-controlled technologies that have rendered past craft-skills obsolete. In other cases, however, the fear that a computer will take over an employee's job has been largely unfounded, and it is important to point out to people that however advanced computer systems become, there are many realms of business activity in which human beings are destined to reign supreme for a very long time to come. As previously noted, whilst computers may come to automate routine decision processes, they will only ever augment the human-centred process of creative decision making. Even when software agents and advanced expert systems[139] come to be employed across industry, they will only ever offer information which people may subsequently choose to ignore. Future managers, sales people, doctors, scientists and administrators are extremely likely to be expected to *consult* a computer before a choice of action is determined. However, ultimately it will be the person, and not the machine, that will actually *make* the decision at the end of the day. Judgement, hunch and intuition based upon human experience will always be of value. Indeed, as computer skills come to be required on top of a traditional discipline training, a great many jobs and associated professions are likely to be upgraded.

ALLAYING EMPLOYEE CONCERNS

Managers and information technology specialists frequently attempt to address the problem of resistance to new technology by explaining that computerized systems will increase efficiency and profits, as well as streamlining the flow of work to be undertaken and improving the quantity and accuracy of information available. Unfortunately, a great deal of technophobia tends to be emotionally founded, and hence rational and logical argument will have little or no effect in allaying employee fears. Indeed in some cases logical argument may even exacerbate the problem.[140]

Emotionally founded cybertechnology resistance is likely to manifest itself via one of three behaviours. Firstly, people may simply play an avoidance strategy, perhaps working figures out on a calculator or by hand when there is a computer sitting idly before them. A second, and extremely common, response is simply to blame the computer system for anything that goes wrong. Granted, we all do this at one time or another (a poor workman always blames his tools!), although it soon becomes obvious when certain individuals state that they are *never* to blame and that their mistakes are *always* the 'computer's fault'. Thirdly, technology resistance may be exhibited in the form of aggressive behaviour, which in some instances can lead toward system sabotage. In addition to these three forms of exhibited behaviour, extreme cases of technology resistance can lead to individuals suffering from a condition known as *cyberphobia*. When this occurs, the 'victim' suffers classic phobia symptoms such as nausea and high blood pressure, and is likely to break into a sweat even if merely prompted to use a computer system.[141]

It can be very difficult to help individuals overcome technology-related fears, especially when logical argument proves to be an unsuitable weapon. Various steps for managers to employ have of course been suggested, such as the following list of recommendations from Robert Callahan and Patrick Fleenor:

☐ Have managers take the lead by buying and using computers to show how they can help performance.

☐ Encourage and reward employees who show an interest in computers.

☐ Establish a PC training centre where employees can learn about and practice with computers.

☐ Provide thorough computer training.[142]

Of the above, the first and the third points are perhaps the most significant to note, given that training in general, and rewarding employee interest in particular, should be components of any competent human resource management strategy. Point one is particularly significant in that in many organizations it has been observed that managers still expect employees to use office technology that they refuse to adopt themselves. Such a 'chauffeured approach'[143] is hardly likely to allay employee fears and to improve their confidence in using computers, and is notable by its absence in many highly successful organizations.[144] Point three is also worth considering, because if people are given the opportunity to experiment and 'play' with computers outside of a normal working environment, then their confidence with computer operation is likely to increase. Even providing a room with a few PCs on which employees can play games during breaks can do wonders to break the 'technological-ice'. Providing such an arcade may at first sound a little offbeat, but if computer gaming decreases technophobia, hence rendering previously fearful employees susceptible to logical persuasion concerning computer adoption, then it may well prove a very sound investment.

It is also worth noting that getting employees involved in the design and implementation of computer systems can greatly decrease their resistance to working with new technology. Research has shown that involving secretaries in the selection of computer equipment can yield considerable benefits, including secretaries with a greater understanding of the technology they employ and with far higher levels of commitment and competence.[145] Similarly, in a study of user involvement and user resistance pertaining to fifty-six new decision support systems, it was found that when end-users helped initiate the new system, there was significantly less resistance encountered when it was finally introduced.[146]

PROTECTING EMPLOYEE HEALTH

Even if none of the employees of an organization exhibit signs of technology-resistance and a resulting technostress or cyberphobia, stroll around any large, computer-populated office and you are likely to hear workers voicing complaints concerning eyestrain, headaches, back pains, finger pains and various other aches attributable to long-term computer usage. However much toil computers liberate us from, there is definitely still a price to be paid in terms of physical comfort. With more and more people using computers, either in a communal office or at home via network links, the related health risks have to be taken extremely seriously. After all, many of today's school-leavers are likely to be exposed to daily computer interaction for well over fifty years.

Newspapers now regularly headline test cases regarding the risk of developing debilitating conditions such as *repetitive strain injury* (RSI) in the fingers, hands and forearms when working at a computer keyboard for long periods. In the USA, the National Institute of Occupational Health has claimed that 40% of employees working predominantly with computers have suffered RSI symptoms.[147] These may arise in the form of either tenosynovitis (swollen muscles) or carpal tunnel syndrome (swollen tendons). The multiple-dangers that may be associated with a long-term exposure to CRT display screen radiation also receive increasing publicity, with some (debated) studies linking cancer, cataract formation and skin sores to computer display screen emissions.[148] If only because companies may find themselves liable for damages claimed by employees suing them for occupational injury compensations, all organizations must be aware of these health concerns and undertake a programme of suitable precautions.

Across the European Community, Directive 270/90/EEC specifies minimum working conditions for all those who 'habitually work with display screen equipment'. The document includes guidelines on suitable desks, chairs and general office ergonomics as well as specifics relating to the computer hardware employed. Legally, ethically, and to ensure optimum worker motivation and productivity, managers must strive to ensure that their organizations *at least comply* with the minimum conditions as set out in this Directive. No form of work can ever be entirely safe, but managers surely have an obligation to contain any potential health risks to a realistic minimum, even if profit margins have to be shaved in order to pay for display screen anti-radiation filters, adjustable office furniture, wrist supports and optimal lighting arrangements.

PEEKING INTO THE FUTURE

What have now been outlined are some of the key issues and concerns relating to both the positive and the negative impacts of computer systems upon individual human beings and upon their work activities and aspirations. Whilst some traditionalist stick-in-the-muds are alarmed as to the current penetration of cybertechnologies across our businesses and society, as the old adage goes, it seems likely that 'we ain't seen nothing yet'.

As cyberspace expands, with more and more individuals empowered via network links into its information web, computer hardware is likely to evolve into many fresh guises. Terminals and PCs with display screens and QWERTY keyboards will continue to dominate for many years to come, but alongside them we will find ourselves using integrated computer-telecommunications consoles, interactive, computer-controlled television sets, pocket PDAs, and revolutionary 'reality-engines' that will empower us to be transported into amazing virtual worlds. We are therefore likely to start interacting with computers in many different, non-traditional ways. In particular, with the predicted growth of the virtual reality market over the next decade, our expectations for visual computer output are likely to be heightened. What therefore follows is an investigation into how the interface peripherals that 'link' human beings into computer systems are likely to develop over the coming decades.

DEVELOPMENTS ON THE HUMAN-COMPUTER INTERFACE

The interface peripherals that allow people to work with computer systems are becoming increasingly subtle and complex. With today's generation of hardware and software, no longer do the majority of users have to type programming commands on a keyboard in order to prompt their machines into action. Rather, in the mid-1990s, most of us launch software applications with the movement of a pointer and the click of a mouse button, only resorting to the keyboard for laborious text entry. Watch any group of students entering a computer training lab, and most will initially take the mouse in hand rather than hovering their fingers near the keyboard. Only five or ten years ago, business computer training not solely dependent upon keyboard entry would have been unthinkable.

With the increased adoption of pen-based computers and PDAs boasting handwriting recognition, body-motion input peripherals such as datagloves and eyeball motion sensors, and the development of voice-recognition systems, today's mice may themselves become quaint antiques over the coming decade. As virtual reality interfaces, peripherals and systems develop, no longer will computer output be limited to 2-D video images on 14″ display screens. 3-D graphics worlds projected via head-mounted displays (HMDs) are likely to become extremely common by early next century. Voice synthesis systems allowing computers to speak may also be widespread, should we desire them.[149] We can therefore potentially look forward to a near-future when both computer users and their software agents will be able to converse in natural spoken language, and even via subtle non-verbal communication. By the time this day dawns, however, the race will be hotting-up to realize a new generation of man-machine interface systems that will allow even greater communications subtleties than are possible via today's state-of-the-art virtual reality systems. If we are to learn anything from a study of the history of technology, it has to be that rampant change is the name of the game. As futurologist Daniel Burrus notes: *if it works, it's obsolete.*[150] And as the next section indicates, interface hardwares in the conceptual and developmental pipeline are likely to render many current peripheral genres as extinct as the unfortunate dodo.

BEYOND THE HEAD-MOUNTED DISPLAY

It has been estimated that half of the human brain is used for processing visual information. Hardly surprising, then, that refining means for visual output remains top of the agenda for most cutting-edge innovators of computer output peripherals. Developments in flat screen and low-radiation display technology aside, most research into new visual output systems is now being directed into the refinement of the HMDs as used to 'immerse' wearers in a computer-generated graphics world. As noted in **chapter 2**, these devices work by positioning a small display screen before each eye, usually mounted within a helmet or a set of goggles. A slightly different image is then fed to each of the two screens so that an illusion of 3-D reality may be perceived by the wearer. Head movement is also tracked so that people can 'look around' in cyberspace.

HMDs were first devised by Ivan Sutherland in the 1960s,[151] although early models were extremely cumbersome and so heavy that they could not be worn comfortably for a period of more than a few minutes. Fortunately, with developments in display and other technologies in the latter part of the 1980s, the ergonomics of HMDs have improved considerably. Every major component is also ripe for further improvement. It is therefore confidently predicted that, in around a decade, a lightweight HMD no more cumbersome than a pair of Walkman-style headphones will be available, perhaps connected to a Walkman-sized computer.[152] HMD prices are also set to tumble. At the time of writing there were already four major companies offering viable, low-cost VR headsets for use on PC systems, such as the VFSX1 HMD from Forte retailing at around £600.[153]

As a new generation of HMDs become common PC and games console peripherals, prices will fall drastically and durability is sure to increase. As this occurs and a mass-market develops, the business application of HMDs is likely to skyrocket. The use of visually immersive VR for training and design purposes is obvious, but even in the conventional office environment we are likely to witness colleagues donning light-weight headsets. Imagine flying through a spreadsheet,[154] a 3-D graphical model or your organizational chart or data store. And this is before we remember the likely virtucommuting application of virtual reality systems. Already we are used to people at the next desk using a telephone to converse with somebody on the other side of the world. In five or ten years they could just as commonly be donning a designer HMD and jacking into a broadband network in order to have a meeting in virtual reality with clients from across the globe.

PROBLEMS WITH THE HMD SOLUTION

Even if HMDs become extremely small and lightweight, and even if in future they are worn as icons of fashion or status, portraying an alternative visual reality to the brain by positioning two small screens before the eyes will always be a second-best solution. Health problems have already been identified, one of the major drawbacks resulting from the fact that the eye has to focus for the entire period of immersion on a flat image at a fixed distance. This not only induces eyestrain of the type associated with any continual fixed-distance viewing (such as staring for long periods at a traditional monitor screen), but can send confusing perceptual signals, as the eyes do not have to alter their focus in order for sharp images of both foreground and background objects to be obtained. There is therefore not only the problem that the illusion of 3-D space may be degraded, but also the danger that the HMD wearer may become nauseated and suffer vision problems after a period of VR immersion.[155]

Whilst in theory HMDs *could* be created wherein screen-to-eye distance was altered either optically or physically during long periods of immersion, additional risks linked to long-term HMD usage are likely to emerge. Concern is continuing to grow regarding the potential hazards of staring at conventional computer display screens for long periods. It therefore hardly seems likely that strapping two small displays a few inches before the eyes will in future be considered 'safe'. Longer-term solutions for VR visual immersion may therefore resort to the application of emerging technologies for *retinal imaging* or *phosphotronic stimulation*, and may one day even utilize direct linkages into the human brain.

NON-SCREEN ALTERNATIVES

Retinal imaging, as the name suggests, is concerned with forming an image directly upon the back of the eye without first projecting it upon a screen. Very high resolution images can potentially be portrayed by this method, and there are fewer problems associated with eyestrain and fixed-distance focusing over long periods.

A key player in retinal imaging systems is Thomas Furness, formerly a VR researcher for the US Air Force, who currently works at the Human Interface Technology (HIT) Lab in Seattle. Furness strongly believes that screen-based HMDs may become obsolete 'sooner than you think', with retinal image systems providing a visual computer interface close to matching the capabilities of the human eye. As he explains:

> A laser microscanner will paint realities directly on the retina of the eye . . . [and what's more] . . . The people working on it think we can achieve a resolution of 8000 by 6000 scan lines.[156]

Whilst retinal imaging relies upon stimulating the human eye with a stream of photons emitted by a low-power laser, some researchers are already predicting a technology that will go a 'step further'. Their idea is that *phosphotronic stimulation* will take an even more direct approach than using photons, and will instead employ mild electrical fields which will trigger eye tissues into releasing stray electrons. These freed electrons will then cascade into nerve impulses and hence produce the illusion of vision.

Today phosphotronic (or electron stimulation) technology is still in its infancy. This said, a device called the *phosphotron* has already been developed by Stephen Beck at Lapis Technology. In the guise of a pair of silvered metal goggles, the phosphotron currently produces optic sensations similar to the phosphenes seen if you press on your eyes. Excited by the potential development of the system, Beck notes that 'designer spectacles' based upon the phosphotron principle will offer a high-bandwidth channel directly to the brain without the need to resort to invasive surgery.[157]

ONE BRAIN IMPLANT OR TWO, SIR?

Some scientists, looking even further ahead than developments such as Beck's phosphotron, are already seriously exploring the feasibility of direct electronic implant connections in order to provide the ultimate human-computer interface. With a direct connection into the optic nerve, for example, pictures may one day be directly fed into a computer user's brain to provide them with totally realistic virtual reality experiences. On a more mundane level, users equipped with an optic nerve implant could call up a clock, pager or personal organizer display in the corner of their eye as and when they desired. Whilst this idea may sound like science fiction, it should be noted that auditory electrodes have *already* been implanted in the spiral of the cochlea to enable the deaf to hear, and that electrodes placed directly into the visual cortex have resulted in subjects *seeing* spots of light when these electrodes were stimulated.[158] Certainly direct optical links into the human body are at present only hypothetical, but equally certain is the vision that one day they will be realized.[159]

Even before practical video links into the brain become a reality, cochlear implants may provide extremely useful direct human-computer interface channels. Communications devices, for example, could be made integral to our bodies, with:

> . . . a cochlear implant [that] might even receive telephone calls. To most of us, an implanted telephone initially seems absurd, but for a person who had a cochlear receiver and was accustomed to using a tiny lapel phone, it would seem quite logical. Of course, an implanted phone that could not be *turned*

off would not be a high technology marvel; it would resemble some cruel torture designed by demented engineers. We needn't worry; by the time a cochlear phone can be implanted, screening calls should be easy. There already exists a hearing-aid that is embedded in a tooth and conducts vibration directly along the jaw, so a solid-state answering-machine in a wisdom tooth would not be much of a challenge.[160]

Although researchers such as Stephen Beck may cite one advantage of their visionary inventions as *not* having to be physically connected into the body, when implant computer and communications interfaces arrive there is likely to be a mad rush on the clinics that will provide them. We already have a society in which many will endure the pain and potential inconvenience of having rings and studs inserted through ears, noses, nipples and other body parts for purely aesthetic purposes. It is therefore not hard to imagine people opting for electronic implants that will increase their functionality, and may hence render that essential competitive edge.

NANOTECHNOLOGY

One of the key research areas likely to fuel the development of computer implants is *nanotechnology*. This is the construction science of very small things, whereby physical mechanisms and microchips will be created not out of conventional electronic components, but on an atomic scale. Already IBM have created a microscope that allows scientists to see individual atoms on the surface of a material, and which has a stylus to move atoms around and join them together like building blocks. As nanotechnology develops, the possibilities are likely to be breathtaking. In the words of two cutting-edge professors:

> One of the exciting possibilities of electronic circuits which are on a nanometre scale (and this is one-thousandth of a millionth of a metre in size), is that our brain neuron connections are on the same sort of scale. And if we could put a silicon chip into the brain, and somehow connect our brain cells to that, then we could interact with the silicon chip in the brain, and for

example you could program a silicon chip with all the names and telephone numbers of your friends, implant it into the brain, and you'll never forget a telephone number again.[161]

. . . we are on the verge of a big reform. We can get rid of disease. . . . Maybe we can't cure all the diseases that we have, but we could rebuild our bodies; we could move our brains into new bodies that don't deteriorate and don't age, and we could replace our brain cells by other kinds of machinery that have replaceable parts . . . . Evolution for humans is in fact going to change . . . We are creating these new beings; these are our real children; biological children are just more dressed-up chimpanzees.[162]

Clearly there is the danger of entanglement in a throat-hugging hype of over-zealous, rosy-eyed enthusiasm when discussing the concept and potential of high-tech implants that may allow us to more closely interface with computer and communications systems. Those of us writing about the medium-term future do not, after all, have to defend our predictions the next day, and will have slipped into a safe obscurity if they do not come to pass. But there is also an equal danger of simply not believing that some of the developments that clearly *are* on the horizon will in future be realized. Can we really dismiss the ideas of some of the world's leading thinkers and scientists just because their visions do not equate to our cosy, blinkered view of tomorrow?

As biophysicist Gregory Stock notes, to achieve the union of electronics and humans will not require any fundamental scientific breakthroughs. Rather, it will demand that existing technologies are pushed forward substantially.[163] With the history of the 20th century charting a progression of substantially pushing forward existing technologies, there is therefore no reason to believe that implant computer interface systems will not be achieved in the early 2000s. Already the power of personal computers has exploded exponentially from nothing in twenty years. So why should we smirk at the realization of direct neural connections between human beings and computer systems in a similar or perhaps slightly extended frame of time? The possibilities for implant cybertechnology are tremendous. Just imagine being able to link *directly* into a corporate database; to search a library with your mind; or to learn a new language by plugging a microchip into a socket in your head. To learn to control a directly coupled computer interface would be a great challenge indeed, but then the rewards would be equally great.

THE MARRIAGE OF MAN & MACHINE

Throughout this chapter, the aim has been to focus upon the present and potential impact of increased cybertechnology adoption upon the individual. As has been noted, many people crave information technology, whilst others still cling to the 'old ways' and harbour fears as to how developments in computing will alter the structure of their employment and social relationships. There are also a range of new technological possibilities on the horizon that nobody with an eye to the future should choose to ignore.

Over the last ten years, computers have arrived upon millions of desks across hundreds of thousands of business organizations. Microelectronic devices now also have a significant presence within our homes. Satellite decoders, compact optical disk players, low-cost video recorders, and games consoles capable of rendering complex graphics in hundreds or thousands of colours, now occupy living rooms across the globe. There can be little doubt that as individuals we continue to actively seek a closer and closer marriage with the machines of the late-20th century. They have fostered new possibilities in our lives. Not surprisingly, therefore, as will be demonstrated in the next chapter, cybertechnologies are also transforming the social patterns of our society and the cultures of our business organizations.

The fact that we need computer networks to recapture the sense of cooperative spirit that so many people seemed to lose when we gained all this technology is a painful irony . . .

Howard Rheingold
The Virtual Community

6
Communities, Corporate Cultures & Communications

WITH IMPROVING AND INCREASINGLY widespread computer-mediated communication (CMC), time and distance will cease to be significant barriers in the formation of human relationships. As discussed in previous chapters, current groupwares already allow employees to work together when they are geographically distant, and expected improvements in virtual reality may soon allow instantaneous 'virtucommuting' into computer-generated graphics domains. With the emergence of hot-desk systems, hotelling arrangements and the encouragement of homeworking across many of today's cutting-edge organizations, it seems likely that computers and telecommunications networks will play a central role in mediating many patterns of work in the none-too-distant future. Indeed even outside of the workplace, there are now many so-called *virtual communities* of individuals who 'meet' and socialize principally via computer network links.

As the trend to use cyberspace as an empowering social and business communications medium gathers pace, so our communities, cultures and working patterns seem destined to evolve. Pessimists contend that an increasing reliance on information technology will impede people from entering into social activity. On the other hand, those already bathing in the warm waters of cyberspace parry such argument with an insistence that access to computer network links will simply *alter the nature* of people's relationships. In fact it is possible that CMC may actually *improve* the quality of some individual's social lives. To illustrate this point, network-a-holics note how most of us meet our friends through acquaintance with our families, neighbours, existing friends and colleagues at work. In a world of virtual communities, however, people can forge friendships across the globe, and will be drawn together as they communicate upon topics of common interest, rather than through 'chance' meetings due to physical proximity. Have a passion for *Star Trek* or stick insects or Greek myths? Chances are you won't find many people locally who share your interest. It is almost certain, however, that with a PC and a modem you may quickly get in touch with an array of equally minded individuals. As even a cursory brush with cyberspace demonstrates, most of the communications 'posted' over computer networks have *nothing whatsoever* to do with computers. To illustrate this point, **exhibit 6.1** lists just some of the 'newsgroup conferences' upon which electronic communications are regularly posted, and whose contents may be accessed by anybody with a computer network link.

Whereas **chapter 5** focused upon the relationship of individuals *with* computer technology, this chapter sets out to explore how computer technology is emerging to mediate the relationships of many individuals *with each other*. Initially the focus will be upon the computer network facilities that have already emerged, and upon how individuals worldwide are now using computers to connect together for electronically mediated relationships. Having explored these services and emerging social patterns, attention will be directed toward how the application of groupware and the rise of computer-supported cooperative working is likely to impact upon the corporate cultures of business organizations. Such a focus leads us to question not only how cybertechnologies are likely to be integrated into business task processes, but also how the very atmosphere — *the climate* — of many organizations will change as working links across cyberspace become more common.

MAKING THE CONNECTION

As discussed within the first two chapters, the 'connectivity' of individuals and organizations is proceeding so rapidly that by early next century we are all likely to be interconnected into one global hardware platform. Indeed to some degree we already are. Most telephones can dial any other internationally, and, with the substitution of the telephone with a modem, any computer can, in theory at least, be connected to any other.

Most commonly, the emerging global computer communications network is referred to simply as 'the Net'; a loose and anarchic amalgamation of most of the individual wide area networks that have evolved over the last thirty years. Today, by connecting into the Net (or 'netsurf-

abuse-recovery
agriculture.fruit
alien.visitors
animals.badgers
asian.movies

beer
bigfoot
binaries.pictures.erotica
binaries.pictures.furniture
binaries.sounds-armpit.noises
bitterness
business.misc
butt-key.marmalade

cereal
child.support
collecting.autographs
college.food
comics.batman
cult-movies.rocky.horror
current-events.bosnia
cyberpunk.tech

dads.rights
dear.whitehouse
destroying.the.earth
drugs.caffeine
dreams
drwho.creative

The above was chosen at random from the a-d listing of the 2700+ newsgroups directly available to the author as of 25th July 1994. Note that 'binaries' newsgroups contain data files (most usually of digitized pictures or sounds) that may be downloaded and subsequently decoded by the user.

Exhibit 6.1 A Sample of Newsgroups Available on the Net

ing'), computer users may gain access both to international data stores and to each other. What follows is a brief guide to the Net and some of its component facilities. For the uninitiated, the viscous, acronym-plastered culture of the Net can at first be extremely intimidating. Once the murky oil of its surface has been penetrated, however, the depths of cyberspace are usually found to be surprisingly clear. As many, many millions of users will tell you, those with a Net connection are undoubtably the best-informed group of people in the world.

THE BIRTH OF THE NET

The first computer network — ARPANET — was created by the US military's Advanced Research Projects Agency (ARPA), and went on-line in 1969. As well as permitting data to be communicated between 'host' computers at a distance, ARPANET also allowed for computer-mediated communication between individuals. *Computer conferencing* thereby emerged. This enables individuals to post electronic messages to other users who are usually organized into 'conferences' based upon a common interest. A typical early conference was entitled SF-USERS, involving a group of people who had an interest in science fiction.

A computer conference can be thought of as a room in cyberspace set aside for like-minded individuals. Anybody who wants to say something can post a message to the entire conference, to which others may subsequently respond. Knowledge and research can therefore spread quickly, with 'onlookers' as well as contributors being party to the latest information flow within the conferences to which they subscribe. This ability to enable many-to-many communications is what can turn computer networks into powerful social, business and research tools. Indeed as Jack Hancock, Executive Chief President of Packard Bell noted in 1993, Internet (the 1980s successor to ARPANET) has for years been 'the wings of intelligence for the research and academic communities'.[164]

It is perhaps interesting to note that one key line of thinking behind the creation of ARPANET was to forge a military communication, command and control network that would not be dependent upon a single centre, and hence that would be impenetrable to nuclear attack. The effectiveness of this concept was demonstrated during the Gulf War when computer systems across Iraq continued to operate effectively even when large chunks of network infrastructure were destroyed by allied bombing. With no centre to 'knock-out', computer networks can be extremely difficult to bring under any totalitarian jurisdiction. During the Tiananmen Square upheavals in China in 1989, the Iraqi occupation of Kuwait in 1990, and the Moscow coup in 1991, information continued to be communicated by ordinary citizens over the Net long after most other forms of international communication were suppressed.

By the early 1980s, Internet/ARPANET was being sponsored by the US National Science Foundation (NSF), with non-classified military communications cleaved aside into an associated network entitled MILNET in 1983. In 1986, the NSFNET (a network designed by the NSF to link supercomputers and their users) amalgamated into Internet, offering improved transmission speed between data centres. The original ARPANET infrastructure was decommissioned in March 1990.

Today Internet is the largest collection of computer networks in the world, with over two million 'host' computers linked into its high-speed backbone of dedicated cable, satellite and fibre-optic linkages. At the time of writing there were estimated to be over twenty-five million Internet users in 137 countries, with a new user being hooked up every two minutes.[165]

Although initially a tool and communications facility intended for the military, education and research communities, over the past few years Internet has started to become commercialized. Already multi-million dollar contracts have been handed over to companies such as AT&T who now manage large portions of the system. A group of companies in Silicon Valley have also banded together to create CommerceNet, an electronic marketplace intended to be the new trade medium for high technology organizations. New, mouse-driven 'browser' interfaces such as Mosaic are also becoming widely available. These mask the complexity of the world of network-accessible information from business users previously daunted by Internet access. Secure data encryption for CommerceNet traffic is also in development.[166]

Many users (or 'Netheads') now talk about Internet as if it *were* the Net. This is, however, not strictly correct, as many networks and computer communications facilities have grown up outside of the ARPANET/Internet amalgamation, some of which still have an extensive user base. Whilst a thorough investigation of all the available facilities and resources is not warranted herein, the concepts behind two — namely

Bulletin Board Systems and Usenet — are worthy of at least fleeting attention.

ENTHUSIASTS, BBSs & USENET

As the PC computer revolution took hold from the end of the 1970s, enthusiasts began experimenting with computer modems and the first Bulletin Board Systems (BBSs) were born. Basically, a BBS is a computer linked into the telephone system and running software which enables remote users to dial in to post or retrieve electronic messages, programs or other data. Being analogous to telephone-accessed notice boards, most BBSs limit their contents either geographically or by topic. Today there are literally thousands of BBSs worldwide, regularly accessed by perhaps over one million people.[167] Many of the larger BBSs now also offer their subscribers an Internet connection.

Also developed in the early 1980s was a system called Usenet, a means of managing many-to-many communications on specific topics for users of Unix-based computers.[168] Usenet is not a network or a BBS in the traditional sense, but instead offers a public conferencing service that makes use of, but does not rely upon, other networks. Messages posted to Usenet *newsgroup* conferences 'hitch-a-ride' across cyberspace every time the computer upon which the message has been posted communicates with any other via UUCP (Unix-to-Unix copy), a utility built into the Unix operating system. The receiving computer then checks to see if it carries the newsgroup to which the message has been posted, and if so takes a copy. When this second computer next makes a UUCP communication, the message travels further, and so on. Some Usenet messages can therefore take days to travel the globe, in contrast to Internet postings that proliferate between host computers in mere seconds.

Although initially intended to be the Unix Users' Network, and to be used exclusively for Unix-centred discussion, Usenet has grown to be a source of public information upon thousands of topics. Whilst Usenet cannot provide private electronic mail services, as available over Internet and from some BBSs, it does offer a very effective public conferencing facility. Indeed with over 2.5 million users by 1992, Usenet has been described as the 'largest conversation in the world'.[169] High-speed UUCP links into Internet are now also proliferating, increasing the speed of Usenet postings internationally and making Usenet and Internet newsgroups/conferences available to users of either resource. As this trend continues, the distinction between Usenet and Internet will become blurred and irrelevant for the majority of users.

NAVIGATING THE NET

The amalgamation of computer and communications facilities and resources that comprise the Net are both complex and wide-ranging. Fortunately, navigating the information available across cyberspace is becoming a less daunting proposition as graphical user interfaces and hierarchical menu systems proliferate. *Gopher* programs are available which function like 'intelligent maps' that automatically point to the source of the data being sought. Even more significantly, a project started at CERN (the European Lab for Particle Physics), has led to the creation of the *World-Wide Web* (WWW), which describes itself as a 'wide-area hypermedia information retrieval initiative aimed at giving universal access to a large universe of documents'. With its own body of software and communications protocols and conventions, the WWW uses hypertext[170] and multimedia[171] techniques to allow anyone to roam, browse and contribute to its wealth of network-accessible information.

Accessed most commonly via the graphical software interface Mosaic, the WWW (also known as W3) is extremely easy to use. Not surprisingly, it is therefore becoming extremely popular, allowing even computer novices access to a tremendous variety of digital media in a simplified fashion. Even the WWW, however, is only a first step toward universal, user-friendly cyberspace access. Soon software agents, as discussed in **chapter 4**, will also become available to ordinary individuals, offering further keys to the cyberspace powers previously locked in the clutches of a technically gifted minority.

CYBERSPACE & VIRTUAL COMMUNITIES

The emergence of the many-to-many media now available across cyberspace constitutes a significant watershed in the development of human communication. Prior to the arrival of computer networks, all media for the exchange of information — newspapers, books, movies, radio and television and so forth — had been based upon a one-to-many paradigm. In other words, only a very few people have had the opportunity to become broadcasters in these media, even though what they have broadcast has had the potential to reach many. All of the subscribers to a computer conferencing facility, however, are afforded the ability to both read *and to post* (broadcast) messages to all other subscribers. The potential for group social relationships to evolve therefore presents itself. Not surprisingly, a great many *virtual communities* have already emerged wherein multiple-minds synergize via network links to solve problems as well as to engage in social banter.

In his trail-blazing book *The Virtual Community*,[172] Howard Rheingold reports how groups of computer users from the USA to Japan have embraced the medium of computer-mediated communications as a new 'social conduit' with its own set of community codes and practices. Howard himself reveals how he has become 'colonized' by the other members of the WELL (the Whole World 'Lectronic Link), a dial-up conferencing facility in the San Francisco Bay area which he accesses via a PC and modem link. For two hours a day Howard tours the 'social petri-dish' of cyberspace, fishing for information and making friends within the 'self-sustaining, on-line saloon' of his virtual community.

In common with other virtual communities, the WELL offers its members support in times of illness and crisis. As an example, Rheingold describes in detail how an electronic 'parenting conference' time and again shared the pains and tribulations of child raising. Another example recounts how WELLites once mobilized their 'knowledge-sharing leverage' to arrange for an ex-community member with liver failure to be flown home from Asia. Perhaps not surprisingly, many early WELL members were knowledge workers (freelance writers, producers, designers, researchers and their ilk), all of whom tended to be 'lone wolves' until they discovered the social unity and community support available across the Net.[173] Just to know that there will always be somebody, somewhere on-line with whom you can communicate can be extremely comforting.

We all need forums in which to air our views and in which we can experiment socially. In the 1960s Marshall McLuhan predicted how new media would 'extend Man', and coined the now-famous phrase the 'Global Village' to encapsulate the scenario of an interconnected world shrunk by global telecommunications.[174] With the rate at which Internet registrations are now accumulating, the Global Village is fast becoming a reality. In the 1980s tens of thousands became hooked on Usenet, BBSs, the interactive communications facility Internet Relay Chat (IRC), and upon MUDs (Multi-User Dungeons) in which they could play out fantasy lives in worlds crafted solely out of text-based network communications.[175] Now hundreds of thousands of new converts are joining these early enthusiasts and network pioneers. During the 1990s, interactive audio and video network facilities will become available, whilst virtual reality links-ups will make cyberspace communications even more exciting as the century turns.

It takes a leap of imagination to embrace the concept of social interaction with people who are not physically present. But as informal public spaces continue to disappear, people are sure to hunger for the chance to participate in virtual communities to order to fulfil potentially frustrated social needs.[176] Already in France there is a strong 'chat-culture' between the millions who communicate over the government-provided *Minitel* network.[177] In under a decade, global many-to-many computer-mediated communications are likely to be as commonplace as telephone calls are today.

EMPOWERMENT, PREJUDICE & LIBERATION

Access to a broad, virtual community of networked companions is both enlightening and empowering. The knowledge and experience of others is constantly available at your fingertips. Between virtual community members, geopolitical as well as geographic boundaries also cease to exist. Perhaps more significantly, even mental barriers disperse. Over a network, people may only be judged upon how they *communicate*, rather than in reference to the age-old prejudices of physical appearance, sex, race and social background. Cyberspace communications mask most facets of real-world identity, and whilst this may create its own set of troubles, many people are more than happy to leave behind normally irreconcilable attributes as they enter into network communications. To those with speech impediments, physical disabilities, disfigurations or perhaps with a fear of going out alone, a link into cyberspace may equate to a link into a new world of liberation. For perhaps the first time in their lives, *they* can contribute as equals within a 'normal' social discourse.

As well as enabling social empowerment, cyberspace access also permits a hitherto unknown freedom for widespread communication and self-expression. As an almost ridiculous number of media analysts will not let us forget, the emergence of computer bulletin board and newsgroup conferencing facilities has given *everyone* the potential ability to become a publisher. Can't get anybody interested in publishing your memoirs, that novel you once scrawled in crayon, or your thousand best tips for houseplant care? Then download the text files to a bulletin board or computer conference and the chances are that somebody, somewhere, sometime, will read it. In the information age, the freedom of the press has given way to the freedom of those with network access.

NEW RELATIONSHIPS,
NEW CUSTOMERS & NEW SERVICES

In 1992, John Quarterman, historian of the Net (or as he terms it the Matrix) predicted that by 1994 there would be more network users than residents of any state in the US, and by 1997 more users than citizens of any single country except India or China.[178] This widespread interaction of individuals across cyberspace clearly points toward radical new social patterns and forms of computer-mediated human relationship, both of which will inevitably come to impact upon business organizations as they become widespread. Most obviously, if your customers regularly 'netsurf' into cyberspace, then this could well be the perfect medium in which to appraise them of your wares. It is also likely that the wares of many organizations will be accessed or at least routed directly though cyberspace. Money is already an electronic phenomenon. Most media are also converging toward the digital. Soon home shopping, home banking and video-on-demand will arrive en masse.[179] Knowing how people will behave in cyberspace — knowing the culture and norms of the Net — will therefore be crucial for the successful marketing of these kinds of services.

As computer-supported cooperative work systems proliferate, the social patterns emerging amongst the enthusiasts of today's virtual communities will spread across the national and multinational corporations by whom they are employed. With face-to-face meetings no longer guaranteed as the norm, acquiring the 'netiquette' necessary for business meetings across cyberspace will become essential. As these changes gather momentum, the corporate cultures of most business organizations will begin to evolve to reflect both new social patterns and the need to acquire new business skills. Business values are also likely to change as companies embrace a new infrastructure of work for the 21st century.

CORPORATE CULTURE & BUSINESS SUCCESS

Perhaps the single most important facet of any community, real or virtual, is its *culture*. Certainly ever since Tom Peters and Robert Waterman published *In Search of Excellence*[180] in 1982, the *corporate culture* of a business organization has been highlighted as a critical factor in determining its overall success or failure. The success of the Japanese, for example, is now firmly associated with the existence of strong, holistic cultures across their business organizations. Although intangible and hard to define, culture is one of those 'soft' things that may be manipulated to deliver 'hard' results.[181]

It is increasingly recognized that most companies are more akin to political entities rather than to rational, productive machines. It therefore seems highly plausible to propose that a strong culture may well be the key to motivating their workforce toward quality and commitment in both the short- and long-term. Tools and management styles that may allow the culture of an organization to be manipulated towards greater success have been sought and debated with vigour over the past decade. Indeed it could be argued that the study of corporate culture has now become the single most important active research area in management.[182] But exactly what *is* organizational culture, and how may *Cyber Business* developments as detailed in previous chapters impact upon its nature, its management, and its future direction?

ICEBERGS, ONIONS & SOCIAL GLUE

Cultures are possessed by all groups and communities in society. They are not just a facet of business organizations, and hence the concept of a 'culture' has attracted a range of definitions. Popular organizational theorist Gareth Morgan describes a corporate culture as:

> . . . the intangible 'social glue' that holds everything together; how . . . language, norms, values, rituals, myths, stories and daily routines form part of a coherent 'reality' that lends shape to how and what people do as they go about their work.[183]

Morgan also asks us to consider corporate culture as an iceberg (with what you see on the surface hiding the bulk of deeper reality); as an onion (with layer upon layer of rituals, ceremonies and symbolic routines); and as an umbrella (with arching values that unite the individuals and groups beneath). Other writers provide similar lists, noting that culture is 'manifested' in the form of organizational symbols, heroes, rituals, values and practices;[184] and with its 'contents' including artifacts, community-specific language, member behaviour patterns, heroes, symbols, beliefs, values, history and ethical codes.[185]

COMMUNICATIONS TECHNOLOGIES & CULTURAL CHANGE

By examining how the adoption of cybertechnologies is impacting and may further impact upon organizational artifacts, language, symbols, behavioural patterns, values and beliefs, the emergence of a 'business cyberculture' can be explored. To take a common scenario, consider what happens when an electronic mail system is introduced into an organization. Immediately the PCs or terminals used to access the system become more prominent organizational *artifacts*, as they transform into important new communications nodes. Before electronic mail arrived, the value of computer skills and access may have been considered minimal by some techno-sceptic employees. When electronic mail is introduced, however, the *beliefs* of such individuals are likely to change, with a realization dawning that they will *need* their own computer in order to remain in touch. As a consequence, a PC or terminal may become a power *symbol* within the organization's culture.

The *language* used within communication usually also evolves when a new information medium is introduced. The style and candour of most people's electronic mail postings is very different to that of their typewritten or telephone communications. In general, electronic mail messages tend to be more formal than those delivered over the telephone, although more relaxed than those sent via conventional letter or memo. Freed of the constraints of both social politeness and formal letter writing, electronic mail therefore has the power to be a very direct and effective means of employee communication. A certain language surrounding its usage — a local 'netspeak' — emerges in most organizations. For example, phrases such as 'management by e-mail' may become part of informal discourse. A small linguistic token perhaps, but a subtle harbinger of the *values* prevalent across the organization. Although a wonderful tool to a wonderful medium, in organizations where face-to-face communications are still possible, electronic mail messaging can be taken too far. A manager who will *only* communicate by electronic mail with an employee in the office next door is likely to become marginalized and less effective.

Employee *behavioural patterns* are also likely to evolve when electronic mail is introduced. Most electronic mailed workers get into the habit of logging-in to the network when they arrive at work in the morning to see if they have any messages. Hence it may be appreciated that even the introduction of a comparatively simply computer-mediated communications system, such as private electronic mail, will impact upon many of the elements that combine together to convey the impression of an organization's unique working atmosphere. Managers need to be aware of this. Just because the social effects of new working practices and infrastructures are sometimes hard to foresee, it doesn't mean that they can be played down. Writing 'way back' in 1986, social psychologist Sara Kiesler noted that, where new technology is concerned:

> . . . we tend to exaggerate the technical changes and the significance of the transient issues, and we underestimate the social effects. . . . The long run effects of a new technology are not the intended ones, but have more to do with the technology's indirect demands on our time and attention, and with the way it changes our work habits and our interpersonal relations.[186]

As lovingly described by Gareth Morgan, the culture of an organization may be considered the 'social glue' that binds its members together. Increasingly, new technologies, such as electronic mail and other groupwares, are adopting a similar and synergetic 'social role'. With CMC, people may work at home or with others in different offices across the world. Today technology itself therefore also constitutes a kind of social glue, a layer of the company onion, or a key arch under one of Morgan's metaphorical cultural umbrellas.

BREAKING DOWN BARRIERS

Behavioural patterns, beliefs and values also change as and when computer communications technologies break down the hierarchical and departmental barriers that sub-divide the members of traditionally structured organizations.[187] In **chapter 3** it was noted how the bounds *between* organizations are now becoming blurred, with cyberspace links and software agent 'employees' soon to permit the emergence of virtual organizational forms across more traditional working structures. Electronic mail and computer conferencing facilities will also make the internal divisions *within* organizations increasingly hard to delineate. Today, no attempt need necessarily be made to locate the employees working on a particular project within offices with any degree of physical proximity. Indeed they don't even need to be in the same building, or even the same country. As project-centred working, sub-contracting and joint-venturing activities increase, in many instances the geographically tidy delineations between the employees and facilities of different organizational departments or divisions will be lost entirely. Work *structures* as well communications will increasingly tend toward computer mediation. Indeed there are already projects underway with the objective of representing organizational structures and data stores as 3-D VR models through which corporate planners and designers may 'fly'.[188]

BUILDINGS, CULTURES & VIRTUAL REALITY

As more and more employers persuade their employees to adopt working practices involving hot-desk arrangements, hotelling, telecommuting and groupware-empowered team working, the artifacts that make up physical and social working environments may radically change. In particular, the traditional, sky-scraping office building may cease to be the icon of corporate cultural focus for many administrative workers. What will replace it is still far from clear.

The architecture of corporate buildings has been noted to have a major influence on human behaviour in terms of how we interact, communicate and perform our work tasks.[189] Improve the layout and furnishings of their office, and most employees will become more productive. It's almost common sense. Buildings, however, also serve organizations as totems or uniting symbols of corporate identity, as symbols of strategic profile — why else would pictures of buildings appear in annual accounts? — and will be inevitably tied up with the history and development of an organization. A building is a major corporate cultural artifact: it encapsulates organizational environment. Indeed:

> . . . even the nature of an empty meeting room conveys something about the general organizational culture, since these rooms generally reflect and reproduce the structures of interaction expected in an organization. Straight lines of chairs and note pads, each guarded by a water glass as erect as a sentry, communicate a sense of conformity and order. The friendly chaos and casualness of more informal meeting rooms extend a more open invitation to self-organization.[190]

Bearing the above in mind, it is interesting to hypothesize what will happen to the culture and corporate focus of organizations as multi-user, computer-mediated virtual realities become widely available business and social tools over the next ten to twenty years. The day is not that far away when it will be possible to hold meetings in cyberspace with geographically distant individuals donning head-mounted displays, datagloves and/or other VR-immersion clothing. Without leaving their home or office, people will simply materialize in virtual graphics worlds programmed with the appearance of any location they choose, and populated with only those objects they desire.

With mounting pressure from corporate accountants, shareholders and environmental lobbyists to cut down on the vast sums expended on oil-burning travel, many managers will have to learn to live with VR as a medium in which they will do some (though certainly not all) of their day-to-day business. By harbouring a headset rather than jumping on a jumbo jet, executives will save a great deal of time as well as money. Many managers and reps spend a very large proportion of their working life travelling from A to B and back again. As already noted, future transportation to corporate graphical environments (CGEs) will be instantaneous. No more waiting in airports or stations or traffic jams. People will therefore be able to spend more time *in* more meetings rather than geographically chasing between them.

THE INFINITE ARCHITECTURE OF THE CGE

The design of the corporate graphical environments, in which the employees of an organization will present themselves in virtual reality, will become a critical weapon in the armoury of the corporate image maker. Network service providers are likely to emerge offering custom CGEs which may be hired for business meetings in the same way that hotels hire out suites for business conferences today. It seems likely, however, that many large organizations will seek total and exclusive control of the CGEs which they will utilize, as in many cases CGEs will be the only means by which prospective clients and customers will gain their first impression of the company.

No longer will buyers be able to be cossetted by plush lobbies, smiling receptionists, strong handshakes and hot coffee. In their droves they will no longer be coming through the real front door. They will never see the actual concrete carbuncle which houses the corporate databanks, reality engines and row-upon-cost-effective-row of employee hot-desks. Instead their first impressions will be cast with reference to the environment they experience when they join with representatives of the company in its very own virtual reality domain.

Whilst the level of 'realism' achievable in virtual reality may be poor for many years to come, cyberspace does offer the possibility for architectures bounded solely by the imagination. A meeting room created by the Virtuosi[191] project researchers, for example, is situated at the nexus of several archways over a swimming pool. Meetings in VR do not have to take place in four-walled offices. They can happen high in the treetops, under the sea, in outer space, or amongst the orbiting atoms of a molecule. A company could have CGEs created with corporate logos emblazoned a mile high in fluorescent neon on distant mountains. Software agents could be programmed to appear in the bodies of famous film stars or as servant fauna or flora (imagine sending Lassie to search a remote database). Indeed, even the VR bodies of company employees will have to be selected and programmed, with the choice of these also likely to be determined by corporate image makers. What's more, programmers and image makers will not only be free to choose your suit, but also your hairstyle, your face, the sound of your voice, and even the number of limbs with which you will be endowed (legs tending to command a rather high and unnecessary computer-processing overhead in a VR environment in which you can fly anywhere by simply pointing your finger). When it comes to meetings held in virtual reality, *how* we appear, *where* we appear, and hence how our *organizations* appear, will be limited solely by human imagination.

Think that companies won't bother to manipulate VR to look good? Think again. Most large organizations today invest phenomenal sums in visual identity and image enhancement programmes. From British Airways to British Telecom, ICI to IBM, the corporate coffers never seem to be exhausted when the colour and typeface of the logo is in doubt. With companies today spending *millions* on getting their symbols stylistically 'correct', it seems unlikely in the extreme that they will not fling their accounts wide open when faced with the possibility of designing the look of their very employees and the environments in which they will meet their customers. Across cyberspace, corporate vanity, corporate image, is likely to become a very big business indeed.

THE MANAGEMENT OF CULTURE & TECHNOLOGY

When managing the continuous cycle of technological change facing businesses today, managers need to be aware that the new systems that they have no choice but to implement will alter not only their business *processes*, but also key components of the *cultures* of their organizations — cultures that may be partly responsible for their present and future success. Additionally, the introduction of new cybertechnologies may lead to the creation of organizational technocultures based around either the individuals and groups who work with these technologies, or around those who actually understand the hardwares and softwares and have a vision of their potential. In some instances, sub-cultures exhibiting technology-resistance may also become apparent. Whilst any employee factions harbouring such an ethos may require careful managerial attention in the short-term, over time they are likely to be consumed by the other groups across the organization who are undaunted by the power of the Net. As the early CMC enthusiasts in the 1970s and 1980s demonstrated, computer network links empower individuals with a group leverage that can be hard for traditional structures to quell or control. It is pointless to resist increasing computer interconnection, and it has to be remembered that what most people fear is not computer technology but the unknown. Once this fear is overcome, and with the application of a little imagination, the magic of technology tends to consume latent technophobias.

When computers were used primarily as information *processors* their use could be avoided. Now that they are becoming tools for *communication*, your voice, or your text message, is far less likely to be noted or even registered if you choose not to adopt some form of computer-mediated communication. Could you stay in business today without a telephone? Indeed even without a fax machine? Almost definitely not in both cases. Equally, in future, no organization, large or small, will be able to stay in business without both internal and external computer-mediated communication links. Over the past two-and-a-half decades, computers and computer networks have become inextricably woven into the social fabric of humanity itself.

As Robert Heller reported after his study of the 'office revolution', nowhere is life changing so rapidly and fundamentally as in the office. New technologies that have existed for only a decade or two are not just speeding up the flow of work, they are radically altering the processes and structures of management.[192] With instant group or individual communications available anywhere, anytime, a global village — a 'global office' — is now emerging. As a consequence the cultures of many organizations are also evolving. Computer-mediated communication facilities, in particular those permitting a many-to-many dialogue, are now bringing more and more people together into previously impossible social patterns. The culture of the societies and communities, and hence the *markets*, in which business organizations operate is thereby set to change. Just how far these changes will go, and in what direction, is extremely hard to predict.

Perhaps the only group of individuals who have explored the possible extremes of social and working relationships across potential future technocultures are science fiction writers. As Jonathan Waldern, managing director of virtual reality systems supplier Virtuality (formerly W Industries), once stated, if you want to know about the future, 'look to science fiction writers, not writers'.[193] Not wishing to ignore the advice of a successful VR industry guru, the next chapter delves into the future as predicted through the typewriters and word processors of the cybertech masters of fantasy and cyberpunk. At times the journey is disturbing, with some novelists and moviemakers presenting us with a future society in which many would choose not to live. What is at times most startling, however, is how much of what was once proposed as pure fiction has *already* metamorphosed into solid fact. Brace yourselves, then, as **chapter 7** attempts to separate the *Fact* from the *Fantasy*.

Our minds help create the world we think we inhabit . . .

Marge Piercy
Body of Glass

7
The Fact
& the Fantasy

THROUGHOUT THE PREVIOUS SIX chapters, constraint has been exercised in all attempts at predicting the implications of our ever-rampant adoption of cybertechnologies. The emergence of global connectivity, virtual working patterns, software agents, and a range of other developments, have all been discussed on the basis of extrapolations of current organizational practice, and research into cutting-edge hardware and software development. The purpose of this penultimate chapter, however, is to allow a little space for the bounds of existing practicality to be relaxed. As a light aperitif to the final discussion of *Evolution, Transition & the Dawn of a New Age*, the following pages therefore detail cybertechnological developments as portrayed within the fictions of leading 'cyberpunk' novelists and movie makers.

SCIENCE FICTION & THE FUTURE

Sculptors of fantasy have almost certainly explored the potential social and cultural implications of cybertechnology adoption most radically. Unlike research scientists, science fiction (SF) writers do not have to focus tightly for long periods upon specific and complex technical hurdles. Instead they can simply let their imaginations roam free. Such quests of imaginings, however, have already prompted technological breakthroughs and provided the scientific community with new and wide-reaching concepts. Perhaps most notably, the term 'cyberspace' itself was first introduced in William Gibson's award-winning novel *Neuromancer*,[194] only in the wake of which did a spectrum of governments, corporates and academic researchers take an express interest.[195]

It should be noted that some of the best SF gurus also write technical non-fiction, whilst almost all conduct comprehensive research before constructing sagas set in future societies. What's more, even when works of science fiction do not reflect realistic potential technologies and social patterns, they nevertheless provide foci for discussion upon what actual futures may really be like, and how we may or may not choose to employ technology in the years ahead. As visionaries, innovators, researchers and philosophical catalysts, the creators of science fiction have come to play an important role in the development of both our popular and emerging technocultures.

The fact that so many people — and especially so many scientists — read science fiction serves as an indication of our yearning to know what is to occur in the years ahead. As Francis Hamit so elegantly notes in Part I of *Virtual Reality and the Exploration of Cyberspace*:

> Science fiction [has] taught its readers not to accept limitations. The budding scientists, engineers, and computer hackers who cut their teeth on science fiction learned that all things were possible, even when those in authority said that they weren't. They learned to dream impossible dreams, and then to try and implement them. Such technological romance made heroes of us all, imbued us with the desire to explore new realms of thought, and taught us persistence in the face of adversity.[196]

CYBERPUNK & CYBERTECH

The science fiction genre concerned with the development and impact of new technologies upon individuals and their societies is most commonly referred to as 'cyberpunk'. Under this banner there is now a plethora of work, which in its widest sense 'embraces technology, revels in the complexities of an imperfect world, and grapples with the journey to the underworld'.[197] As is the case with most fantasy genres, however, a state of confusion prevails as to exactly what ought or ought not to be included under the 'cyberpunk' banner. A comprehensive survey of cyberpunk SF is therefore 'not only materially impossible but methodologically dubious'.[198]

Rudy Rucker, whose acclaimed novels *Software*[199] and *Wetware*[200] concern the first sentient robots and bioengineered 'meatbops', argues that cyberpunk is mainly about the fusion of humans and machines. It is the fictional genre offering new 'thoughtforms' to represent our fears and hopes concerning the *present* period of man-machine symbiosis, wherein computers are taking over many human functions and where in turn humans are being fed more machine-processed information.[201] Cyberpunk has also been described as an attempt to tie the development of postmodern culture to technological developments, with its writers operating as 'techno-urban-guerilla artists' announcing technological dreams and nightmares.[202]

In the preface to *Mirrorshades: The Cyberpunk Anthology*,[203] Bruce Sterling comments upon how cyberpunk writers have emerged from the first generation to grow up in a truly science-fictional world. They are therefore creating fiction from a standpoint that simply could not have been adopted by the SF writers of old. For 'New Age' writers, and for its readers, cyberpunk is helping to crumble the traditional 'yawning cultural gulf' between the sciences and the humanities. Its proponents are turning rebel pop culture inside out until artists at the cutting edge also 'become cutting edge technicians into the bargain'. Cyberpunk is marked by visionary intensity, almost clinical objectivity, a telling use of detail, and a willingness to extrapolate future vision into the fabric of daily life. Central themes include invasion of the body and invasion of the mind, with new hardwares empowering individuals whilst offering multinationals and governments fresh tools for oppression and control.

It should be noted that the cyberpunk genre is not exclusively concerned with detailing future computer and communications technologies and their impact upon society. Frequently the 'punk' ethos of anarchy and rebellion is also in evidence, whilst some tales revolve around advancements in biochemical, genetic or cosmetic engineering. Within this chapter, the decision has therefore been taken to focus upon SF detailing computer-based cybertechnology — cybertech — rather than upon the broader categorization of cyberpunk. As a result, certain cyberpunk 'classics' (such as *The Naked Lunch*[204] and *Videodrome*[205]) come to be excluded.

Even with the cybertech cleaved from the cyberpunk, limitations of space inevitably constrain the array of fictions that may be covered within this chapter. Fortunately this restriction proves to be largely irrelevant, as common themes quickly become apparent after scrutinizing even a handful of sources. It should be noted, however, that whilst the following review of literature and movies provides a flavour of cybertech, it is also intended as a selective route map to SF which readers are strongly encouraged to seek out if they wish to gain an increased understanding of the ambience — the *feeling* — of *Cyber Business* developments. To this end, a list of further reading and viewing appears towards the end of this book.

THE MASTER OF CYBERSPACE

The undisputed master of cyberpunk/cybertech is William Gibson. No apology is therefore made for the fact that just under half of the books mentioned within this chapter have been written by this author alone. Read Gibson carefully and you will come across all of the major themes of the cybertech/cyberpunk genre. Indeed, some critics contend that perhaps we ought to stop talking about 'cyberpunk SF' and instead note that there is simply one writer (Gibson) and a couple of expert PR men who have recognized the commercial value of his label.[206]

Gibson's first novel, *Neuromancer*, burst onto the science-fiction scene like a supernova, its technopoetic prose detailing the sleazed-out global village of the near future.[207] It is in *Neuromancer* that we are first introduced to cyberspace as the 'consensual hallucination experienced daily by billions'; as the 'graphic representation of data abstracted from banks of every computer in the human system. Unthinkable complexity. Lines of light ranged in the nonspace of the mind, clusters and constellations of data. Like city lights, receding . . .'.[208]

Ten years on, and *Neuromancer* is widely heralded as *the* definitive cyberpunk novel. Its hero, Case, is a burnt-out software cowboy, a cyberspace hacker down on his luck and manipulated into one last job in order to avoid death by mycotoxin. The female lead — Molly — has surgically implanted sunglass visors behind which lurk electronic eyes. Eyes through which Case can arrange to see when jacked into cyberspace via a key-operated 'deck' in combination with the forehead (elec)'trodes used for total immersion in the matrix.

None of the characters in *Neuromancer* appear totally sane or totally stable. All have had their lives altered by technology, whether by accident or design. Immersive cyberspace access has become natural for human beings. Artificial intelligences also roam the matrix, even though they have been legally banned. Manufacturer brands have come to mean everything — cyberspace decks being referred to as 'Hitachis' or 'Ono-Sendais' — and power always equates to the corporate power of the zaibatsus, the multinationals, that have 'transcended old barriers' and shaped the course of human history.

The real agendas of *Neuromancer*, however, run far deeper and darker than the intricate prose and plot twists used to caress characters and technology into cold life. The contrast between 'meat and metal', the denaturing of the body, the transformation of time and space in post-industrial society, the primacy of information, and the 'overarching demiurge' that individuals are being manipulated, are what the book is really all about.[209] As in all of his work, Gibson is at pains to explore the impact of cybertechnologies upon the human condition. He's far from being the only writer to attempt this, yet the scalpel with which he cuts his prose is certainly one of the sharpest. As Gibson himself has pointed out, his books are not 'hard and glossy', but are instead about 'what being hard and glossy does to you'.[210]

Three years after *Neuromancer's* arrival came *Count Zero*,[211] a slower and less dense novel which allows more time for character development. The plot comes in three interweaving strands. Presented in entwining rotation, these involve the defection of a Maas Biolabs scientist, the quest of an aspiring console cowboy keen to cut his teeth in cyberspace, and a young woman, Marly, who is directed by a hologram to search for a piece of art that may bring new meaning to the matrix. For somewhere there are those who believe that cyberspace is now populated by ghosts, by voices. And why not?

> Oceans had mermaids, all that shit, and we had a sea of silicon, see? Sure, it's just a tailored hallucination we all agreed to have, cyberspace, but anybody who jacks in knows, fucking *knows* its a whole universe.[212]

The theme of sentience in cyberspace continues into the final instalment of Gibson's cyberspace trilogy, *Mona Lisa Overdrive*.[213] Characters and themes from the previous two novels come together in this masterpiece, which continues to explore the very nature of the medium of pure information. We hear of black lacquered cubes that contain the recorded personalities of deceased executives and corporate directors, and from which modern managers seek advice. And there are those amongst the living who are obsessed with cyberspace, with finding its shape, with discovering its God-like nature, and who can now connect into the 'iconics' of the sum data of the human system without even needing to use a cyberspace deck. A versatile novel with a mature blend of character and cybertechnology, *Mona Lisa Overdrive* has the pace of *Neuromancer* with the maturity of *Count Zero*.

BURNING CHROME & VIRTUAL LIGHT

Many of the themes explored within Gibson's first trilogy stem from earlier short stories now published collectively in a book entitled *Burning Chrome*.[214] Three of the *Burning Chrome* tales are worthy of particular note, each involving a by-now-familiar dark, chrome-and-black-plastic future in which popular culture and technology have become synonymous, and in which corporations across the matrix have attained a kind of immortality.

In *Johnny Mnemonic* we meet a guy who rents out his brain to store information. Multinationals entrust him with secure data encoded in his head just as they now trust couriers with paper documents in wrist-chained briefcases. The power of corporations across a global computer-communications infrastructure is a central theme of the story, with connectivity empowering the control and surveillance of individuals whose actions are inevitably:

> . . . reflected in numbered bank accounts, securities transactions, bills for utilities . . . it is impossible to move, to live, to operate at any level without leaving traces, bits, seemingly meaningless fragments of information. Fragments that can be retrieved, amplified . . . . [215]

In *The Winter Market* a young woman seeks immortality in computer software, desperate to throw away her 'poor, sad body' and to be free of the 'bonds of hated flesh'. Following this chilling tale there is *Burning*

Chrome itself, the story from which the collection takes its title, and in which many of the elements used in Gibson's later trilogy can be found. Bobby Quinn is a cowboy, a hacker, a cracksman:

> . . . casing mankind's extended electronic nervous system, rustling data and credit in the crowded matrix, monochrome nonspace where the only stars are dense concentrations of information, and high above it all burn corporate galaxies and the cold spirals of military systems.[216]

Virtual Light,[217] Gibson's latest solo novel to date, is set in a far nearer future than those of his previous trilogy. Its characters therefore come to utilize a range of cybertechnologies clearly extrapolated from the present day. Indeed, the 'virtual light' of the title is a term coined by VR researcher Steven Beck, and relates to the non-photon stimulation of the optic nerve that can be achieved by use of his phosphotron device as described in **chapter 5**. The plot of *Virtual Light* concerns the recovery a stolen pair of virtual light sunglasses, and again the power of a large corporation verses low-life individuals is a central theme.

In places *Virtual Light* is rather disturbing. It's all just a little too close to the present for comfort. For some believers, television has evolved into a sort of religion, whilst society in general has sub-divided into the very rich and the very poor. 'There used to be a middle class inbetween, but no more.' Hardware now in betatest development is in widespread application. People play video laser disks on VR 'goggle sets' and pocket screens, use eyephones for telepresence, carry 'virtufaxes' in their purses, make VR telephone calls, and employ pen-operated notebooks (PDAs) that translate either handwriting or the spoken word. All such devices will be commonly employed in practice before the turn of the century. It is therefore hard not to believe Gibson's accompanying predictions, which include the fact that in future all white-collar crime will be computer-related, and that those who can 'do things with computers won't have to worry about the cops'.[218]

Although not as complex and deeply atmospheric as the books of the earlier trilogy, *Virtual Light* is definitely one of the best novels available involving emerging cybertechnologies in action. It also carries many warnings. Do we really want a society in which the rich all live inside security compounds, people avoid hospitals so that they will not be 'checked out by computers', and history itself is 'turned into plastic' as its digital patterns are manipulated by those who control the archives? Unfortunately, if we are not careful, such a society could well prove the downside of *Cyber Business* developments.

CYBORGS & ROBOTS

Cyborgs[219] and humanoid robots have played centre stage in science fiction tales for many years. It is therefore hardly surprising that many novels of cybertech involve robots and other forms of artificial humanoid life. Whether software patterns will ever achieve sentience is a matter of debate. However, as noted in **chapter 5**, it is quite likely that software agents and artificial intelligences will soon *appear* intelligent. They will also soon become capable of performing many functions that could previously only be accomplished by human beings. We will therefore need to decide how we are to both treat and employ such 'entities', together with what 'rights' (if any) they will be granted.

In *Body of Glass* by Marge Piercy (also published in the USA as *He, She and It*),[220] we learn of Yod, a cyborg created in the 21st century to protect a Jewish enclave from multinational corporations. Concurrently we are also told the tale of a golem (a man of clay) brought to life in a ghetto of the 1600s. Both Yod and the golem serve as intelligent weapons created to do the bidding of their human masters. An ethical proposition? Almost certainly not, with the creation of any conscious being as a tool likely to lead toward disaster.

In addition to addressing the dilemmas posed by the ability to create 'artificial life', *Body of Glass* also builds upon Gibson's concept of the cyberspace matrix. Meetings, for example, take place in virtual reality for reasons of both convenience and safety:

> They had been given a conference room by the Net computer.
> In the spacial metaphor that was the Net, they requested
> coordinates at the entrance map, and their conference room
> was highlighted. Moving around in the Net used different
> controlling imagery at different times. Lately the Net had been
> using escalators and moving walkways, so they mounted and

> moved swiftly into position. They dismounted in an area
> marked Conference Room 147 Z-18. What they saw was a
> room. Inside double doors stood a doughnut-shaped table with
> chairs all about it. No one was there. They sat down. They
> waited. [221]

Within *Body of Glass*, humanity has evolved to a point such that people cannot even *think* without computer access, such a proposition 'being like asking someone to walk to California or cross the Atlantic on a raft'. Just as nobody can do arithmetic without a calculator, so 'who can think with just their own brain?'. Piercy also highlights the fact that, once plugged into a computer system, immersed human beings may become vulnerable to potentially lethal mental attacks.

Another entertaining novel that explores the creation of an intelligent, person-like machine is Amy Thompson's *Virtual Girl*.[222] This book tells of Maggie, a self-aware software life-form created in a computer landscape of virtual reality, and then embodied within a mechanical frame resemblant of a young woman. Maggie is the product of the obsession of Arnold Brompton, a computer genius who has lived on the streets ever since AIs were legally prohibited under the Neural Computer Interface Laws. In a sense, Maggie is presented by Thompson as another example of technology created in a 'companionship role' for a socially incapable individual.

In *Virtual Girl* 'Net Police' programs patrol cyberspace looking for viruses and illegal program forms. Amy Thompson also provides a new perspective on why humanoid robots may one day be created. Popular science writer Gregory Stock once commented that we are unlikely to see people-like androids as there would be little point in mimicking human capabilities with robot technology. Rather, Stock suggested that intelligent computer companions would be far more useful if they were pocket-sized rather than 'clunking along beside us in a humanoid frame'.[223] After reading *Virtual Girl*, however, we may speculate that, even though *human beings* may not come to value robotic humanoid bodies, AIs almost certainly will. For an artificial intelligence 'trapped' in cyberspace, an independent humanoid frame would offer liberation and the chance to participate in society as an 'equal'. If software does ever achieve sentience, then it may well ask or cajole Mankind into providing it with a mechanical body for the purpose of its own sanity.

SOCIETIES OF THE FUTURE

A great deal of cybertech SF attempts to predict the form of future
societies by examining the impact of technology upon our daily patterns
of life. Across a range of books from the likes of Bruce Sterling, Philip
K. Dick, Greg Bear, Rudy Rucker and William S. Burroughs, we are
presented with futures wherein society has come to be mediated by the
supremacy of information, and in which human beings enjoy or fight
against technologically-mediated relationships and employment structures,
share their worlds with artificial life in a myriad of forms, and frequently
come to be manipulated by large technology-empowered corporations or
other oppressive regimes. Bruce Sterling's *Islands in the Net*,[224] for
example, presents us with a future in which nuclear weapons have been
banned and in which information is the most valuable commodity. In Alan
Dean Foster's *Cyberway*,[225] Detective Vernon Moody employs a
methodology of criminal investigation involving the use of computer webs
and databases. Meanwhile in Don H. DeBrandt's fantasy '*The Quicksilver
Screen*',[226] control of the fantasy 'information nexus' of infinite range
television (IRTV) renders 'infinite power', whilst virtual reality is used
for business and recreation, brain implants allow direct connection into
TV channels, and implant technology may animate corpses into
telepresence controlled 'zomborg' slaves. If, however, you are looking
for the ultimate tale of the most distant technologically-mediated society
imaginable, then *the* novel to revel in has to be *The City and the
Stars*,[227] by Arthur C. Clarke.

An old master of SF, Clark wrote *The City and the Stars* way back in
1956. The book tells the tale of Diaspar, the final city on earth, which
houses the last ten million members of the human race. Diaspar's citizens
spend their lives playing out VR-style leisure sagas, crafting matter into
artistic creations with their minds, and engaging in telepresence-style
meetings. The latter sometimes take place in vast virtual amphitheatres
that 'slumber in the computer' until called into existence, and which allow
millions to attend the pronouncements of a single speaker.

Although a city of future technological wonder and harmony, Diaspar
is a sad reflection of past glories. The spirit of ancient humanity has long
since ebbed from its citizen's lives. In order to avoid over-population,
most of Diaspar's inhabitants are encoded as disembodied patterns in a
central memory store, only to emerge from the Hall of Creation in
physical bodies once every hundred thousand years. Clark beautifully

sculpts the resulting 'frozen culture' held in timeless perfection by eternally perpetuating technology; a culture that has resulted from living out of contact with reality for far too long. *The City and the Stars* therefore presents the reader with a totally different technologically mediated future than that found within most novels of cybertech, even though the involved elements and themes are extremely similar. Perhaps the future does not have to involve vast corporate regimes controlling downtrodden individuals caught in gritty, drug-and-crime-infested street cultures. This said, the price to be paid for using technology to 'overcome' our current social tribulations could well prove to be an unpleasant stagnation of the human condition itself. Early next century, people will not be slumbering in a computer matrix within an eternal city. However, many may live a solitary existence whose highlights solely involve interaction with cyberspace technologies accessed from the isolated honeycombs of an increasingly cellular society.

CYBERTECH ON THE BIG SCREEN

Whilst novels offer the creative space to flesh out the detail of future times and places, SF movies allow their audience to actually *see* what the future may be like. Due to its highly visual nature, the technology of virtual reality is arguably that with greatest potential for celluloid exploitation. It is therefore unfortunate that, owing to the expense and technical complexity of creating cinema-quality computer-generated images, very few films to date have successfully delved into the VR arena. Thankfully those that have — most notably Brett Leonard's *The Lawnmower Man*[228] — have been spectacular.

Barely two minutes into *The Lawnmower Man*, and we have been presented with a subject (admittedly an augmented chimpanzee) clad in a VR helmet and cybersuit, and gyrating in a full-motion girosphere whilst being battle-trained in virtual reality. The technology of VR is visible in abundance throughout the film — and not technology created by special effects technicians. Although the film is a fantasy, the headsets, datagloves and so forth worn by the actors are the real thing. Just a cursory glance at the closing credits serves to illustrate how many of the big names of the VR industry were involved.

Dr. Larry Angelo (Pierce Brosman) plays a scientist disillusioned with military VR research. Subsequently, he employs 'the new medium that holds the key for the evolution of the human mind' in an attempt to augment the mental capabilities of Jobe (Jeff Fahey), a simple gardener known locally as 'the lawnmower man'. Under the influence of neurotropic drugs, and after several 'cyberlearning' experiences in virtual reality, Jobe does indeed start to get smarter. Alarmingly so. As the film progresses toward its stunning climax, Jobe even develops telepathic abilities, as latent psychic powers and ancient brain capacities are awakened.

Fantasy aside, *The Lawnmower Man* makes us witness once again to the age-old battle of technoaddict verses technosceptic. Dr. Angelo is clearly obsessed with the potential of virtual reality. His wife is certainly not. As she retorts in one argument: 'it may be the future to you Larry, but it's the same old shit to me'. What *The Lawnmower Man* best illustrates, however, is the look and feel of both VR peripherals (helmets, couches and cybersuits) and the computer graphics worlds to which they permit access. If you haven't seen virtual reality in action then rent the video of *The Lawnmower Man*. It is certainly the best film available to demonstrate what the dawning and almost incomprehensibly powerful medium of VR will look like in application.   The forthcoming *Lawnmower Man II* (in production at the time of writing) should also prove stimulating viewing.

Although often overlooked, another film worthy of a screening if you wish to gain an insight into what virtual worlds may look like, is Walt Disney's *Tron*.[229] This SF fantasy takes place largely inside the hardware of a corporate mainframe, with many of the film's characters being computer programs portrayed in human form. Computer in-jokes abound, with characters having names such as 'Bit' and 'Ram'. Although largely irrelevant, the plot of *Tron* involves the schemes of the Master Control Program (the MCP) which is trying to take over all the computers in the world. When ace programmer Kevin Flynn is sucked down into the computer 'game grid', however, the MCP's plans start to go wrong and his plans for cyberspace domination are thwarted.

Although initially a rather drab and run-of-the-mill film in the old 'a-computer-is-going-to-take-over-the-world' mould, *Tron* builds into a visually spectacular movie whose graphics landscapes provide an excellent illustration of what near-future VR environments may well look like. It's not a film to be taken that seriously, although there is a strong underlying theme regarding the danger of putting the control of a corporate computer system into the hands of just one senior executive.

TERMINATORS & ROBOTIC POLICEMAN

Like their counterparts in the world of literature, many movie makers have presented us with cybertech futures in which robots and cyborgs play a prominent role. Paul Verhoeven's *Robocop*[230] is one of the best of the genre, and is set in a very near metropolitan society in which the US has space 'peace platforms', and there are TV adverts for replacement artificial hearts.

As in many fictions of cybertech, key players in the drama are the executives of a powerful, technology-empowered multinational, in this case Omni Consumer Products (OCP). The company has plans to build an entire new city in place of old Detroit, but first the 'cancer of crime' has to be cut from the streets in order to guarantee the safety of its construction workers.

Initially OCP intends the future of law enforcement to lie with a series of robots coded ED-209. However the ED-209 enforcement droids prove dangerously unstable, and hence OCP's back-up 'robocop' programme is initiated. After being horrifically shot to pieces in the line of duty, Police Officer Murphy (Peter Weller) is consequently turned into the first cybernetic policeman, the majority of his body now an armoured machine and his mind erased for fresh programs.

Murphy/Robocop soon goes into action to stamp out crime across the city. Old memories begin to surface, however, and he goes in search of his previous identity, his family, and the felons who gunned him down. In doing so Murphy also comes up against the executives of OCP, their corporate politics, and revitalized ED-209 enforcement drones.

Although in *Robocop* we see few new hardware developments aside from Robocop himself and the ED-209 drones, the downside of technology empowerment, and in particular the potential power of future multinational corporations, are chillingly demonstrated. Indeed when asked if he has access to military weaponry, one OCP executive replies, 'we practically *are* the military'. As in many cybertech fantasies, technologically empowered 'good' (in this case Murphy/Robocop) ultimately triumphs over a faceless and oppressive technological 'evil'

(OCP). Unfortunately, success only leads the poor man-machine to endure two lacklustre sequels.

Throughout its grim and violent forays, the original *Robocop* is a hard-hitting and gritty cybertech movie which pulls no punches in its assessment of the implications of achieving the ultimate in man-machine synthesis. Based so closely on the present, in places the film conjures forth a very worrying vision of how we may employ cybertechnology in the years ahead.

Much more of a cybertech fantasy than *Robocop* is James Cameron's *The Terminator*.[231] The film opens in the ruins of Los Angeles in 2029, with hunter-killer robots pursuing the remnants of humanity. The action then moves to 1984 where a Cyberdine Systems 'Terminator' cyborg (Arnold Schwarzenegger) arrives in a shower of blue lightning. His mission is to kill Sarah Connor, who will later become the mother of a renegade leader. Minutes later Sergeant Kyle Reece (Michael Biehn) also materializes, his mission to protect Sarah from the Terminator and hence to safeguard the future of Mankind.

A highly successful film of the genre, *The Terminator* spawned one of those rare sequels worthy of attention. *Terminator II: Judgement Day*[232] is set a decade after the action of the original film. Again a cyborg comes back from the future, this time to strike at renegade leader John Connor whilst he is still a child. The twist, however, is that a cyborg is also sent back *by* John Connor to protect both himself and his mother. Unfortunately, the cyborg sent to murder John is more advanced than the Schwarzenegger model, made of a metal alloy capable of metamorphosing into any form. The stage is therefore set for a spectacular battle which is littered with computer-generated, virtual-reality-style special effects. A battle that predicts little of what the future may actually look like, but within which the ethos of cyberpunk and technology empowerment always remains centre stage.

FUTURE SOCIETY IN CELLULOID

When it comes to portraying future technologically-plastered societies, few films can match the intensity of sparkling high tech and refuse-strewn low-life as portrayed in Ridley Scott's *Blade Runner*.[233] If *Neuromancer* is the definitive cyberpunk novel, then *Blade Runner* has to be the definitive cyberpunk movie.

Based upon SF guru Philip K. Dick's novel *Do Androids Dream of Electric Sheep?*,[234] *Blade Runner* takes place early in the 21st century. Synthetic people known as 'replicants' can now be created, although after a bloody mutiny they have been banned from earth under penalty of death (or, as it is termed, 'retirement'). Teams of 'blade runner units' therefore have the task of hunting down renegade replicants, their orders to shoot to kill.

Once again we find ourselves in a future Los Angeles, this time the year being 2019. The night skyline is a choking maze of concrete and high tech, with bursts of flame randomly erupting into the air across a landscape of black. Closer, fluorescent neon bathes the streets as flying vehicles soar amongst concrete monoliths splattered with tens of thousands of windows and decked with video wall displays.

Harrison Ford plays Deckard, a retired blade runner pressed back into service when a group of highly advanced replicants return to earth in search of their maker. The future society through which Deckard moves is steeped in technology. Buildings have voice-print identification systems, voice-control of domestic appliances is common, and video telephones are the norm. As in Gibson's novels, a central theme concerns the conflict between the streets where 'technology finds its own uses', and the corporations who control technology and its innovation. We also come to question who is more 'human'; Deckard, the legally empowered killer, or the replicants whom he is seeking to gun down. *Blade Runner* is a masterful and disturbing work of cinema.

When it comes to viewing day-to-day future technologies in action, *Total Recall*[235] is also well worth a screening. Again inspired by a work of Philip K. Dick (in this case a short story entitled 'We can remember it for you wholesale'), the first 30 minutes of the film provide a superb vision of a future 80 years hence. We are party to a world of large, flat-screen TV walls, video telephones, nail varnish that alters its colour with the touch of a stylus, automatic x-ray style security screening, video advertisements on tube trains, holographic tennis partners, and taxis with cheery, shop-dummy-style robotic drivers.

A company called Recall sells its customers the memory of a 'vacation they've never had', saving them the trauma of travelling, lousy weather and lost luggage. The option is even available to 'take a holiday from yourself', with alternative identities available to adopt within your very own 'ego trip'. This is mind-linked virtual reality with a difference!

In order to try and unlock hidden memories from his nightmares, Douglas Quaid (Arnold Schwarzenegger) elects to take a 'trip' with Recall. Things go wrong, however, when a memory block is encountered in his mind and it is revealed that he was once a secret agent. 'Sorry Quaid, your whole life was just a dream', pouts Lori (Sharon Stone), the woman hired to play his wife. As in *The Lawnmower Man*, the power of computer-induced reality as the ultimate psychological tool for mind control, is carefully explored. Evading the secret police in a violent and bloody succession of gun battles and chases, Quaid eventually ends up heading for the Federal Mars Colony in order to thwart Cohaagen, the tyrant of yet another of the oppressive multinational corporations so often portrayed in cybertech SF.

***

EXTRAPOLATING FROM FICTION

In its rendition of future times and places, most cybertech SF provides some insight into potential future *hardwares*, individual cybertechnological *empowerments*, and the means by which corporations may come to exercise increased *control* over their employees and society. Examples of most of the cybertechnology hardware in development today (virtual reality peripherals, video telephones, smart notebook computers, software servants and so forth) can be found within many works, with the books of William Gibson and films such as *The Lawnmower Man* and *Total Recall* providing probably the best illustrations of future technology in application.

Through the eyes of cybertech SF writers, individual cybertechnological empowerment may be seen to be occurring at two distinct levels. For the law-abiding members of the general populace, technology simply becomes interwoven into business and social activities in order to make life 'easier'. With space and time negated, there is less travelling to be endured, less waiting, and less decision making taking place under conditions of incomplete information. As a result, cybertechnological societies will have the potential to become increasingly stressful, with the natural breaks and punctuations of daily routines increasingly curtailed.

For anarchists and criminals with a technical knowledge, future societies and organizations are usually portrayed as manipulable so long as you can arrange access to a computer terminal. Perhaps more significantly, an almost universal SF prediction is that in future organizations themselves will have wide-ranging powers enabling them to monitor and manipulate any individuals they choose. Organizations will be able to be trace people via the data history of their cyberspace transactions (a process in development even today). Giant corporations are invariably portrayed in cybertech as the real controllers of the world, more powerful than governments and law enforcement agencies. Already we can observe this trend in actuality. Who now controls the international currency markets? Certainly not governments. Commit a crime and most multinationals, as portrayed in cybertech SF, will be able to fix things for you. Upset one of these future corporations and you will be in serious trouble.

Perhaps the fact that vast corporations are invariably portrayed as oppressive in most works of cybertech SF is just a coincidence. Or maybe all cyberpunk/cybertech writers are anarchistic rebels with something against Big Business. Almost certainly neither of these scenarios is completely the case. Rightly or wrongly, as demonstrated across previous chapters of this book, proliferating cybertechnologies are almost certain to provide corporate executives with a great deal more power to monitor and control their organizations, and their employees, than they have available today. As businesses entangle in an enmeshment of network connections and software patterns, such power will transcend into a *potential* weapon that may be directed at other organizations and/or individuals across entire industries or even economics. This need not, of course, imply that employee exploitation, monitoring and manipulation *will* occur. That depends upon how society itself evolves, a topic well beyond the scope of this book.

As this chapter draws to a close, it is interesting to highlight a final theme resulting from its cursory review of cybertech SF. It is a theme concerning the human *fear* of technological advancement. In the fictional societies of the future, artificial intelligences and humanoid robots are almost universally feared, and in a great many they are even outlawed. The evolution of human physiology made possible via technological developments also arouses great anxiety and resistance. Yet despite such deep-rooted apprehensions, there never seems to be any question of

Mankind moving to curtail his technological advancement. So it is in reality. As a species we are instinctively curious. We yearn to invent new machines, new means of communicating, and hence new technological structures to mediate our fantasies of work and play and education. Like a global science fiction writer, we, as a race, seldom if ever accept the bounds of anything but our own limitless imagination.

The final chapter of the book tries to address where the business organizations of human kind are impatiently headed. Many analysts across a range of disciplines now place us at the dawn of a new 'wave' of technological and hence organizational and social development. How this next phase of postindustrial evolution will turn out nobody yet knows. And maybe that's just as well. Hypothesis as to the road ahead is invariably far more rewarding than actual definitive knowledge. Possession of knowledge, after all, invariably leads toward stagnation. Hypothesis, on the other hand, fuels curiosity and hence the fresh patterns of creation and innovation necessary for our very survival.

In his play he had found the ultimate, deadly toy which might wreck what was left of civilisation — but whatever the outcome, to him it would still be a game . . .

Arthur C. Clarke
The City and the Stars

8
Evolution, Transition & the Dawn of a New Age

AS CYBERTECHNOLOGIES PROLIFERATE TO form the infrastructural backbone of the global business community, so radical social and organizational transformations are being triggered upon many levels. The offices within which over half of the labour force are employed have already started to evolve. With a great many work activities now reliant upon cybertechnological interaction, computer screens and keyboards reside upon desks that ten or fifteen years ago knew no more technology than an early electronic calculator. Computer skills have become paramount prerequisites for many employees. Remote working is also a common reality. Millions of people already undertake 'traditional' office work either at home or out in the field, and as technologies such as video-conferencing and wide-area virtual reality improve, millions more are destined to join their dispersed ranks.

A level up from the grass-roots, the internal structures of a great many organizations have also entered an evolutionary state of flux. Whilst this transitory phase may not be attributed purely to cybertechnological developments, new technologies are nevertheless playing an important role in the shift toward the more cost-competitive industrial arrangements now necessary for organizational survival. In place of traditional hierarchies and rigid job demarcations, companies are seeking flexible working practices and fluid employment and control relationships. Computer networks prove pivotal to the establishment and successful operation of many of today's innovatory employment patterns, and partially as a result, static lines of organizational communication are ceasing to be the norm. In their place, knowledge-driven networks and project-based teams are arising, their members technologically empowered into new 'virtual' working patterns as discussed in **chapter 3**.

Across entire industries and economies, the way in which organizations interact to do business has also started to alter. Electronic communications media have already negated the restrictions of time and distance across many multinationals and between countless other organizations. EDI now permits information and resource transactions to take place without the need to relocate physical goods or pieces of paper. Money has for years been a virtual commodity, and as the world goes digital, more and more information products and services will be traded solely across the webs of cyberspace. With business practice increasingly software-mediated, and the infrastructural hardware of industry converging toward unity, entire industries, economies and other information network components may now be analysed not just as single entities, but as amalgamated and evolving *metasystems*. Technological advances are therefore not only altering the way in which we do business, but also the means and platforms by and from which business activity may be analysed.

A PERIOD OF TRANSITION

With radical, technology-mediated transformations occurring in so many guises, it is hardly surprising that a great many analysts contend that we are now caught in a transitionary phase of business and social evolution. A *New Age* is emerging which will exhibit not only revolutionary new organizational structures, employment trends and working relationships, but in addition fresh patterns and norms of human civilization itself. The scope of this cycle of change has become so enormous that is it extremely difficult to step back far enough in order to view current transformations with any degree of even moderate subjectivity. This does not imply, however, that there is no point in attempting to predict the challenges that lie ahead. Far from it. In future, placing yourself even just *a little* ahead of your competition will be likely to result in a *considerable* competitive advantage. As information becomes widely and instantly available to everybody in the business community, so *foresight*, rather than information itself, will become the basis of a great deal of corporate power and success.

Nobody woke up one morning in the 18th century and cried 'Let's start an industrial revolution!' Instead, we only note the incredible impact of that period of Western mass-industrialization with hindsight. So it is with

Cyber Business developments as we approach the dawn of a fresh millennium. Every manager, every employee, and every organization, is now inextricably part of the potentially volatile liquid lava of the future. And every PC that becomes networked into Internet, every child weaned on video games, and every transaction routed through cyberspace, advances the technology-driven evolutionary cycle that we are caught within an infinitesimal stage further.

The *Great Work* as some New Age radicalists now term it, is so big that nobody alive can really put a name on it. What the Great Work is concerned with, however, is getting people more and more 'mixed up with machines', whilst breaking down old barriers through the adoption of digital media. The Great Work also has to do with the end of the old style of politics,[236] together with a future beyond the extrapolation of past experience. Not for many years will corporate tomorrows be even vaguely related to corporate todays, for the world has entered new territories of the psyche and the intellect as well as of material progress. Many of the traditional grounds for historical judgement, such as seeking precedents from past events, may therefore no longer be valid.[237]

MANAGEMENT BY WIRE
IN NETWORKED ORGANIZATIONS

With computer network links commonplace across many organizations, the buzz-phrase 'management by wire' has found its way into the New Age lexicon of business. As discussed in previous chapters, some computer systems are already programmed to facilitate automatic restocking, or to calculate insurance premiums based upon a number of risk factors. In these circumstances, 'management by wire' may be said to be occurring, an analogy being made with the way in which airline captains 'fly by wire' when they let the autopilot take control during the mundane portions of a flight. As software agents develop and are widely adopted across the business community, so the trend for electronically instigated business dealings will continue. However the 'management by wire' concept may go far further than the mere computer automation of run-of-the-mill business processes. It is predicted that *enterprise models* of organizational functioning will soon be developed, which will represent the operations of an entire business in a computer software mirror world. With a click of a mouse button, or the sweep of a dataglove, a manager will be able to change the nature of such a model, which will be rendered in 2-D or 3-D virtual reality. Simultaneously, their actions will also change the operation of the *real* organization whose data constantly feeds the software model. In other words, managers will become empowered with the 'management by wire' capacity to run their business by manipulating an information representation of the company from their computer terminal.[238]

In some instances, management by wire may become like playing with a *real* version of the computer game *Sim City*.[239] In such cases, as datafeeds across organizational networks allow real-time enterprise models to constantly reflect reality in software, so the software representation of the company will become an integral, interactive component of the organizational reality upon which it is based. The boundaries between the real and the virtual components of the organization will thereby become indistinct and highly interdependent. Clearly the hurdle in creating such a management by wire system will be in creating a robust model of the business concerned from the on-line data available. However, many companies have already spent decades automating and networking their information sources, media, locations and employees, whilst elaborate data models have proved valuable to a range of major banks, airlines, retailers and food manufacturers.[240] The creation of 'corporate cockpits' from which executives may control many company operations via software manipulation may therefore not be that far away.

Even today, before the emergence of full 'autopilot' and 'remote-control' management by wire, computer network facilities allow information to 'fuzz' the linear communications pattern of a traditional corporate hierarchy. Often bypassing hierarchical levels, information routed through computers can increasingly pass freely and instantaneously between the people who actually need it. It may also be provided to its different recipients in a variety different formats, each suited to the receiver's purpose and role within the organization.

A CEO, for example, is unlikely to want to know the daily performance of every sales area or individual representative in the company. With an executive information system (EIS) linked into the sales computer network, however, he or she may well become interested in glancing at a daily amalgamation of total sales figures, which may quite possibly be presented graphically and sub-divided by major strategic business units (SBUs). Before the 'hardwiring of business', aggregate information had to be laboriously (and expensively) collated from individual transaction sources. In 'wired organizations' this is no longer the case. Simultaneously, as sales are processed, the CEO will be able to view figures for the entire organization; area managers will extract results for their particular divisions; marketing managers will be presented with information by product, and individual reps will tally their own performance. Everybody will be viewing figures based upon the same raw sales data, but the collated information with which they will be presented will be different in all cases, based upon particular user requirements.

As management by wire continues to speed the process of cutting information slices from 'the old wedding-cake of bureaucracy', so the nature of the managerial function will inevitably evolve.[241] Tasks that used to involve a great deal of time-consuming data collection will be able to be left in the hands of computer software. Estimates will increasingly be replaced by hard facts. Additionally, with video-conferencing and virtucommuting used to hold meetings both internally and externally, nowhere near as much managerial time will be wasted on the road or in a jet airliner.

Across wired organizations, the 'wired executive' will have more time available to concentrate upon creative and innovative activities. Computer network facilities have already been noted to 'supercharge' organizations, with hierarchical and functional boundaries often short-circuited as interdepartmental problem-solving teams spontaneously form. In computer-networked organizational environments, people with relevant knowledge invariably get drawn into any kind of discussion, with employees forming together into little 'virtual departments'.[242] It is therefore perhaps not surprising that using computer network facilities to permit electronic brainstorming (EBS) has been shown to be a highly effective means of generating, disseminating, and evaluating new ideas.[243] Participants, whether they are in the same room or scattered across continents, sit at computers and enter ideas which are automatically transmitted to all other parties for evaluation. Unlike in conventional brainstorming sessions, parallel entry negates the problem of having to wait your turn, whilst guaranteed anonymity encourages openness and the evaluation of ideas based upon their merit rather than their proposer.

As with other initiatives reliant upon computer-mediated working practices, problems can arise with electronic brainstorming if individuals will not embrace, or cannot operate, the technology involved. Indeed across the spectrum of management by wire developments, it is essential that new technical, data handling and interpersonal skills are taken on board by a whole range of employees, in order to cull the greatest advantage from working within a computer-networked organization. Not only will training programmes be required toward this end, but additionally the role in which some workers are pigeonholed may also have to be revised.

TECHNICIANS ON THE FRONT-LINE

Already most large organizations are entirely dependent upon the continuous and reliable functioning of their computer systems. Companies have grown so large, with the transactions between them so numerous, that it is barely possible to even *imagine* the operation of a financial institution, accounts department or stock control system, that is not totally reliant upon computer technology. With the boom in groupware, most notably electronic mail, a great many organizational communications and data-access facilities are now also computer-reliant. Vast sums of money have therefore been expended to ensure that organizational computer hardware and software is as reliable as possible. What many companies have failed to invest in, however, have been the technicians who both conceive and maintain their systems. Indeed, many firms are now not even attempting to maintain a pool of specialist computer employees. Rather, they simply contract services from the marketplace. It is therefore agencies who have to worry about the constant battle to recruit and retain skilled programmers and hardware technicians.[244]

Staff with high-level technical computing competencies are now like gold. As the farmhand was to the agrarian economy, and the machine-operator became to the era of electromechanical industrialization, so computer and telecommunications technicians are now the core employees of the information age.[245] Once boffins in the backroom, programmers and hardware engineers are fast becoming front-line workers whose efforts will be directly responsible for improvements in customer service. Computer technicians keep the information-blood pulsing through the cyberspace arteries of the new organizational forms of modern business. Companies must therefore make sure that those with technical skills are extremely well trained and rewarded. Managers are also increasingly likely to have to give technical workers a much greater say in how the company is actually run. One of the best ways to really get to know an organization is via a technical understanding of its information infrastructure. Control its cyberspace, and you can control a company.

Traditionally, research scientists, systems analysts and computer programmers have been isolated from front-line company operations. They have had no contact with customers, and hence have not needed training in customer liaison. However, with many organizations now downsizing away from remote mainframes, and with cybertechnology being used by a greater and greater number of employees, this scenario is changing. Across many institutions, technical employees, and the computer systems and interfaces they create and maintain, are becoming the first point of contact. Take banking as an example. Many customers now never actually go into a bank at all. They deal with the whole organization totally via interaction with its hole-in-the-wall machines. Such a trend will explode as home banking, home shopping and other interactive television services become available. Just as companies now spend money training sales reps, marketing personnel and other customer representatives, so in future attention will need to be focused upon the non-technical capabilities of technicians, as their contributions to organizational success emerge from the backroom and into the harsh light of the front-line. All employees will require some degree of customer training. Similarly, future managers may well require a high level of technical expertise if they are to reach for the top. A powerful ethos of the New Age is *convergence* in a myriad of guises. Across industry, demarcations are being decimated on all levels.

Some companies now specify the mastery of a technical skill as a prerequisite for career growth. At Union Pacific, for example, all aspiring managers must spend a year as a 'data integrity analyst'.[246] Under such a policy, all employees are forced to obtain a mastery of how the company really operates. As the writers of cybertech SF almost unanimously predict, in future those who understand corporate computer systems will wield the ultimate in organizational power. Times they are rapidly a-changing. No longer will an MBA, or many years working diligently up through the ranks, count significantly if you desire top-notch promotion. Almost certainly, it is those with the best technical, software, or data handling skills who will become tomorrow's corporate executives.

INDUSTRIAL ORGANIZATION IN TRANSITION

Since the dawn of the 1980s, the structures of a great many industrial organizations have known nothing but continual transition and pain. New concepts in organizational form feeding constant business process re-engineering, coupled with wave after wave of mergers and demergers, have landed company after company in the uncertain quagmire of chaos. Even today, ten years after the cost-conscious corporate shake-outs of the mid-1980s, only one thing seems certain. Traditional, bureaucratic hierarchies will not survive. They can't cope with even current levels of market complexity. They can't react quickly enough to hypercompetitive conditions. They are also, quite literally, being torn apart by the plague of computer connectivity; their bureaucratic delineations no longer recognized by knowledge-empowered workers utilizing cybertechnologies across the bounds of traditional industrial organization.

If grass-roots employees think that the impact of organizational evolution is being felt worst in the traditional environment of the office, then a brief glance upwards into the corporate jungle ought to convince them otherwise. At least office environments and the working practices of administrative employees are now evolving toward clear and specific targets. Many people may not like the idea of homeworking, hot desks, virtual teams and virtucommuting, but at least these and other future developments have been specifically identified *as* the future. Corporate planners, seeking to guide the lumbering skeletal dinosaurs within which most employees work, don't have the advantage of anywhere near as much foreknowledge. Few visions have as yet crystallized as to the likely shape of a great many organizations to come.

Despite the *availability* of a great many new technologies and market opportunities, industrial development is arguably still sulking in the doldrums. The majority of corporations, large and small, are apprehensive as to the best long-term direction. Whole departments of long-range planners have been made redundant left, right and centre. 'Long-range plans can't be made in an uncertain world where technology is constantly changing can they?' Perhaps not traditional long-range plans. But to abandon far-sighted strategic planning, simply to replace it with two- to five-year horizon spans, is simply to stick one's head in the sand. Uncertainty may make long-range planning difficult, but it also makes it even more important. Even airline captains capable of flying blind or on autopilot need to be told the direction in which they are headed. The same holds true for the management of even the most sophisticated wired organizations.

In 1984, Michael Piore and Charles Sabel hypothesized that periods of industrial confusion and uncertainty, when existing institutions no longer secure an adequate match between production and consumption, signal the end of periods of industrial stasis and the emergence of new eras of organizational evolution. They noted that such crises involve technological uncertainties, and went on to term the 'moments when the path of technological development itself is at issue' as *industrial divides*.[247] Specifically, Piore and Sabel's contention is that we are now caught within the *second industrial divide*, wherein traditional organizational structures are meeting the limits of industrial development founded upon mass production. Organizations therefore need to seek new operational paradigms, moving towards what Piore and Sabel term 'flexible specialization' — ie the flexible coupling of specialist resources into production networks only as and when required.

When mass-production techniques first took hold in the mid- to late-19th century, so the first industrial divide was triggered. Massive social and industrial unrest soon ensued. As the turbulence of the period receded, however, the breakthroughs in the use of labour and machines that had driven the first industrial divide led to a period of expansion and increased prosperity. Providing that we do not shy away from today's analogous challenges of new organizational forms empowered by cybertechnological developments, such a term of expansion and prosperity awaits us post the second industrial divide.

Whereas, in the 19th century, the choice for organizations to make was between newfangled mass production or tried-and-tested craft skills, so the choice today is between the old-fashioned ideology of mass production and the new paradigm of flexible specialization. If comparisons with the first industrial divide hold true, then it is clear which pathway must be chosen. Today's companies have to opt to become more flexible; to downsize from vast hierarchies toward dynamic, cybertechnology-empowered production networks and virtual organizations as discussed in **chapter 3**. Such change is easier said than instigated, however, with the technology upon which the future stability and prosperity of organizations depends itself being in a state of flux. Which computer systems should organizations install? Which groupware packages and systems for EDI? Should video-conferencing facilities be adopted now, or in five years when the costs will have fallen and the performance will have improved? And will adopting the infant technologies of virtual reality lead to real competitive advantages today? Unfortunately, there are as yet no clear-cut answers to these and many other questions. All that is clear from historical precedent is that it was the companies which adopted new philosophies and technologies who survived the last phase of major industrial transition.

Embracing change nearly always equates to embracing survival. Change is essential to Mankind. Change is life itself.[248] Unfortunately, in the short-term, embracing change frequently leads toward the adoption of the most painful short-term route ahead. Indeed many organizations will have to go through the pain barrier if they are to survive the second industrial divide. And we don't even know how long it will last. It may even prove to be the case that when a period of stability does emerge, it will merely signal the eye of the storm and not the end of the current period of transition. All that seems certain is that current developments across both industry and society do signal the end of one era of organizational practice and the transition to the next.

PRESTIGE, WEALTH & WISDOM

Shumpei Kumon, a highly respected Japanese professor and government adviser, has suggested that the key impacts of technological periods of transition come to influence the sources of power that govern civilization. As with Piore and Sabel, Kumon suggests that humankind is experiencing the end of the second and the beginning of a third key phase of industrial history. In his framework, the first phase of human civilization is defined as that in which men played a *Prestige Game*, using military force and threat to maintain power positions. Then came the industrial revolution, and a paradigm shift toward a society based upon a game of *Wealth*, with financial might rendering ultimate power. Such a Wealth Game is still in its final throes, with many powerplays still focused exclusively upon economic amalgamation and industrial concentration. However, Kumon predicts that as information technologies proliferate we are now entering a period of history based upon a game of *Wisdom*, wherein *knowledge*, rather than money or military might, will reign supreme.[249]

An analysis of current industrial trends (downsizing, demergers, and risk-averse R&D joint-venturing) seems to support the Japanese professor's proposition. Certainly, technological transformations are now enabling possession and control of information and derived knowledge to challenge the might of traditional wealth, just as wealth came to challenge the might of military force in the transition from the Prestige Game. We need only look to the computer industry for an illustration. Five years ago IBM, Apple and other industry giants were in fierce competition to maximize profits, each espousing their own computing solutions as the *only* sensible alternative. In the mid-1990s, however, whilst the large computer companies are still competitors, they are also cooperating upon developments such as the creation of the PowerPC. As the 'big is best' decades of 1960s and 1970s demonstrated, nobody can hope to win the Wealth Game. With cybertechnological resources evenly matched, even the emerging Wisdom Game may lead to a great many stalemates. But they will be stalemates that will be far less likely to bankrupt their losers. There will also always be the opportunity for foresight and experience — perhaps past 'ghost' experience encoded in computer software — to empower a clear winner. In the Game of Wisdom, there will be real paybacks for creativity and innovation.

THE THIRD WAVE

Although the theories of Piore and Sabel, of Kumon, and of a range of other future gazers, have been influential in certain circles, almost unquestionably it is Alvin Toffler's writings upon the great transitions of industrial civilization that have had the most impact. In *Future Shock*, his book of a quarter of a century ago, Toffler explores the 'shattering stress and disorientation that we induce in individuals by subjecting them to too much change in a short space of time'.[250] He also argues that visions of the future provide us with valuable intellectual tools for today, and that society will continue to 'quiver and crack and roar' as it suffers the jolts of the high-energy discharge of the 'super-industrial revolution'. However it was not *Future Shock* but *The Third Wave*,[251] Toffler's work of a decade later, that became the early bible to the technoculture of the emerging New Age of cybertechnology.

Yet another label for the Great Work, the Wisdom Game, or the period post the second industrial divide, Toffler describes the *Third Wave* as a 'powerful tide surging across the world', bewildering businessmen as they swim against highly erratic technological and economic currents. As with

Piore and Sabel, Toffler offers hope for a brighter future beyond our present period of transition, providing of course that we embrace the 'crashing waves of technological change' causing the conflict and tension around us:

> Old ways of thinking, old formulas, dogmas, and ideologies, no matter how cherished or how useful in the past, no longer fit the facts. The world that is fast emerging from the clash of new values and technologies, new geopolitical relationships, new lifestyles and modes of communication, demands wholly new ideas and analogies, classifications and concepts. We cannot cram the embryonic world of tomorrow into yesterday's conventional cubbyholes.[252]

> Humanity faces a quantum leap forward. It faces the deepest social upheaval and creative restructuring of all time. Without clearly recognizing it, we are engaged in building a remarkable new civilization from the ground up. This is the meaning of the Third Wave.[253]

Few analysts concerned with assigning a label to the current period of industrial transition — a transition that all agree involves fresh technological creations and hence patterns of work and socialization — produce works awash with answers as to what the 'new future' will be like for Mankind. The fact that a New Age is dawning is not in question. The fact that the New Age concerns convergence is also undisputed. Convergence of the sciences and the arts. Convergence of physical, technical and biological research and development. Convergence of cultures and social patterns across our emerging 'global village', 'information age' or 'post-industrial society'. Through the medium of cyberspace — the medium of the totality of information in the human system — *everything* seems to be coming together, with the focus for the future concentrated within the raw data of the global system, and the resultant realities empowered by such data.

The implication of the convergence of technologies, disciplines and cultural patterns across the globe is that managers at any level of an organization can no longer ignore what is happening in the technologist's research lab. Conversely, those creating technological wonders need to be made aware of the huge social and cultural implications of the daily miracles that they conceive for an unsuspecting world. Whatever label we choose to adopt for the New Age, a new unity of Mankind will inevitably be the result *if*, or more optimistically *when*, we emerge from the current period of transition. Technologies, languages, cultures and social and working patterns are all destined to mix together. The boundaries between our current tight geographical concentrations of individuals will also cease to be of great significance in a world of global connectivity, and in which organizations utilize flexible employment patterns which often technologically link remote human beings to engage in cooperative work.

The industrial revolution led humankind to concentrate in the cities that still require vast and complex individual infrastructures to support their crowded populations. Such cities will continue to exist in the New Age, but as we increasingly become inhabitants of a planet rather than of a town or a country, so the need to concentrate within cities for either occupational necessity or out of a requirement for cultural empowerment is likely to decline. Mankind will come to live *across* his first planet. The focus of humanity will thereby shift to become the global hardware platform — the unified worldwide infrastructure — that will both support and mediate our continued existence and evolution.

BIRTH OF A METASYSTEM

In his quest for the new cultural rituals likely to become entrenched in a future society of global connectivity, anthropologist David Tomas tries to envisage 'the outlines of post-organic forms' that will develop in the context of cyberspace.[254] Such information entities may well be enormous. Indeed, with cyberspace becoming the focus for the business and social dealings of humanity, the potential now exists to analyse a single *metasystem* involving human beings, software infomachines and computer systems.

As noted in the first chapter, Gregory Stock has named the community of technologically interrelated organisms that make up the 'thin planetary patina of Mankind' as *Metaman*.[255] Metaman is a single living being, a 'super-organism' of which every human being is a cellular component, with the physical and information infrastructures of the New Age holding each of its human cells together for collective activity. Stock notes that the 'birth' of Metaman is only a recent development. It is also a development which constitutes a *fourth* evolutionary transition in the progression of life on earth. For Stock, the previous evolutionary phases of life equate to the initial tight association of biochemicals into primitive bacteria, followed by the combination of these bacteria into complex eukaryotes, and their subsequent amalgamation into multicellular organisms. This latter progression, whereby complex cells combined into synergistic animal bodies, occurred around 700 million years ago, and has provided the basic structure for organic life ever since. Within Stock's terms of reference, the dawn of the New Age permitting Metaman to come into existence thereby heralds the most significant event upon earth *for over 700 million years*. The industrial revolution occurred but a second or two ago by comparison.

Whilst the sheer scale of Stock's analysis is breathtaking, his proposition that the impact of new technologies upon global societies, organizations and business infrastructures is leading toward a fresh stage in the 'natural' development of life itself, is both compelling and ablaze with enlightenment. We need only look to mother nature to witness a wide variety of metasystems in action. Termite and ant colonies, for example, can be analysed as single life-system entities even though they comprise hundreds of thousands of apparently independent, individual insects. The body of a human being is also a metasystem of individual biological cells with their own random behaviours. View a cut under a powerful microscope, and the patterns of movement of any particular blood cell cannot be predicted. What *is* certain is that cells of the body will eventually form some sort of scab across the wound *in amalgamation*.

THE METAMAN PERSPECTIVE

In viewing Mankind, his business communities, and his emerging global information infrastructure, as a single entity, the randomness of the current period of New Age transition becomes masked. Mankind as Metaman adapts amazingly quickly to both internal and external developments impacting upon the nature of his super-organism. Resources are mobilized, and systems changed, at an incredible pace in relation to the sheer size of the lifeform concerned. A transition period of perhaps fifty years is but a blip in time for Metaman. As a race we are utilizing our new technological arteries to react at top speed to challenges such as global warming and over-population. It is simply unrealistic to expect an organism spread over the surface of a ten-thousand-kilometre globe to mobilize with respect to such causes in a matter of years rather than decades.

Although adopting a radically different standpoint to Piore and Sabel, Kumon or Toffler, Stock also paints for us a very rosy future. He also agrees with other analysts that regional cultures, languages and communications patterns will increasingly blend into a cosmopolitan pot. Such a human potpourri is *inevitable* as computer-mediated communications systems spread. As knowledge disseminates via many-to-many interaction through cyberspace, so the walls of individual societies, like the levels of classical hierarchies, will inevitably crumble. Existing cultures will explode, to be reconfigured out of elements that will be electronically drawn into them from outside.[256]

As noted in **chapter 6**, the Global Village will soon be the largest country in the world. Inevitably, hyperprotectively insular cultures, such as those of the Japanese and the French, will become part of a global whole as and when they embrace large-scale access to the world-wide net of cyberspace. No country (nor multinational for that matter) can fight this trend. No country or company should even *want to*. In the New Age, the super-organism of Metaman will consist of hundreds of thousands of sub-cultural islands in a sea of global, technologically distributed, shared experience. This will not represent a losing but a *gaining* for humanity. It is evolution that has kept Mankind alive for so many hundreds of thousands of years. Cybertechnological developments are now part of Man's evolution — an evolution that may ultimately lead to the emergence of group consciousness across the cyberspace information nexus.

OF GOLDFISH & GROUPMINDS

Two of the key individual themes of *Cyber Business* are global connectivity, and the ever closer synthesis of human beings and computer systems. Each of these concepts presents us with many potentially powerful new applications in its own right. Put the two sets of developments together, however, and the results may be not only be spectacular, but potentially beyond living comprehension. To explore the fusion point of global connectivity and man-machine synthesis, we will therefore utilize the metaphor of the goldfish and the groupmind.

Consider all items of information and all of the ideas in the world to be tiny, tiny goldfish. Within this analogy, water therefore becomes cyberspace (the medium in which goldfish live), whilst computers equate to the metaphorical aquaria in which information may be caged. In the early days of their development, computers were not connected together. It was therefore impossible for the goldfish within their individual tanks to move freely from one to another. Each fish therefore had to remain within its own particular cyberspace; its own particular water tank within its own native computer system.

Then one day somebody invented rubber tubing, allowing pipelines to be constructed to *network* the information tanks of different computer systems. Goldfish suddenly had a whole new world opening up before them, with the ability afforded to visit the information aquaria of many different computers aside from their own. Since computer networking emerged, wider and wider tubing has been used to connect more and more computers together. The ease with which our metaphorical goldfish have been able to swim *between* computer information tanks has therefore been continually increased. As the New Age dawns, and every computer becomes networked with every other, it will be as if the open information tank of every computer in the world has suddenly been thrown into the sea. Cyberspace will become an enormous single ocean of information. Any goldfish within its depths will be able to visit any computer. Ideas and information will no longer know any bounds or restrictions. This is what is really meant by global connectivity across a single global hardware platform. A common ocean in which all our datafish may swim free.

But remember, in our analogy goldfish not only represent packets of data, they also symbolize *ideas*. Therefore, whilst goldfish may be found living in the aquaria of computers, they can also be discovered residing in their multitudes within the water bowls of all human brains. Whilst most literatures only consider cyberspace as the information space found within and between networked computer systems, we should never forget that each of us possesses our own information space inside our very own heads. To date, there has been little point in noting this fact, as each biological cyberspace has only ever been accessible by the individual human being to whom it belongs. With New Age developments this lonely state of affairs may change.

In **chapter 5**, developments in man-machine computer interface systems were explored. In particular, the future development of *direct mental links* into computers was discussed. Great. The goldfish in our heads will one day be able to swim out into our desktop PCs. We will no longer need to translate our thoughts into clumsy symbolistic language in order to convey them to a computer. Want to write a letter? Think it, and it will appear on your screen, or even a mile high in your own personal virtual graphics world.

But hold on a second. We've just thrown all the computers in the world into the sea. By definition, therefore, once you have the technology to link your own mind into your computer, then you also have common mental access to the ocean of cyberspace made possible via global connectivity. Therefore, with a direct brain-computer link, you could access not just every computer and piece of information in the world, *but also the mind of every other human being connected into the system.*

As global connectivity and man-machine synthesis achieve their ultimate convergence, our mental goldfish will be able to swim freely from one mind to another. New species of goldfish will also be created and manipulated *across multiple minds*: across the *groupminds* of the cyberspace ocean. A potential for group consciousness will thereby emerge. By definition, *nobody* at present can even start to *imagine* what this may mean. Suddenly Stock's Metaman could be afforded the ability to *think globally*. Governments or boards of directors could connect together to allow their multiple experiences to synergize in the ultimate form of *collective* decision making.

Mankind is a social animal who has achieved incredible feats even though direct mental contact between human beings has hitherto proved impossible. As this changes, who knows what future men — future metamen — will become capable of. Organizations themselves may actually achieve consciousness. Suddenly the tribulations of New Age transition seem worth embracing in their turgid totality. Casualties may include the watering down of distinctive cultures such as those of the Far East, together with the slow death of French and other minority languages. However, they are casualties of almost insignificant proportion compared with the New Age wonders and evolutions that potentially lie ahead.

POWERS OF THE CYBERPANOPTICON

Whilst the concepts of groupminds and metasystem consciousness excite the brain cells as potential far-distant wonders of technological magic, the power of business organizations to survey, and potentially to manipulate, the activities of their employees and their customers looms before us in reality in the very near future. As many writers of SF cybertech have predicted, a 'cyberpanoptic society' may emerge, wherein information technology systems enable governments and multinational corporations to control and to manipulate the populace.

The concept of a Panopticon — of a prison or other institution whose architecture enables every inmate to be under perpetual observation — was conceived by moral philosopher Jeremy Bentham in the late 18th century. His plans were put into effect in Russia in 1787, when a polygon-shaped factory was built, sheathed in glass, around a central tower. Mirrors were positioned to alleviate shadows and to provide additional lines of sight, allowing those at the top of the tower the opportunity to continually observe all workers. 'Universal transparency' was therefore achieved, with the resulting Panopticon inducing a conscious state of permanent surveillance upon its members. What's more, the visibility of the central tower and the perfection of the surveillance available within the panoptic structure made the actual exercise of continual monitoring unnecessary.[257]

Every inmate of a panoptic structure knows that they have the *potential* to be monitored at all times. That knowledge alone is usually more than enough to allow the exercise of an incredible degree of control by those in authority. It may therefore be of concern that cybertechnological systems, that can translate, record, display and communicate data, now have the potential to become 'cyberpanopticons'. Such potential surveill- ance systems are not only freed of the constraints of space and time, but also of the physical arrangements of buildings, the mutual presence of the observer, or regimes of laborious record keeping and administration.[258] Indeed, the entire global Net may become a Panopticon in disguise. After all, the cables that bring information into our homes and businesses will equally have the power to take information away. Select one of four hundred interactive encoded television channels, and somebody, somewhere, will *know* that you have selected it. The potential for the totalitarian abuse of our emerging global hardware platform is thereby significant.[259] Already, across companies and educational institutions, the supervisors that control local and wide area networks often have the ability to call up details pertaining to exactly what any particular user is doing, and at which terminal they are situated. As cable and satellite network links spread across the industrialized world, the power of 'global network supervisors' could potentially become extremely wide-ranging.

The most significant factor to distinguish cyberpanoptic architectures from those of previous institutions and police states is that of invisibility. Whereas the central tower of Bentham's initial conception served as an icon of potential and continual surveillance, there is no obvious evidence of central monitoring associated with the use of many information technology systems. Today, people are even *inviting* panoptic arteries — such as fibre-optic cabling links for new television services — right into their homes. They even pay for the privilege. We have in fact come to accept and to demand other elements of cyberpanoptic machinery by the 'back door'.

Visiting a supermarket which employs a barcode-scanning checkout, and which allows payment by debit or credit card, certainly speeds the pace of shopping. You return home with a printed, itemized receipt, and subsequently receive bank statements that indicate where and when you spent your hard-earned 'cash'. In engaging in electronically mediated activity, however, you are also leaving an electronic trail of your spending habits across the computer network of both the supermarket and many financial institutions. With rapidly decreasing information storage costs, it is now perfectly possible that a supermarket computer may be programmed to contain a record of every single item that you have ever bought, when, and at what price. This data *could* subsequently be correlated by a third party with information from other sources (employment records, vehicle licensing information, medical records and so forth) in an almost infinite variety of ways.

As the speed and connectivity of network databases increases, it will become not only possible, but cost-effective, to track entire electronic lives across cyberspace. Corporations will have the ability to know the nature of every transaction you have ever undertaken in your life. And there is no way out of this system. Fortunately, today's data protection systems are relatively effective, although the potential will always exist for cybertechnologies to 'turn privacy into a commodity'.[260] It is therefore hardly surprising that the science for encrypting computer data to protect both privacy and intellectual property is receiving a great deal of attention, and is likely to spawn a very large sub-niche of the telecommunications marketplace in the future.

DANGERS OF THE HYPER-REALITY CHARADE

Increased computer connectivity will potentially not only enable the panoptic surveillance of individual activities, it will also allow the masters of cyberspace to manipulate the parameters of common reality. Already across the Western world we can witness such a trend. Television programmes, and the adverts between them, distort our perceptions of what life is really like and what goods we need. They raise expectations and alter the way in which we process information. They unconsciously foster aspirations toward dreams only available within a hyper-real world of beautiful people, shiny cars, happy endings, and powders that wash whiter-than-white.

Clearly the emergence of immersive computer-generated graphics worlds will enable us to experience new forms of 'reality'. Cyberspace VR worlds will become incredible training and education tools, as well as forums for business meetings and leisure. However, for a very long time to come, we will know that computer VR environments *are* merely charades. After all, having to stop and put on the headset and other bodywear will always give the game away. We are therefore extremely unlikely to confuse reality with computer-generated VR, even though we might discover skills and experiences in VR that will come to alter our forms of behaviour in the real world. There is, however, a very serious danger that the use of far more basic, non-immersive cyberspace medias in our daily lives, may erode our perceptions of reality itself.

The term *hyper-reality* has been coined to refer to a state of affairs wherein data abstraction masks the actual nature of the world from its citizens. When this occurs, reality becomes denatured and the values of both individuals and society are likely to be perverted. As witnessed in the Gulf War in 1991, high technology already has the potential to make military conflict hyper-real. Masked by the current battle hardware of war, mass killing has become faceless. Metre-accurate missiles can be guided on-screen by infra-red as if they were playtime rockets within the video game *Space Invaders*. Across the world, TV audiences marvelled as buildings crumpled under the impact of computer-guided weapons controlled from on high. The videotape of the kill became as important as the kill itself, and somewhere along the line many people conveniently forgot the fact that the new toys of the military were actually taking human lives.

In a similar fashion, the more we come to abstract business and social patterns across cyberspace, the more hyper-real our perceptions may become. Output too high? In a future wired or even 'virtual' organization, a manager may simply sweep his or her dataglove in a software mirror world to decouple 'surplus' employees from the company. *Cyber Business* developments clearly have the potential to make control of reality far too easy. The decision to fire some employees would surely be taken far less lightly if workers were known to the manager as individuals, and if they had to be called into their office and made redundant face-to-face.

Across cyberspace, even with video-links coming on-line, people have the potential to become as abstract as the future companies who will employ them. Those in positions of power will have to be made especially aware of this. A homeworker is just as much a human being as those 'real, live, flesh-empowered people' who work in the office next door. Some future managers will undoubtably have employees working for them whom they have never actually met, and whom they are unlikely ever to encounter in 'reality'. Treating such individuals with equity may well prove quite a challenge. We will therefore all have to be careful that the people whom we come to know through computer-mediated links are not perceived as a different kind of being — as a lower kind of lifeform — than those individuals we experience with a real physical proximity. Similarly, we need to ensure that the artificial constructions of cyberspace do not come to be treated as reality, or as more real than items in the physical world or even human beings themselves.

Cyberspace as a medium will empower us with many new social tools, but it will inevitably mask elements of reality from our individual and group perceptions. Mediated information may become our 'enemy' as much as our 'friend'. Already many Western dreams have been corporately manipulated to become hyper-real. Approaching dangerous levels of abstraction, the dreams of hyper-reality will always be subject to selective mutation by the dreamer (we witness the explosion yet filter out the human devastation it causes). And as long as we embrace hyper-real visions, 'no atrocity will be past us, for we will have kicked the Reality Syndrome once and for all'.[261]

DARK DILEMMAS & NEW HORIZONS

As we stand on the brink of the 21st century, the human race faces the dilemma of avoiding the downside of increased technological adoption, whilst retaining the benefits of technological dependence.[262] Some technosceptics and change-resistant traditionalists still harbour a hope that Mankind will one day cast aside his recent shackle of technoaddiction. They argue that computers have been 'overdressed in fabulous claims', which have been deliberately propagated by those elements of our society who are adopting some of the most 'morally questionable' uses of computing power.[263] However, despite the potential risks of reality perversion and the rise of oppressive, all-seeing cyberpanoptic corporations, there are no signs at present that a backlash against technological society is on even the distant horizon. For a decade the most popular children's toys have been home computers and video games, with around a third of households in the UK now owning a personal computer.[264] Whatever some slide-rule and pen-and-paper brandishing stick-in-the-muds may preach, the battle is already lost if we think we can vanquish the near primeval desire to utilize the fruits of human innovation from the minds of the next generation. Children are already the true masters of virtual reality. They manipulate the laws of fantasy every day of their lives, glorying in role-play and drama and the creation of storylines. Adult fantasies, so the psychologists tell us, are all depressingly similar. Only children are conceptually free. Hardly surprising, then, that it has been suggested that one way to solve many of the world's difficulties would be to get all children on-line via a computer network conference over which problems would be posted.[265]

Across the economies of the world, information itself, rather than oil, land, minerals or industrial plant, has now become the key global resource. A great many organizations rely upon continuous and rapid technological advancement to enable them to compete successfully for global resources. Even companies outside of the high technology industries need to make the development of sophisticated data gathering and storage methods a priority, as collecting specialized marketing information has become a prerequisite for business success.[266] Whether we all like it or not, it is indisputable that the world has become utterly dependent upon many forms of cybertechnology in order to both maintain present living standards and to generate future wealth. To try and turn the clock back at this critical stage in our history would be to condemn billions to enforced and permanent misery.[267]

There can be no doubt that Mankind will push the boundaries of all technological innovation to their extreme. The spirit of invention is instinctive to our race, and once any Pandora's box has been prised open, it is but folly to suggest that it can subsequently be quietly closed and left out-of-sight in a dark corner. Mankind will embrace immersive virtual reality technologies, computer-mediated communications, virtual working patterns, and the many other developments of the *Cyber Business*. As highlighted by the analysis of Gregory Stock, New Age developments constitute an integral pathway in Mankind's evolutionary progression. Such progression may one day come to completely re-engineer the social patterns of humanity, yet as a race we will keep experimenting with smarter and smarter machines.

Whilst emerging cybertechnologies are, and will continue to be, responsible for social changes and fresh patterns of civilization, at the same time our culture itself increasingly drives technological development.[268] It is simply not the case that computer enthusiasts are pushing society in their own selfish, narrow-minded direction. Just as equally, society fuels the process by inciting researchers to advance their innovatory undertakings in order to conceive further wonders for the picking of the mass-populace. In this sense, everyone living and working within an industrial society is partly responsible for the acceleration of *Cyber Business*.

Precisely because of the inevitability of technical advancement, this book has tried to avoid entanglement in the moral and political debates that surround much of the academic discussion of immersive VR technologies and new systems for computer-mediated communication. Whatever the 'rights' and the 'wrongs', we are irrevocably caught in the struggle to emerge into a New Age in which 'smartness' will be endowed into objects from alarm clocks to automobiles, and from buildings to bombs. The period of transition is painful, and by the time stability returns to our economies and society the fabric of our daily lives will have altered in a great many respects. Beneath the surface, however, we will still be just as *human* as we were way back before the current divide between the present and future technological waves. Indeed, across industry, people will be permitted far greater freedom to exercise the spirit and creativity of the human condition. As cybertechnology empowers the business community not only with data, but also with smart software agents to seek the valuable information they require from the cyberspace 'infobog', so companies will no longer be able to waste the creativity of their human employees. Quite to the contrary, creativity itself will increasingly become the key factor that creates long-term competitive advantage.[269]

Many enthusiasts bemoan the fact that cyberspace is fast becoming a commercial domain. This trend need not be feared, however, as the realm of information will still continue be used as a social space by virtual communities engaging in friendly exchange across its electronic nothingness. There may be teething troubles as new structures are introduced to control and regulate a vastly *improved* Internet. What is certain, however, is that Big Business will not want to drive all enthusiasts from the world of information. Such a proposition (and it has been loudly voiced over the Net) is akin to suggesting that all of the stores in a shopping mall would ever seriously adopt a policy of locking out all of their customers. Successful and hence innovative businesses can't evolve in a vacuum. By definition, they need to attract resources and to draw in capital, partners, suppliers and customers to create the cooperative networks necessary in order to survive.[270] Companies evolving across cyberfrontiers will desire as many human beings and other organizations to be involved in cyberspace as possible. Unlike the physical territory of our planet, cyberspace is unique in that its terrain is infinitely expandable. There will always be room for everyone. We will therefore all be at liberty to share the domain of pure information, each making our own contribution to enable the virtual medium to become a richer and an even more useful common resource for the whole of humanity.

As cyberspace evolves into a future marketplace as well as a military, research and communications nexus, so large multinationals will come to dominate the computer networks of the world. Again, however, this is a natural development that need not be feared. Lumbering bureaucracies already dominate our society, so there should be little for either individuals or smaller companies to fear as they also come to 'control' the infrastructure of cyberspace. As new means of 'control' and 'regulation' emerge, so new tricks and shortcuts will be invented to buck the system when it is perceived to be unfair. Whatever the level of technology involved, learning how to survive in new forms of social and technical environment is human nature. And human beings have become extremely adept at engaging in such a Wisdom Game. We will certainly not be witness to a utopian future of mass individual cybertechnological empowerment as dreamt of by the idealists of the 1960s, but nor will the majority become party to mass-authoritarian cyberpanoptic oppression. There will be winners and there will be losers, across both the business community and wider society, as we continue to bridge the technological chasm toward the promise of the New Age. Governments will undoubtably have less and less power in comparison to multinationals and knowledge-empowered individuals. Yet people will still be people, and computers will still be the boxes of electronics that we curse and swear at as we continually wish they were more intelligent, more adaptable, and capable of processing our requirements at least twice as quickly.

QUESTIONS, ANSWERS & DREAMS

This book, like all others, has used the medium of sequential, printed text as the syringe to inject its ideas and information into your mind. Future cybermedia will be far less clumsy, allowing direct mental transfers from one person or one group to another. Computers are, and will always remain, merely tools to be brought to life via human action and desire. Computers are significant, however, in that they serve to facilitate access to the medium of cyberspace. Just as a sculptor works with a chisel but in stone, so many future employees will work *through* computers to craft their creations in the domain of pure information.

As its Epilogue approaches, **Cyber Business** leaves a great many questions unanswered. This is both inevitable and intentional. Just exactly how will virtual organizational working patterns spread across the business community? Will virtucommuting become a common genre of homeworking? Will the native inhabitants of cyberspace — its agents, ghosts and other virtual monsters — ever achieve true intelligence or even sentience? And perhaps most importantly, what kind of timescale will mediate the patterns of business and social evolution that surround the concepts, ideas and technologies paraded herein, but which are still as intangible to the majority as the glass-encased exhibits of an ancient and dusty museum?

The answers to the above lie not in the hands of research scientists or academics, nor in those of journalists or futurologists or computer programmers. They instead depend upon the visions and the dreams that current business practitioners will forward into action across their organizations. It is up to managers today to create the organizations of tomorrow.

How we choose to shape our future, and how we choose to realize our dreams, greatly depends upon where we decide to draw the line between present and future fantasy and reality. If we do not believe that some of the predicted developments of the New Age will be achieved, then our closed minds will inevitably condemn them to remain as residents of the Land of Fiction. Across the cyberspace medium, new 'virtual' realities will soon come to be experienced. New social patterns will also emerge, whilst new forms of business organization will rise to craft the information of the world toward the accomplishment of previously undreamt of crusades. In the New Age, *Cyber Business* developments will not only change how we perceive reality, they will also alter the nature of reality itself.

Epilogue
The Reality

GRANT GAZED OUT OVER the new landscape, content with the realization of yet another dream. It was perfect. Then the software crashed, rolling satin clouds vaporized, and his temporal colleagues were once more back in their own domains.

His agent surveyed their thoughts. All was well. Even with the Japanese bankers. A continent away Samantha smiled. Grant smiled back, glad that he had accepted her marketing provision, and trucked his vision in to a close-up of the young lady at her console. Perhaps that was too forward? Perhaps not. After all, she had already granted him the use of over two hundred idle gigabytes.

The public domain freak in the arctic excitedly reported the first booking. Grant hurriedly requested a myriad of infomachines to de-bug the software and to prepare his new virtual resort for incoming tourists. He also requested a tactful v-mail to the guy in the polar wastes stating that if he posted him again with such a tacky animation then he would terminate his connection. After all, Samantha might be monitoring his files, and he hardly imagined her as the sort of girl to respect those who still used keyboards and studied sixty four bit assembler.

He didn't have to imagine for long, however, as an instant later Samantha was there beside him. And what a nice location she had chosen for a stroll. Even if it wasn't one of his own creations. They talked for a few hours, sharing the vastness of cyberspace, and parted with their agents on personal terms. Grant smiled as he logged-out and lay back in bed that night. Perhaps he would catch a shuttle tomorrow. After all, despite what the multinats advertised over the Net, there were still some encounters not quite as enjoyable when mediated via computer . . .

Glossary

AI *Artificial intelligence.* The encapsulation of intellect into computer software.

Applications program Any computer software used for productive activity. The most common examples of applications programs are word processors, spreadsheets (electronic ledger tables), databases, communications packages and graphics programs.

Backbone (network) One of the high-speed communications links forming the data transmission 'arteries' of a wide-area computer network such as the Internet.

BBS *Bulletin board system.* A computer network facility allowing people to 'post' public electronic messages, software programs and data so that they may later be 'picked up' and utilized by others.

Bodysuit A virtual reality peripheral that allows all of the motions of the human body to be registered and 'tracked' in cyberspace. May include devices for providing 'tactile feedback' so that the wearer can actually *feel* objects in a virtual reality simulation.

CD-ROM *Compact disk read only memory.* An optical disk, the same size as a standard audio CD, on which computer software, data or video images may be supplied.

CLI *Command line interface.* A means of interacting with a computer which requires the user to type in exacting keyboard commands.

CMC *Computer-mediated communications.* The use of computers and computer networks for communications purposes.

Connectivity Pertaining to the interconnection of computer systems across networks.

CSCW *Computer-supported cooperative work.* Relating to the use of computer technology to enable people to work together. Most commonly, computer-supported cooperative work involves linking together two or more employees over a computer network.

CTI *Computer telephone integration.* When telephones and computers are combined, negating the need to have separate telephone and computer hardware, and offering the potential for 'smartphones'.

Cyberholic Somebody who is addicted to computer and network technology and the use thereof.

Cyberphobia A deep-rooted fear or mistrust of computers that can result in physical/medical symptoms.

Cyberpunk A rebel of the New Age, embracing the notion that 'information wants to be free'. Many so-called cyberpunk science fiction writers have fuelled the creation and discussion of new technological developments and their impact upon society.

Cyberspace The realm of pure information used for computer processing, communications and data representation. Cyberspace is the electronic space inside computers and across computer networks.

Cybertech SF *Cybertechnology science fiction.* The branch of the fictional genre of cyberpunk defined herein as dealing with future developments in electronic and computer hardwares together with their impact upon society.

Cybertechnologies A compound term for all information technologies that utilize the electronic medium of cyberspace. Computers and computer networks, telecommunications systems, video links, virtual reality peripherals, and telephone and fax devices, are all examples of cyber-technology.

Dataglove A computer peripheral enabling the motion and position of the hand and fingers to be 'tracked' in virtual reality.

DOS *Disk operating system.* The operating system or 'control program' that enables applications programs to be executed on an IBM personal computer. Amongst other things, DOS controls the allocation of computer memory for other programs, and coordinates disk drive operations.

Downsizing With respect to computers, the shift toward using smaller and smaller machines. Usually downsizing involves using a network of personal computers rather than a mainframe or minicomputer accessed via a remote terminal. In a general business context, downsizing refers to the trend toward re-engineering organizations into smaller and smaller units.

EBS *Electronic brainstorming.* The use of networked computer facilities to enable many individuals to engage in the process of idea generation.

EIS *Executive information system.* A computer application enabling top managers to extract amalgamated information upon the business in an easy-to-access fashion. Executive information systems are said to be used as much for problem finding as for problem solving.

Gigabyte (Gb) Just over one thousand megabytes of computer data storage; ie around one billion characters of information.

Global hardware platform The system of business infrastructure that will result when global connectivity is achieved and all computer systems are networked together.

Gopher A menu-based 'intelligent map' application which can assist computer network users in locating resources over the Internet.

Groupware A genre label for the many types of computer software which are designed to enable group rather than individual computer usage. Most groupware systems allow for common data access by many individuals and/or provide a means of communicating via computer.

GUI *Graphical user interface*. A means of interacting with a computer whereby small pictures (or 'icons') are used to represent functions and data. A mouse is used to move a pointer to select icons or control menus, hence making a GUI far more 'user-friendly' than a command line interface (CLI).

Hierarchical structure A form of organization exhibiting clear and rigid chains of command from its lowest to its highest levels. Each member of a hierarchical structure will have just one boss on the next level above to whom they are directly responsible.

HMD *Head-mounted display*. A virtual reality peripheral that positions a small display screen before each of the wearer's eyes in order that he/she may perceive a stereophonic, 3-D image of a computer-generated graphics world. Most HMDs also track the position of their wearer's head so that he/she may naturally 'look around' in virtual reality.

Homeworking Using computer and communications technologies to enable individuals to work from home. Also known as teleworking or telecommuting.

Host (network) A computer through which other computers connect in order to access network resources.

Infomachine An *active* 'entity' of computer software.

Internet The *International network*. A loose amalgamation of thousands of interconnected computer networks, all using the same communications standards, which together constitute the largest computer network in the world.

IRC *Internet relay chat*. A system whereby two or more computer network users may enter into interactive, two-way communication over an Internet channel.

ISDN *Integrated services digital network*. A high-speed communications link that may be used for transferring data in a variety of formats such as text, graphics, audio and video.

LAN *Local area network.* A means of interconnecting personal computers for short-distance communications and program sharing. Most office PCs are now connected into LANs.

Management by wire Pertaining to the use of computer and communications technologies in the management of an organization. True management by wire systems will allow a manager to run a company or section thereof purely by manipulating a software model.

Megabyte (Mb) Just over one million characters of computer storage (in actuality 2^{20} bytes, where one byte is a single character of information stored within a computer).

Metaman A term coined by Gregory Stock to embrace the entirety of Mankind. Metaman is a single 'super-organism' or metasystem in which every person on earth is treated as a just one small component of the whole system. Some 'cyberians' refer to the Metaman concept as 'Gaia'.

Mirror world The concept of an interactive representation of reality created in computer software. When reality changes, so will the computer software mirror world on which it is based. Conversely, when a mirror world itself is changed, the reality on which it is based will also be altered.

Modem *MOdulator/DEModulator.* A device enabling a computer to connect into the telephone system to enable network communications.

Mosaic A graphical, user-friendly interface which allows Internet resources to be 'browsed' via the World-Wide Web.

Network (computer) Any system involving the interconnection of two or more computers for communication and/or resource sharing.

Network (organizational) An organizational network involves a central 'core' body which allocates sub-tasks to network 'nodes' or 'agents'. A hierarchical structure is thereby not exhibited. Network organizational forms frequently involve a great deal of outsourcing (sub-contracting) and are inherently flexible. Also known as dynamic or organic networks.

Optical disk A computer storage medium using laser technology to enable vast quantities of data to be recorded upon a single computer disk.

PC *Personal computer.* A stand-alone, desktop computer system with its own internal processing capacity and storage system. PCs may be networked to communicate with other computer systems.

PCMCIA *Personal computer memory card international association.* A standard for credit-card-sized computer peripherals. Most PCMCIA cards are used for data storage.

PDA *Personal digital assistant.* A small, hand-held computer and communications device, usually operated by writing and drawing with a pen directly upon its screen.

Pentium At the time of writing, one of the most powerful PC microprocessors on the market, and used as the heart of top-of-the-range IBM and compatible personal computers.

Peripheral (computer) Any device that connects into a computer.

PowerPC A new and extremely powerful generation of personal computers. PowerPCs are produced by both Apple Computer and IBM.

Reality engine The computer hardware used to generate virtual reality graphics environments. Head-mounted displays, datagloves and so forth are all connected into the reality engine.

Smartcard A credit-card-sized device packed with electronics to enable it to hold data or to enable it to be used as a security or identification tag or a repository for electronic money.

Sniffer A computer program used by the criminally minded to attempt to discover the passwords of legitimate users in order to forge access to a computer system.

Software agent A 'smart' computer program (or *infomachine*) that will 'serve' its human master in cyberspace. Software agents protect their users from the complexity of computer and network operations, and may engage in database searches and transactions based upon a knowledge of their user's 'profile'.

Telecommuting *See* Homeworking.

Telescript A software agent control language created by developer General Magic.

Terabyte (Tb) Over one thousand gigabytes (one million megabytes) of computer storage.

Virtual community A group of individuals who interact via communication over a computer network.

Virtual organization Any pattern of organization based around information technology systems that enable geographically distant individuals to work together. Most virtual organizations will involve people linked by computer and telecommunications networks, hence permitting them to run groupware, and perhaps even virtucommuting applications.

Virtucommuting The concept of virtual reality homeworking, wherein individuals will don VR clothing and link into a home reality engine in order to be 'transported' to a computer-generated working domain.

Virus A maliciously created form of computer program whose sole function is to disrupt normal computer operations and/or to corrupt computer data.

VR *Virtual reality*. A representation of the real world, encoded in computer software, with which computer users may freely interact. The term virtual reality is most commonly used to refer to *immersive* VR systems whereby peripherals such as head-mounted displays, datagloves and bodysuits are used to allow people to become enveloped in a computer-generated graphics world.

WAN *Wide area network*. Any system allowing the connection of computers for communications over long distances.

Wand A peripheral whose movement in space may be used to control a computer system and to manipulate objects in virtual reality.

Windows™ The graphical user interface created by Microsoft® and used upon IBM and compatible personal computers. A 'window' is an area on a computer display screen in which computer software executes. In *Windows*, more than one program may operate at a time, each appearing within its own area upon the display screen.

World-Wide Web A graphical and extremely user-friendly Internet interface based upon 'hypertext' style information links. Often abbreviated to 'W3' rather than WWW.

Further Reading & Viewing

Whilst the full compilation of endnotes follows, the sources listed below are particularly recommended in providing further coverage upon many of the topics discussed within this book

FACT

Computers as Theatre, Brenda Laurel (Reading, MA: Addison-Wesley, 1993).

Cyberspace: First Steps, Michael Benedikt (ed) (Cambridge, MA: MIT Press, 1993).

Glimpses of Heaven, Visions of Hell: Virtual Reality and its Implications, Barrie Sherman and Phil Judkins (London: Hodder & Stoughton, 1992).

Metaman: Humans, Machines and the Birth of a Global Super-organism, Gregory Stock (London: Bantam Press, 1993).

MONDO 2000: A User's Guide to the New Edge, Rudy Rucker, R. U. Sirus and Queen Mu (London: Thames & Hudson, 1993).

Technotrends, Daniel Burrus with Roger Gittines (New York: Harper Collins, 1993).

The Third Wave, Alvin Toffler (London: Collins, 1980).

The Virtual Community, Howard Rheingold (London: Secker & Warburg, 1994).

Virtual Reality and the Exploration of Cyberspace, Francis Hamit (Carmel, IN: Sams Publishing, 1993).

FICTION

Body of Glass, Marge Piercy (London: Penguin, 1992) — also published in the USA as *He, She and It*.

Burning Chrome, William Gibson (London: Victor Gollancz, 1986).

Count Zero, William Gibson (New York: Ace Books, 1987).

CyberWay, Alan Dean Foster (London: Little and Brown, 1992).

Islands in the Net, Bruce Sterling (New York: Morrow, 1988).

Mirrorshades, Bruce Sterling (ed) (New York: Arbour House, 1986).

Mona Lisa Overdrive, William Gibson (London: Victor Gollancz, 1988).

Neuromancer, William Gibson (New York: Ace Books, 1984).

The City and the Stars, Arthur C. Clarke (London: Frederick Muller, 1956).

The Quicksilver Screen, Don H. DeBrandt (New York: Ballentine, 1992).

Virtual Girl, Amy Thompson (New York: Ace Books, 1993).

Virtual Light, William Gibson (London: Penguin, 1993).

MOVIES

Blade Runner (Director: Ridley Scott, Warner Bros, 1982; Director's cut, 1991).

Robocop (Director: Paul Verhoeven, Orion, 1987).

Terminator II: Judgement Day (Director: James Cameron, Carolco, 1992).

The Lawnmower Man (Director: Brett Leonard, First Independent, 1992).

The Terminator (Director: James Cameron, Carolco, 1984).

Total Recall (Director: Paul Verhoeven, Carolco, 1990).

Tron (Director: Steven Lisberger, Walt Disney, 1982).

References &
Notes to All Chapters

Chapter 1: Prelude

1. For a wide-ranging exploration of the advantages of distributing organizational processing across small computer systems, *see* Dan Trimmer *Downsizing: Strategies for Success in the Modern Computer World* (Reading, MA: Addison-Wesley, 1993).
2. Malcolm Wheatley 'The Flight from the Mainframe' *Management Today* (June 1993).
3. Thomas Stewart 'The Information Age in Charts' *Fortune International* (4th April 1994): 58.
4. *New York Times* (13th December 1991).
5. Andrew Kupfer 'Augmenting Your Desktop with Telecom: phones and PCs start to merge', *Fortune International* (11th July 1994): 58-61.
6. Daniel Burrus with Rodger Gittines *Technotrends: 24 Technologies that will Revolutionize Our Lives* (New York: Harper Collins, 1993): 64-65.
7. Monica Horten 'Big Potential for Smart Phone Systems' *Financial Times: Computers in Finance* (8th November 1993): 11-12.
8. For a general discussion of dynamically networked organizational forms, *see* Raymond Miles and Charles Snow 'Organizations: New Concepts for New Forms' *California Management Review* XXVIII(3) (1986): 62-73. For a brief illustration of networked organizational activities in the fashion industry, *see* Gareth Morgan *Creative Organization Theory* (Newbury Park, CA: Sage Publications, 1989): Chapter 27, and for an exploration of the concept across the television industry, *see* Christopher Barnatt and Ken Starkey 'The Emergence of Flexible Networks in the UK Television Industry' *British Journal of Management* 5(4) (1994): 251-260.
9. Gregory Stock *Metaman: Humans, Machines and the Birth of a Global Super-organism* (London: Bantam Press, 1993).
10. Richard Wheeler in *Brokers Monthly and Insurance Adviser* (November 1993), for example, notes how 24 insurers in the UK are now receiving live business electronically from brokers, and that, with the encouragement of large insurers, the adoption of such systems is set to rise.

11. Paul Taylor 'Valuable Boost for Efficiency: electronic data interchange and electronic mail', *The Financial Times: Technology in the Office* (Tuesday 26th October 1993): VI.

12. The United Kingdom video games market has been calculated at six times the total budget of the Department of Education. *AUI* (March-April 1994): 22.

13. Thomas Stewart; op. cit.: 55.

14. Michael Benedikt (ed) *Cyberspace: First Steps* (Cambridge, MA: MIT Press, 1993): 3.

15. William Gibson *Neuromancer* (New York: Ace Books, 1984).

16. William Gibson *Count Zero* (New York: Ace Books, 1987).

17. William Gibson *Mona Lisa Overdrive* (London: Victor Gollancz, 1988).

18. For example, eighteen leading writers in the field of computer technology and human computer interaction, from professors to software engineers, industrialists to artists, contribute to *Cyberspace: First Steps* edited by Michael Benedikt (Cambridge, MA: MIT Press, 1993), now in its fifth printing. Respected technology writer Howard Rheingold is also perfectly happy with the term, stating that cyberspace is a place: 'But what kind of place . . . is a big question' — *Virtual Reality* (London: Mandarin, 1993).

19. Barrie Sherman and Phil Judkins *Glimpses of Heaven, Visions of Hell: Virtual Reality and its Implications* (London: Hodder & Stoughton, 1992).

20. The research, started in the 1970s, in Rank Xerox's Palo Alto Research Centre, California, is famous in the field of human-computer interface design. In particular, the use of graphical representations to mediate the interaction of users with computers was central to their design philosophies, leading PARC researchers to create the first desktop WIMP (windows, icons, menus and pointers) environments.

21. Howard Rheingold, for example, in *Virtual Reality* (London: Mandarin, 1993) devotes a chapter to 'Teledildonics and Beyond'. Douglas Rushkoff, in *Cyberia: Life in the Trenches of Hyperspace* (London: Harper Collins, 1994): 62, also discusses some of the more outlandish possibilities of virtual sex, such as the potential ability for virtual lovers to program the feel of their bodies, perhaps to make themselves appear furry. Indeed, most books in the field of VR discuss the currently fictional topic of cybersex with a plethora of references. *See also*, for example, Barrie Sherman and Phil Judkins *Glimpses of Heaven, Visions of Hell: Virtual Reality and its Implications* (London: Hodder & Stoughton, 1993), and Francis Hamit *Virtual Reality and the Exploration of Cyberspace* (Carmel, IN: Sams Publishing, 1993).

22. Francis Hamit *Virtual Reality and the Exploration of Cyberspace* (Carmel, IN: Sams Publishing, 1993): 36.

23. Barrie Sherman and Phil Judkins; op. cit.: 276.

24. Philip Manchester 'Virtual Reality: Glimpse of Alternative Worlds' *Financial Times A-Z of Computing* (26th April 1994): 17, citing the forecasts of market researcher Frost & Sullivan.

25. Christopher Barnatt *The Computers in Business Blueprint* (Oxford: Blackwell Business, 1994): 165-166.

26. Gregory Stock; op. cit.: 136-140.

27. Herbert Girarde 'The Mega City Syndrome' *Clean Slate: The Magazine of Sustainable Technology*, Issue 9 (Winter 1992).

28. Cited from Sheila Hayman *The Electronic Frontier*, transcript of BBC TV *Horizon* documentary (London: BBC, Broadcasting Support Services, 1993): 14.

29. Steve Pruitt and Tom Barrett 'Corporate Virtual Workspace' in Michael Benedikt (ed) *Cyberspace: First Steps* (Cambridge, MA: MIT Press, 1993).

30. Francis Hamit; op. cit.: 33-35.

31. Led by British Telecom, and funded for three years by the SERC and the DTI CSCW programme (UK), Virtuosi involves the development of metaphors, models and distributed systems architectures for two major pilot systems: the 'Virtual Factory' and the 'Virtual Catwalk'. Aside from British Telecom, the partners include leading European VR systems supplier Division, GPT and the GEC-Marconi Research Centre, BICC Ltd, Nottinghamshire County Council, and researchers at the Universities of Nottingham, Lancaster and Manchester. The discussion of the projects in the text is based upon information supplied by Dr. Steve Benford, Department of Computer Science, University of Nottingham, UK. *See also* Benford, S., Bowers, J., Gray, S. Roden, T., Ryan, G. and Stanger, V. 'The Virtuosi Project' in *Proceedings of VR 94*, held in London as part of Virtual Reality Expo (February 1994).

32. As explained by Professor Bob Stone, Managing Director of ARRL, at the BIT'94 Virtual Reality and its Applications conference held at the University of Leeds, 24th March 1994.

33. British Gas, for example, now offers a service entitled 'Kitchen Reality' in some of its showrooms. Once measurements have been provided, customers are able to see a VR representation of exactly what their new kitchen will look like once it has been installed. Doors and drawers may even be opened, whilst lighting can be adjusted for day or night 'inspection'.

34. These latter three examples are just some of those listed by Dom Pancucci in 'The Real Thing' *Which Computer* (August 1993): 38-43.

35. E. Brodie 'Virtual Reality Takes Fund Managers into Cyberspace' *The Independent on Sunday* (1st August 1993).

36. As reported by John Browning and Phil Barrett 'Hype or Reality?' *Focus* (December 1993): 27.

37. Management Science America Ltd 'Excellence and the IT factor: information technology inside excellent companies in Britain' *Journal of Information Technology* (March 1990): 41-48.

38. Stephen H. Haeckel and Richard L. Nolan 'Managing by Wire' *Harvard Business Review* (September-October 1993): 125.

Chapter 2: Embracing the Technology

39. Jon and Jack B. Rochester *Computers for People: Concepts and Applications* (Homewood, IL: Irwin, 1991): 247.

40. Peter J. Bird *LEO: The First Business Computer* (Wokingham: Hasler Publishing, 1994): 12.

41. Dirk Hanson *The New Alchemists* (Boston: Little Brown & Co., 1982): 59-60.

42. Jon and Jack B. Rochester; op. cit.: 462.

43. H. L. Capron and John D. Perron *Computers and Information Systems: Tools for an Information Age* 3rd end (Redwood City, CA: Benjamin/Cummings, 1993): 547-548.

44. *Financial Times: Companies and Markets* (14th March 1994): 17.

45. William Davidow and Michael Malone present this intriguing analogy in *The Virtual Corporation: Structuring and Revitalizing the Corporation for the 21st Century* (New York: Harper Collins, 1992): 76.

46. Several analysts have written about organizations more keen to outsource their IT functions than to invest in internal facilities. *See*, for example, Mary Lacity and Rudy Hirschheim 'The Information Systems Outsourcing Bandwagon' *Sloan Management Review* (Fall 1993); Mel Mandell 'Corporate Computers: How Necessary?' *Across the Board* (March 1991); and Maris Martinsons 'Outsourcing Information Systems: A Strategic Partnership with Risks' *Long Range Planning* 26(3) (1993).

47. From the final chapter of Brenda Laurel's *Computers as Theatre* (Reading, MA: Addison-Wesley: 1993): 200, in which the anatomy of the VR fad is discussed in the aftermath of the hype of the early 1990s.

48. At the British Information Technology BIT'94 conference: *Virtual Reality: Applications and Implications* (24th March 1994, University of Leeds), several speakers, including Charles Grimsdale, Managing Director of leading VR system supplier Division, were at pains to point out that 'VR is not hype'. Instead, VR is simply in an early, but stable, stage of its development.

49. For a review of the Malatron keyboard, 'an effective deterrent to the dreaded RSI' (repetitive strain injury), *see* Catherine Eade 'PCD Malatron Keyboard' *Personal Computer World* (December 1992): 183.

50. In *Caligari24*, for example (Octree Software Inc., Mountain View, CA: 1993), a VR rendering and animation system for the Amiga range of PCs, the user can move objects around in 3-D via mouse movement. Holding down one mouse button tracks their motion in the X and Y planes, whilst holding down the other allows movement up and down a further Z axis. Control of motion in 3-D space is thereby easily achieved with only a 2-D motion-tracking peripheral.

51. For an illustration of the footmouse (and other peripherals), *see* Jenny Preece *A Guide to Usability: Human Factors in Computing* (Wokingham: Addison-Wesley, 1993): 62-64.

52. The SpaceBall™ is produced by Spatial Systems, Inc.

53. Created by Thomas Zimmerman and marketed by VPL Research, the original DataGlove™ is considered by many to have triggered the 'explosion' of research into virtual reality.

54. Surprisingly, this voice-recognition system works with a tiny telephone-speaker-and-microphone combination, called an EarPhone, which is worn in the ear, and which picks up the operator's voice from the vibration of the bones in their head as they speak. The EarPhone and voice-recognition dialling software sell for just $169. *See* Andrew Kupfer 'Augmenting Your Desktop with Telecom' *Fortune International* (11th July 1994): 60.

55. For a more comprehensive discussion of voice-recognition systems, *see* H. L. Capron and John D. Perron *Computers and Information Systems: Tools for an Information Age* 3rd edn (Redwood City, CA: Benjamin/Cummings, 1993): 87-89.

56. For a comprehensive review of current telepresence displays and other VR peripherals, see 'Appendix A: Virtual Reality Toolkit' in Francis Hamit's *Virtual Reality and the Exploration of Cyberspace* (Carmel, IN: Sams Publishing, 1993): 345-364.

57. For a brief description of Dr Tom Furness' work in this area, *see* Barrie Sherman and Phil Judkins *Glimpses of Heaven, Visions of Hell: Virtual Reality and its Implications* (London: Hodder & Stoughton, 1993): 63.

58. It is interesting to note that many of the Amiga range of PCs from Commodore Business Machines have been equipped with hardware-based text-to-voice synthesis since the early 1980s. However, the feature has been so sadly neglected by software developers that it has been dropped from some of the latest models.

59. This view was expressed by Professor Bob Stone, Technical Director of the Advanced Robotics Research Centre (ARRC), at the BIT'94 *Virtual Reality:*

Applications and Implications conference held in March 1994 at the University of Leeds.

60. 'Power PC/Pentium: Giants line up for a battle royal' *Financial Times A-Z of Computing* (26th April 1994): 13.

61. Louise Kehoe 'Apple Launches Assault on Intel' *The Financial Times: Companies & Markets* (14th March 1994).

62. As reported by Dom Pancucci in 'The Real Thing' *Which Computer?* (August 1993), a complete high-end VR system, based upon a Silicon Graphics workstation, cost in the region of £250,000.

63. The actual theoretical capacity of a 3.5″ high-density floppy disk is 2.0 Mb (with 1 megabyte equal to 2^{20} bytes of information, or 1,048,576 characters of storage). Once formatted to hold data, however, IBM PC and compatible DOS systems only allow 1.44 Mb of data to be contained on a single HD 3.5″ disk.

64. Typically CD-ROM drives can only load around 0.3 Mb of data per second into a computer, compared to the several megabytes per second data transfer rate attainable from modern hard disk drives and some other forms of optical media.

65. Using complex algorithms for data compression, the MPEG-1 standard can store around 70 minutes of full-motion video, together with a hi-fi stereo soundtrack, on a single 5″ compact disk. The quality of the images attained is similar or superior to that achieved from conventional VHS video tapes. An MPEG-2 standard for data compression to professional broadcast quality requirements has also been established.

66. A company called Westpoint now sell a 100 CD 'jukebox' (providing 60 gigabytes of storage), 28 of which can be linked together to give 5-second access to almost two terabytes of data. *See* '10 Year Old Baby' *AUI* (February 1994): 29.

67. The Mondex smart card will be 'loaded' with money from either a dispenser in the side of the bank, or from one of the smartphones being developed by British Telecommunications. Money held upon the card will be able to be 'locked' by slipping the Mondex into a special wallet and entering a PIN (personal identification number). If the card is stolen it will subsequently prove worthless.

68. In 'Along the Right Lines' *Personal Computer World* (August 1992): 286-292, Eric Doyle notes how computer technicians have turned computer networking into a 'Black Art' masked in jargon and protected within the 'inner sanctum' of the centralized mainframe or minicomputer department.

69. As reported in *The Financial Times* (22nd March 1994): 1.

70. H. L. Capron and John D. Perron; op. cit.: 168.

Chapter 3: From Hierarchy to Virtual Organization

71. *For example, see* Andrew Baxter 'Virtual Factory Takes Shape' *The Financial Times* (London: 8th February 1993).

72. *For example, see* Alan L. Porter 'Virtual Companies Reconsidered' *Technology Analysis & Strategic Management* 5(4) (1993): 413-419.

73. *For example, see* Alison Sprout 'Moving into the Virtual Office' *Fortune International* (2nd May 1994): 67.

74. *For example, see* William H. Davidow and Michael S. Malone *The Virtual Corporation: Structuring and Revitalising the Corporation for the 21st Century* (New York: Harper Collins, 1992).

75. Alfred Chandler's classic study charting the rise of large-scale, multidivisional organizational structures post the 1930s depression is contained within *Strategy and Structure* (Cambridge, MA: MIT Press, 1962).

76. Colin Hastings *The New Organization: Growing the Culture of Organizational Networking* (Berkshire: McGraw-Hill, 1993).

77. Henri Fayol and Frederick Winslow Taylor, both proponents of the 'task school' of management, saw rigidly defined patterns of authority and specialization as central to successful employee coordination. In particular, Taylor was keen to divorce muscle power (labour) from brain power (management), whilst Fayol listed unity of command (each worker having only one boss with no other lines of command) and unity of direction (people engaged in the same kind of activities having a single goal) as key management principles to be achieved via an implementation of a clear scalar chain of command. *See* Frederick Winslow Taylor *Scientific Management* (New York: Harper & Row, 1947) and Henri Fayol *General and Industrial Management* (London, Pitman: 1949); translation by Constance Storrs from the original *Administration et Générale* (1916).

78. In their seminal *The Second Industrial Divide* (New York: Basic Books, 1984) Michael Piore and Charles Sabel suggest that we are now in a transition between organizational structures based upon vertical integration and inflexible technologies, and those employing disaggregated modes of production utilizing flexible technologies and working practices reliant upon economies of scope rather than of scale.

79. Tom Burns and G. M. Stalker *The Management of Innovation* (London: Tavistock, 1961).

80. Most notably Joan Woodward lead a team in south-east Essex in the UK in an investigation of 100 manufacturers spanning a range of industries, technologies and workforce sizes, whilst Paul Lawrence and Jay Lorsh studied firms in the plastics, wood and container industries in the USA in an investigation of the way that organizations develop separate departments, divisions or functions

to solve environmental problems. *See* Joan Woodward *Industrial Organization: Theory and Practice* (Oxford: Oxford University Press, 1965) and Paul Lawrence and Jay Lorsh *Organization and Environment* (Harvard University Press, 1967).

81. Raymond E. Miles and Charles C. Snow 'Organizations: New Concepts for New Forms' *California Management Review* XXVIII(3) (Spring 1986): 62-73.

82. Gareth *Morgan Images of Organization* (Newbury Park: Sage, 1986): 51.

83. S. A. Bergen *R&D Management: managing projects and new products* (Oxford: Basil Blackwell, 1990): 145.

84. Gareth Morgan *Creative Organization Theory: A Resourcebook* (Newbury Park: Sage, 1989): 67.

85. Christopher Barnatt and Ken Starkey 'The Emergence of Flexible Networks in the UK Television Industry' *British Journal of Management* 5(4) (1994): 251-260.

86. Gareth Morgan *Creative Organization Theory: A Resourcebook*; op. cit.

87. David Gelernter *Mirror Worlds: The Day Software puts the Universe in a Shoebox . . . How it will happen and what it will mean* (New York: Oxford University Press, 1992): 185.

88. James E. White, Director of Apple Computer spin-off, General Magic, describing the concept of the 'agent' as conceived in the telescript project. Cited from the transcript of the documentary *Horizon: The Electronic Frontier*, produced by Sheila Hayman (London: BBC TV Broadcasting Support Services, June 1993): 14.

89. Philip Judkins, David West and John Drew *Networking in Organizations: The Rank Xerox Experiment* (Aldershot: Gower, 1985).

90. Thomas A. Stewart 'The Information Age in Charts' *Fortune International* (4th April 1994): 56.

91. Andrew Emmerson 'The Virtual Office' *FT Survey: Telecommunications in Business* (15th June 1994).

92. Claire Gooding 'Homeworking: Benefits outweigh problems' *Financial Times A-Z of Computing* (26th April 1994): 8.

93. Louise Kehoe 'Computers Come Face to Face' *The Financial Times* (28th January 1994).

94. Sheila Hayman *The Electronic Frontier*, transcript of BBC TV Horizon documentary (London: BBC TV Broadcasting Support Services, 1993): 6-7.

95. *Business Update* Issue 7 (Digital Equipment Corporation, 1993).

96. Christopher Barnatt *A Prelude to the Cyber Business* (Working Paper, School of Management & Finance, University of Nottingham, UK: 1993.XIII): 14.

97. Santa Raymond and Roger Cunliffe 'At home in the office' *The Financial Times* (9th March 1994).

98. Alison Sprout 'Moving into the Virtual Office' *Fortune International* (2nd May 1994): 67.

99. Ibid.

100.John Kavanagh 'The Groupware Revolution' *Financial Times Review: Software at Work* (Spring 1994).

101.Ibid.

102.David Kirkpatrick 'Groupware Goes Boom' *Fortune International* (27th December 1993): 63.

103.Ibid.

104.Malcolm Brown 'BT on the Beam' *Management Today* (January 1994): 73.

105.Steve Pruitt and Tom Barrett 'Corporate Virtual Workspace' in Michael Benedikt (ed) *Cyberspace: First Steps* (Cambridge, MA: MIT Press, 1993): 409.

106.Ashley Cotter-Cairns, 'A Real Fantasy?' *AUI* 8(2) (February 1994).

107.Bruce Lloyd, 'Office Productivity - Time for a Revolution?' *Long Range Planning* 23(1) (1990): 66-79.

108.Andrew C. Boynton 'Achieving Dynamic Stability through Information Technology' *California Management Review* (Winter 1993): 71.

Chapter 4: Agents, Ghosts & Other Virtual Monsters

109.Created in 1945 to calculate mathematical tables, the electronic numerical integrator and computer (ENIAC) was the world's first electronic computer.

110.UK market researchers expect the $37m market for agent software to expand to be worth $2.6bn by the year 2000. *Source:* Philip Manchester 'Agent Software' *Financial Times A-Z of Computing* (26th April 1994): 3.

111.Whereas conventional computer processing techniques rely upon the manipulation of a single stream of symbolic data, neural networks use a processing paradigm known as *connectionism*. In effect, they attempt to model the processes of the human brain, being composed of many independent cells (or neurons) which connect in patterns in response to input stimuli. No symbols are therefore stored within the network, with interpretations instead being assigned to each input stimulus in order to make sense of the resulting connectivity pattern. Neural network computer systems therefore don't store digital information in conventional 'memory', but instead hold patterns of weights of interconnection throughout the total neural web. Nor does programming in the traditional sense take place, with the systems instead being 'trained' to recognize and respond to certain data patterns. For example, a neural network used in geological analysis may be fed data upon sites where oil has been found in the past, and from this data will establish a connectivity pattern enabling sites with similar characteristics to be recognized in the future.

112. Barrie Sherman and Phil Judkins *Glimpses of Heaven, Visions of Hell: Virtual Reality and its Implications* (London: Hodder & Stoughton, 1993): 29.

113. One problem in defining the attainment of true 'artificial intelligence' is in deciding upon the involved yardstick. The famous Turing test for machine intelligence, for example, requires a remote computer communicating with a person via a screen and keyboard to be able to fool the person into believing that the computer is actually a remote human being. Whilst at first this may sound a reasonable acid test, why should we assume that intelligent computers will be indistinguishable from human beings? More likely, artificial computer minds will constitute a different race entirely. We may therefore question whether an 'intelligent' entity has to behave and think like a man in order to be classed as intelligent. Almost certainly the answer is that it does not. As Professor Donald Michie of the Turing Institute notes: 'If a machine becomes very complicated then it becomes pointless to argue whether it has a mind of its own. It so obviously does that you had better get on good terms with it and shut up about the metaphysics' (cited in Barrie Sherman and Phil Judkins, op. cit.)

114. *The SUREFAX PLUS User Guide: What's that little blue and white box?* (Mercury Communications, London).

115. David Gelernter *Mirror Worlds: The Day Software Puts the Universe in a Shoebox . . . How it will happen and what it will mean* (New York: Oxford University Press, 1992).

116. Ibid.: 39.

117. As reported by Andrew Kupfer 'Software Agents will Make Like Easy' *Fortune International* (24th January 1994): 54.

118. Philip Manchester 'Agent Software' *Financial Times A-Z of Computing* (26th April 1994): 3.

119. For an illustration of Eager agent operations *see* Brenda Laurel *Computers as Theatre* (Reading, MA: Addison-Wesley, 1993): 110-111.

120. Cited in *The Electronic Frontier*, text adapted from the BBC TV *Horizon* programme transmitted 7th June 1993 (London: BBC TV Broadcasting Support Services, 1993).

121. *See* Barrie Sherman and Phil Judkins; op. cit.. Howard Rheingold in *The Virtual Community* (London: Secker & Warburg, 1994): 106, also explains the potential use of specialist knowbot 'agents' which will use the tools of the Internet in research tasks such as searching for data within the US National Library of Medicine.

122. *See* 'Artificial Life' in Rudy Rucker, R. U. Sirus and Queen Mu (eds) *Mondo 2000: A User's Guide to the New Edge* (London: Thames & Hudson, 1993): 30-35.

123. Bryan Clough and Paul Mungo *Approaching Zero: Data Crime and the Computer Underground* (London: Faber & Faber, 1992): 85.

124. Christine McGourty 'Highway to the Global Netropolis' *The Daily Telegraph* (4th May 1994): 20.

125. Katie Hafner and John Markoff *Cyberpunk: Outlaws and Hackers on the Computer Frontier* (London: Corgi, 1993).

126. Quoted from Rudy Rucker, R. U. Sirius and Queen Mu (eds) *Mondo 2000: A User's Guide to the New Edge* (London, Thames & Hudson, 1993): 55.

127. Ibid.

Chapter 5: The Marriage of Man & Machine

128. Daniel Burrus with Roger Gittines *Technotrends: 24 Technologies that will Revolutionize Our Lives* (New York: Harper Collins, 1993): 279.

129. David Gelernter *Mirror Worlds: The Day Software Puts the Universe in a Shoebox . . . How it will happen and what it will mean* (New York: Oxford University Press, 1992): 1-2.

130. Sheila Hayman *The Electronic Frontier*, transcript of BBC TV Horizon Documentary (London: BBC TV Broadcasting Support Services, 1993): 7.

131. Example from Christopher Barnatt *The Computers in Business Blueprint* (Oxford: Blackwell Business, 1994): 97.

132. For a more thorough review of the respective automation and augmentation of routine and creative work processes, *see* Richard W. Larson and David J. Zimney *The White Collar Shuffle: Who Does What in Today's Computerized Workplace* (New York: AMACOM, 1990): 3-65.

133. Brenda Laurel in *Computers as Theatre* (Reading, MA: Addison-Wesley, 1992) provides a fascinating, in-depth study of engagement, flow and dramatic interaction on the man-machine interface.

134. In *The Virtual Community* (London: Secker & Warburg, 1994): 33, Howard Rheingold reports how addict Blair Newman couldn't tear his hands from the keyboard and his eyes from the screen long enough for him to ingest the cocaine crystals left beside his computer.

135. The Musical Instrument Digital Interface (MIDI) standard is now universal for the computer control and interlinkage of electronic instruments. Using a suitable software package, a user can have as many attempts as they like to play each section of a tune correctly, with the computer helping out by correcting minor timing errors in a processes called quantanization. It is also possible for musicians to record difficult sections slowly and then to have the computer play them back at full speed. The computer may even be made to play instruments

directly by entering musical notation or programming commands into appropriate MIDI sequencing software.

136. Abraham H. Maslow 'A Theory of Human Motivation' *Psychological Review* 50 (July 1943): 370-396.

137. Howard Rheingold *The Virtual Community* (London: Secker & Warburg, 1994): 4.

138. Dan Trimmer *Downsizing: Strategies for Success in the Modern Computer World* (Reading, MA: Addison-Wesley, 1993): 53.

139. Expert systems use a knowledge base and a set of predetermined rules (or *heuristics*) to help solve problems in narrow, predefined areas such as medical diagnosis or geological forecasting. Most systems ask the user questions, for example regarding what symptoms are being suffered by a patient, which are then compared with previous cases from the knowledge base in order to come up with a 'diagnosis'. Across business, expert systems are starting to be employed in areas such as risk analysis. A client seeking insurance, for example, will provide answers to the questions posed by an expert system (concerning age, weight, eating, smoking and drinking habits, occupation and so forth), allowing for the best insurance policy to be ascertained and tailored for each individual's requirements and factors of risk. Expert systems are also starting to be employed in areas such as vision recognition, in order that security systems may identify authorized users.

140. Paul R. Tim, Brent D. Peterson and Jackson C. Stevens *People at Work: Human Relations in Organizations* 3rd edn (St. Paul, MN: West Publishing, 1990): 393.

141. H. L. Capron and John D. Perron *Computers and Information Systems: Tools for an Information Age* 3rd edn (Redwood City, CA: Benjamin/Cummings, 1993): 5.

142. From Robert E. Callahan and Patrick C. Fleenor 'There Are Ways to Overcome Resistance to Computers' *Office* 106 (October 1978): 80.

143. Jacqueline Senker and Peter Senker 'Gaining Competitive Advantage from Information Technology' *Journal of General Management* (Spring 1992): 38.

144. A survey by consultants Management Science America, as reported in the *Journal of Information Technology* (March 1990): 41-48, noted that in 'excellent' organizations in the UK, PCs could be found upon the majority of manager's desks.

145. Jacqueline and Peter Senker; op. cit.

146. As reported by Steven Alter in *Decision Support Systems* (Reading, MA: Addison-Wesley, 1980).

147. As reported in Paul W. Ross, H. Paul Haidek, H. Willis Means and Robert R. Sloger *Understanding Computer Information Systems* (St. Paul, MN: West Publishing; 1992): 164.

148. Christopher Barnatt *The Computers in Business Blueprint* (Oxford: Blackwell Business, 1994): 132-134.

149. It is now debated as to whether giving many technological devices the power of speech is such a good idea. For example, cars with 'talking dashboards' became available in the late 1980s, although most purchasers quickly dismissed the voice-synthesis as a gimmick and turned it off. Whilst driving at least, people preferred traditional instrumentation rather than being 'talked at' by a computer.

150. Daniel Burrus with Roger Gittines; op. cit.: xvi.

151. Ivan Sutherland conceived the first head-mounted, stereoscopic display system whilst teaching at Harvard. He subsequently became Director of the Information Processing Techniques office at the US Government's Defense Advanced Research Projects Agency, before co-founding his own VR company in 1968. *Source*: Francis Hamit *Virtual Reality and the Exploration of Cyberspace* (Carmel, IN: Sams Publishing, 1993): 57-59.

152. This prediction is made by Benjamin Woolley in *Virtual Worlds* (London: Penguin, 1992): 238.

153. John Bennett 'Virtual Reality Part II' (Update on the VFX1) *PC Review* (June 1994): 40-41.

154. A spreadsheet is the computer software equivalent of a balance sheet. Numbers, text entries and formulas are entered into cells in a grid of lettered columns and numbered rows, and are frequently linked so that a value in one cell (such as a price or interest rate) will influence the values in other cells. Many spreadsheets now also offer a 3-D facility, with cells arranged in a cube matrix.

155. As more and more corporate interest in immersive VR emerges, a great deal of research is being directed into the effects of head-mounted displays (HMDs) on their users. Some of the first doubts as to the suitability of HMDs were raised by researchers in Edinburgh University, who demonstrated user eyestrain lasting for some time after leaving virtual reality. Similar results have been obtained by SRI International in the USA, and the UK Health and Safety Executive has now launched an investigation into the impact of VR on physical and psychological health.

156. Thomas A. Furness III quoted from Howard Rheingold's *Virtual Reality* (London: Mandarin, 1991): 194. Note that conventional computer display screens typically boast a maximum image resolution of 800×600 picture elements or 'pixels'. Furness is therefore confidently predicting future stereoscopic laser microscanners capable of presenting us with images ten times clearer than we are used to seeing on computers today.

157. *See* 'The Phosphotron' in Rudy Rucker, R. U. Sirus and Queen Mu (eds) *Mondo 2000: A User's Guide to the New Edge* (London: Thames & Hudson, 1992): 266-267.

158. M. Bak et al. 'Visual Sensations Produced by Intracortical Microstimulation of the Human Occipital Cortex' *Medical and Biological Engineering and Computing*, No. 28, (1990): 257-259.

159. As reported in Rudy Rucker, R. U. Sirus and Queen Mu (eds) *Mondo 2000: A User's Guide to the New Edge* (London: Thames & Hudson, 1993): 38, a recent computer implant by Dr. Dabelle of the University of Utah featured 64 electrodes with a connecting plug inserted just above the right ear. The subject — a blind man — therefore simply lifted up his hair in order to attach a computer connection lead. In one experiment, the computer was programmed to feed him images of braille letters via the matrix of implants. He got so good that he could read braille eight-times faster than with his fingertips. In a subsequent experiment, a camera was directly linked in and the blind man could make out the difference between horizontal and vertical lines.

160. Gregory Stock *Metaman: Humans, Machines and the Birth of a Global Super-organism* (London: Bantam, 1993): 140.

161. Colin Humphreys, Professor of Material Science, Cambridge University, UK, interviewed in *The Net, Programme 8*, produced by Illuminations Television for the British Broadcasting Corporation (Spring 1994).

162. Professor Marvin Minsky, interviewed for *The Net, Programme 8*, ibid.

163. Gregory Stock, op. cit.: 140.

Chapter 6: Communities, Corporate Cultures & Communications

164. Susan Estrada *Connecting to the Internet* (Sebastopol, CA: O'Reilly and Associates, 1993): xiii.

165. Figures cited from Louise Kehoe 'Doing Cyber Business' *The Financial Times: Media Futures* (6th June 1994): 16.

166. Ibid.

167. In 1993 *Broadwatch* magazine estimated that there were around sixty thousand BBSs in the United States alone, and that every fifty thousand BBSs probably represented around half a million people. *Source*: Howard Rheingold *The Virtual Community* (London: Secker & Warburg, 1994): 132.

168. Unix is a multi-user operating system ('control program'), and was developed as a research tool in AT&T's Bell Laboratories in 1969. In 1983 Unix was commercially released, and remains one of the most sophisticated operating systems available to this day, with versions to run on PCs to Cray supercomputers. *See* H. L. Capron and John D. Perron *Computers and*

Information Systems: tools for an information age, 3rd edn (Redwood City, CA: Benjamin/Cummings, 1993): 237-239.

169. Howard Rheingold *The Virtual Community* (London: Secker & Warburg, 1994): 120; 131.

170. Hypertext, a form of 'nonsequential writing', was developed by Ted Nelson in the mid 1960s. Hypertext documents provide multiple links or 'branches' between their elements. Click upon a keyword, for example, and you will be transported to another part of the document containing more detailed information upon the term. Highly intuitive and extremely popular in educational application, hypertext media free the user from the constraints that limit information presentation upon the printed page.

171. Multimedia simply refers to any system capable of manipulating digital information in many formats. Multimedia documents and presentations can therefore contain not only text and still graphics images, but also sounds and moving video.

172. Howard Rheingold; op. cit.

173. Ibid.: 56.

174. Marshall McLuhan *Understanding Media: The Extension of Man* (New York: McGraw-Hill, 1964).

175. Multi-user dungeons are fantasy worlds crafted within computer databases and accessed by participants over a network. Within a MUD each participant assumes a character — that of a wizard or starship captain, for example — in the guise of which they play out the scenarios before them. MUDs first started in the UK in 1980, and soon attracted many addicts. As MUDders require intense network access and communication, however, they have in many instances been viewed as a nuisance. Indeed in Australia MUDs have been banned in order to curtail excessive Internet satellite connection charges.

176. Howard Rheingold; op. cit.: 6; 26.

177. Minitel terminals, which plug directly into a telephone socket without the need for a PC or modem, were distributed free in France to six million users in the 1980s. The original idea behind Minitel was to replace the French telephone directory with an on-line video text service, but users soon discovered that they could use the terminals for computer-mediated communication as well as for data access. The *messagerie* chat services subsequently became extremely popular, and for some even addictive.

178. John Quarterman 'How Big is the Matrix?' *Matrix News* 2, No. 2 (Austin, TX: Matrix Information and Directory Services, 1992).

179. It should be noted that home banking services utilizing PC computer-modem links have been available for some time. They have mainly been run mainly as experiments, however, and have not been widely advertised. In the UK, the Royal Bank of Scotland claims to have 10,000 home banking

customers for a trial service operating in Brighton, Preston and Dundee, whilst NatWest's Action Line service caters for 935,000 customers. *Source*: Monica Horten 'New Dial-in Services' *The Financial Times* (8th November 1993): 11-12.
180. Thomas J. Peters and Robert H. Waterman *In Search of Excellence: Lessons from America's Best Run Companies* (New York: Harper & Row, 1982).
181. Gerald Egan 'Cultivate Your Culture' *Management Today* (April 1994).
182. Andrew D. Brown *Organizational Culture* (London: Pitman, 1995): 3.
183. Gareth Morgan *Creative Organization Theory: A Resourcebook* (Newbury Park, CA: Sage Publications, 1989): 157.
184. G. Hofstede, B. Neuijen, D. Ohayv and G. Sanders 'Measuring Organizational Cultures: a qualitative study across twenty cases' *Administrative Science Quarterly* 35 (1986): 286-316.
185. Andrew D. Brown; op. cit.: 8.
186. Sara Kiesler 'Thinking Ahead: The Hidden Messages in Computer Networks' *Harvard Business Review* (January-February 1986): 47.
187. Ibid.
188. British Telecom, for example, now has a 3-D 'hierarchic visualization' of its network through which users can move in real time. *See* (eg) *Focus* (December 1993): 27.
189. O. Berg and K. Kreiner 'Corporate Architecture: Turning physical setting into symbolic resources' in P. Gagliardi (ed) *Symbols and Artifacts, Views of the Corporate Landscape* (New York: Aldine de Gruyter): 41-67.
190. Gareth Morgan *Images of Organization* (Newbury Park, CA: Sage Publications, 1986): 135.
191. *See* note 31.
192. Robert Heller *Culture Shock: The Office Revolution* (London: Hodder & Stoughton, 1990).
193. As reported in Barrie Sherman and Phil Judkins *Glimpses of Heaven, Visions of Hell: Virtual Reality and its Implications* (London: Hodder & Stoughton, 1993): 171.

Chapter 7: The Fact & the Fantasy

194. William Gibson *Neuromancer* (New York, Ace Books, 1984).
195. David Tomas 'Old Rituals for New Space: Rites de Passage and William Gibson's Cultural Model of Cyberspace' in Michael Benedikt (ed) *Cyberspace: First Steps* (Cambridge, MA: MIT Press, 1993): 31-47.
196. Francis Hamit *Virtual Reality and the Exploration of Cyberspace* (Carmel, IN: Sams Publishing, 1993): 20.

197. Joan Gordon 'Yin and Yang Duke it Out' in Larry McCafferly (ed) *Storming the Reality Studio: A Casebook of Cyberpunk and Postmodern Fiction* (Durham, NC: Duke University Press, 1991): 199.

198. Darko Suvin 'On Gibson and Cyberpunk SF' in Larry McCaffery (ed) *Storming the Reality Studio: A Casebook of Cyberpunk and Postmodern Fiction* (Durham, NC: Duke University Press, 1991): 351.

199. Rudy Rucker *Software* (New York: Ace, 1982).

200. Rudy Rucker *Wetware* (New York: Avon, 1988).

201. Rudy Rucker 'On the Edge of the Pacific' in Rudy Rucker, R. U. Sirus and Queen Mu (eds) *Mondo 2000: A User's Guide to the New Edge* (London: Thames and Hudson, 1993): 9.

202. Larry McCaffery *Storming the Reality Studio: A Casebook of Cyberpunk and Postmodern Fiction* (Durham, NC: Duke University Press, 1991): 12.

203. Bruce Sterling *Mirrorshades: The Cyberpunk Anthology* (New York: Arbour House, 1986).

204. William S. Burroughs *The Naked Lunch* (New York: Grove, 1962). Alternatively seek out the movie *Naked Lunch* (David Chronenberg, 1991).

205. *Videodrome* (David Chronenberg, 1983).

206. Darko Suvin; op. cit.: 365.

207. Larry McCaffery; op. cit.: 263.

208. William Gibson *Neuromancer* (New York: Ace, 1984): 67.

209. Larry McCaffery; op. cit.: 15.

210. As noted when interviewed by Larry McCaffery; op. cit.: 280.

211. William Gibson *Count Zero* (New York: Ace Books, 1987).

212. William Gibson; ibid.: 170.

213. William Gibson *Mona Lisa Overdrive* (London, Victor Gollancz, 1988).

214. William Gibson *Burning Chrome* (London: Victor Gollancz, 1986).

215. William Gibson 'Johnny Mnemonic' in *Burning Chrome* (London: Victor Gollancz, 1986): 30.

216. William Gibson *Burning Chrome*; op. cit.: 197.

217. William Gibson *Virtual Light* (London: Penguin, 1993).

218. William Gibson; ibid.: 204.

219. Cyborg is short for 'cybernetic organism', a creature part biological and part mechanical. Cyborgs may therefore arrive in the guise of technologically augmented human beings, or in the form of totally synthetic lifeforms utilizing both mechanical and biochemical components.

220. Marge Piercy *Body of Glass* (London: Penguin, 1992).

221. Ibid.: 525.

222. Amy Thompson *Virtual Girl* (New York: Ace Books, 1993).

223. Gregory Stock *Metaman: Humans, Machines and the Birth of a Global Super-organism* (New York: Bantam Press, 1993): 44.

224. Bruce Sterling *Islands in the Net* (New York: Morrow, 1988).

225. Alan Dean Foster *Cyberway* (London: Little & Brown, 1992).

226. Don H. DeBrandt *The Quicksilver Screen* (New York: Ballantine, 1992).

227. Arthur C. Clark *The City and the Stars* (London: Frederick Muller, 1956)

228. *The Lawnmower Man* (Brett Leonard, First Independent, 1992).

229. *Tron* (Steven Lisberger, Walt Disney, 1982).

230. *Robocop* (Paul Verhoeven, Orion, 1987).

231. *The Terminator* (James Cameron, EMI, 1984).

232. *Terminator II: Judgement Day* (James Cameron, 1992, Carolco).

233. *Blade Runner* (Ridley Scott, Warner Bros, 1982). Note that a director's cut was also issued in 1991.

234. Philip K. Dick *Do Androids Dream of Electric Sheep?* (New York: Ballantine, 1968).

235. *Total Recall* (Paul Verhoeven, Carolco, 1990).

Chapter 8: Evolution, Transition & the Dawn of a New Age

236. Rudy Rucker, R. U. Sirus and Queen Mu *Mondo 2000: A User's Guide to the New Edge* (London: Thames & Hudson, 1993): 13.

237. R. A. Buchanan *The Power of the Machine* (London: Penguin, 1994): 255.

238. Stephan H. Haeckel and Richard L. Nolan 'Managing by Wire' *Harvard Business Review* (September-October 1993).

239. One of the most successful computer games across all PC platforms, *Sim City* places a computer user in charge of their own city, giving them the opportunity to experiment with its ecology, politics and resource allocations. As decisions are made, the user watches their city grow or decline in an addictive and never-ending game.

240. Stephan H. Haeckel and Richard L. Nolan; op. cit.

241. Thomas A. Stewart 'Managing in a Wired Company' *Fortune International* (11th July 1994): 20-28.

242. Ibid.: 23.

243. R. Brent Gallupe and William H. Cooper 'Brainstorming Electronically' *Sloan Management Review* (Fall 1993): 27-36.

244. *See* note 46.

245. Louis S. Richman 'The New Worker Elite' *Fortune International* (22nd August 1994): 44.

246. Ibid.: 47.

247. Michael J. Piore and Charles F. Sabel *The Second Industrial Divide: Possibilities for Prosperity* (New York: Basic Books, 1984): 5.

248. Alvin Toffler *Future Shock* (London: The Bodley Head, 1970): 430.

249. For a summary of Kumon's theory, *see* Howard Rheingold *The Virtual Community* (London: Secker & Warburg, 1994): 209-210.

250. Alvin Toffler; op. cit.: 4.

251. Alvin Toffler *The Third Wave* (London: Collins, 1980).

252. Ibid.: 18-19.

253. Ibid.: 26.

254. David Tomas 'Old Rituals for New Space: Rites de passage and William Gibson's Cultural Model of Cyberspace' in Michael Benedikt (ed) *Cyberspace: First Steps* (Cambridge, MA: MIT Press, 1993): 33.

255. Gregory Stock *Metaman: Humans, Machines and the Birth of a Global Super-organism* (London: Bantam Press, 1993).

256. 'Alvin Toffler: Still Shocking after all these Years' *New Scientist* (19th March 1994): 22.

257. Michel Foucault *Discipline and Punishment: The Birth of a Prison* (New York: Vintage Books, 1979): 201-202.

258. Shoshana Zuboff *In the Age of the Smart Machine* (Oxford: Heinemann Professional, 1988): 322.

259. Howard Rheingold *The Virtual Community* (London: Secker & Warburg, 1994): 15.

260. Ibid.: 291.

261. Rudy Rucker; op. cit.: 144.

262. R. A. Buchanan *The Power of the Machine* (London: Penguin, 1992): 236-237.

263. Theodore Roszak *The Cult of Information: A neo-Luddite Treatise on the High-Tech, Artificial Intelligence and the True Art of Thinking* 2nd edn (Berkeley, CA: University of California Press, 1994): xiii.

264. In 1994 a Gallup pole commissioned by IBM found that 31% of UK households owned a personal computer, with 42% of respondents stating that they used a PC either at home or at work. Results as reported in 'Newsfile' *AUI* (March/April 1994): 16.

265. Daniel Burrus *Technotrends: How to Use Technology to Go Beyond Your Competition* (New York: Harper Collins, 1993): 205.

266. Larry McCaffery *Storming the Reality Studio: A Casebook of Cyberpunk and Postmodern Fiction* (Durham, NC: Duke University Press, 1993): 4.

267. Alvin Toffler *Future Shock*; op. cit.: 380.

268. 'Alvin Toffler: Still Shocking after all these Years' *New Scientist* (19th March 1994): 24.

269. Mark Daniell 'Webs we Weave' *Management Today* (February 1990): 81.

270.   James F. Moore 'Predators and Prey: A New Ecology of Competition'
Harvard Business Review (May-June 1993): 75.

Index